D1381277

CREATIVE CAKE DECORATING

Above: Pink daisy cake (see page 102).
Below left: Caramel coffee gâteau (see page 91).
Below right: Feather iced biscuits (see page 165).

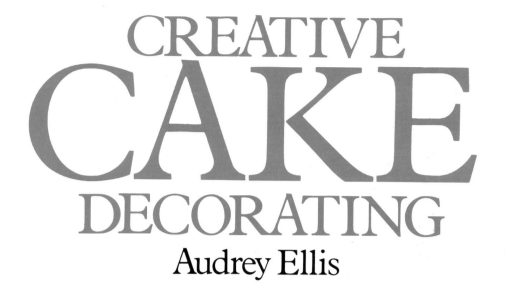

CREATIVE CAKE DECORATING

Audrey Ellis

This edition produced exclusively for
WHSMITH

ACKNOWLEDGMENTS

The author and publishers would like to thank the following companies for their help in supplying some of the photographs for this book:

The Apple and Pear Development Council (pages 78–79)
Bacofoil from British Alcan (pages 164, 175)
Bakewell Non-Stick Baking Parchment (page 142)
Birds Eye Walls Limited (page 133)
British Sugar PLC (pages 30, 45)
Cadbury Typhoo Food Advisory Service (pages 69, 72, 95, 90, 94, 158, 162, 171)
Flour Advisory Bureau (pages 71, 150)
Force Wheat Flakes (pages 29, 78–79)
Gale's Honey (page 160–161)
General Foods (page 63)
The Kellogg Company of Great Britain Limited (pages 184–185)
Lyons Tetley Limited (page 56)
McDougalls Flour (pages 17, 60, 61, 137, 138, 168)
McVite's (pages 66, 166)
The National Dairy Council (page 22)
The Nestle Company Limited (pages 64–65)
Ocean Spray Cranberries (page 77)
Spillers Homepride (page 82)
Tate & Lyle Refineries (pages 146, 152)
United Rum Merchants (page 93)
Wheelbarrow Unsalted Dutch Butter (page 86)
Whitworth's Holdings Limited (pages 35, 37, 38, 52, 53, 54, 101, 106, 107, 121, 172–173, 177)

Line illustrations Kate Simunek

**This edition produced exclusively for
W H Smith**

Published by
Deans International Publishing
52–54 Southwark Street, London SE1 1UA
A division of The Hamlyn Publishing Group Limited
London·New York·Sydney·Toronto

Copyright © The Hamlyn Publishing Group Limited 1985
ISBN 0 603 03717 8

All rights reserved. No part of this publication
may be reproduced, stored in a retrieval system,
or transmitted, in any form or by any means,
electronic, mechanical, photocopying, recording
or otherwise, without the permission of The Hamlyn
Publishing Group Limited.

Printed in Spain

Contents

Useful Facts and Figures

Notes on metrication

In this book quantities are given in metric and Imperial measures. Exact conversion from Imperial to metric measures does not usually give very convenient working quantities and so the metric measures have been rounded off into units of 25 grams. The table below shows the recommended equivalents.

Ounces	Approx g to nearest whole figure	Recommended conversion to nearest unit of 25
1	28	25
2	57	50
3	85	75
4	113	100
5	142	150
6	170	175
7	198	200
8	227	225
9	255	250
10	283	275
11	312	300
12	340	350
13	368	375
14	396	400
15	425	425
16 (1 lb)	454	450
17	482	475
18	510	500
19	539	550
20 ($1\frac{1}{4}$ lb)	567	575

Note: When converting quantities over 20 oz first add the appropriate figures in the centre column, then adjust to the nearest unit of 25. As a general guide, 1 kg (1000 g) equals 2.2 lb or about 2 lb 3 oz. This method of conversion gives good results in nearly all cases, although in certain pastry and cake recipes a more accurate conversion is necessary to produce a balanced recipe.

Liquid measures The millilitre has been used in this book and the following table gives a few examples.

Imperial	Approx ml to nearest whole figure	Recommended ml
$\frac{1}{4}$ pint	142	150 ml
$\frac{1}{2}$ pint	283	300 ml
$\frac{3}{4}$ pint	425	450 ml
1 pint	567	600 ml
$1\frac{1}{2}$ pints	851	900 ml
$1\frac{3}{4}$ pints	992	1000 ml (1 litre)

Spoon measures All spoon measures given in this book are level unless otherwise stated.

Can sizes At present, cans are marked with the exact (usually to the nearest whole number) metric equivalent of the Imperial weight of the contents, so we have followed this practice when giving can sizes.

Notes for American and Australian users

In America the 8-oz measuring cup is used. In Australia metric measures are now used in conjunction with the standard 250-ml measuring cup. The Imperial pint, used in Britain and Australia, is 20 fl oz, while the American pint is 16 fl oz. It is important to remember that the Australian tablespoon differs from both the British and American tablespoons; the table below gives a comparison. The British standard tablespoon, which has been used throughout this book, holds 17.7 ml, the American 14.2 ml, and the Australian 20 ml. A teaspoon holds approximately 5 ml in all three countries.

British	American	Australian
1 teaspoon	1 teaspoon	1 teaspoon
1 tablespoon	1 tablespoon	1 tablespoon
2 tablespoons	3 tablespoons	2 tablespoons
$3\frac{1}{2}$ tablespoons	4 tablespoons	3 tablespoons
4 tablespoons	6 tablespoons	$3\frac{1}{2}$ tablespoons

An Imperial/American guide to solid and liquid measures

Imperial	American	Imperial	American
Solid measures		**Liquid measures**	
1 lb butter or margarine	2 cups	$\frac{1}{4}$ pint liquid	$\frac{2}{3}$ cup liquid
		$\frac{1}{2}$ pint	$1\frac{1}{4}$ cups
1 lb flour	4 cups	$\frac{3}{4}$ pint	$2\frac{2}{3}$ cups
1 lb granulated or caster sugar	2 cups	1 pint	$2\frac{1}{2}$ cups
		$1\frac{1}{2}$ pints	$3\frac{3}{4}$ cups
1 lb icing sugar	3 cups	2 pints	5 cups ($2\frac{1}{2}$ pints)
8 oz rice	1 cup		

American terms

The list below gives some American equivalents or substitutes for terms and ingredients used in this book.

British/American
Equipment and terms
cling film/plastic wrap
deep cake tin/spring form pan
double saucepan/double boiler
flan tin/pie pan
greaseproof paper/ waxed paper
grill/broil
liquidize/blend
loaf tin/loaf pan
piping bag/pastry bag
stoned/pitted
Swiss roll tin/jelly roll pan

British/American
Ingredients
bicarbonate of soda/baking soda
biscuits/crackers, cookies
cocoa powder/unsweetened cocoa
cornflour/cornstarch
cream, single/cream, light
cream, double/cream, heavy
essence/extract
flour, plain/flour, all-purpose
glacé cherries/candied cherries
icing/frosting
lard/shortening
shortcrust pastry/basic pie dough
sultanas/seedless white raisins
yeast, fresh/yeast, compressed

NOTE: **When making any of the recipes in this book, only follow one set of measures as they are not interchangeable.**

Introduction

To make and decorate cakes at home, instead of buying them, is to enjoy a creative art more and more people are coming to appreciate. Bought cakes are often not as delicious to eat, nor do they have the individual touches you alone can add to the design. Also, they are increasingly expensive. Your own time, which passes by on wings when you are happily engaged in an absorbing pastime, costs nothing. But a professional cake decorator would charge a great deal to produce the same stunning creations.

This book is planned to help you make beautiful cakes. To achieve complicated designs, using the expert's techniques, which are not difficult to master if you have a steady hand, an eye for form and colour, and enough enthusiasm. Finally, to tackle cakes for grand occasions; birthdays, exam successes, engagements, marriages, christenings and the yearly celebrations when families gather together at the festive table.

Some of the most beautiful effects are produced with very simple devices. For instance, if you can flat ice a round cake and use a writing tube to make dots, you can decorate your own creation just like the flower-decked beauty on the cover. Apart from the centre decoration, the only extra item needed is a piece of narrow ribbon. The professional touch comes from measuring the circumference carefully, dividing this measurement to space out the loops accurately round the side of the cake, and pricking out the places at which you will secure the loops with iced dots. Of course, you will also measure the ribbon and mark the length of each loop exactly. These small calculations take little time; then you can be sure the result is perfectly even and looks like the work of an expert. A tiny vase filled with fresh flowers and anchored with a dab of icing fills in the centre prettily.

On the other hand, if you enjoy building up your repertoire of icing, piping and modelling techniques, you can create a far more elaborately decorated cake. It is not difficult, but you do need time and patience, two ingredients often lacking in this busy age. For those who want to develop their creative talents with this fascinating hobby to the full, my book takes you through all the necessary stages. It deals first with collecting the right tools for the job and goes on to instructions for making cakes of every size. Of course, you can buy them ready-made, even if this means putting in a special order, if you are really only interested in the art of decoration.

The next stage is to prepare your cake for icing, if necessary using a first covering to produce a good, smooth surface. This is most important to justify the painstaking work you will now put in, and just as essential as the artist's canvas for oils or special paper for water-colours. One word of advice here; don't rush. Allow the time specified for icing to dry, and run-outs or modelled flowers to harden. Follow the advised order of carrying out the scheme to avoid damaging the early stages. Never proceed when you are tired and your hand is not quite steady; set the work aside. This may be a

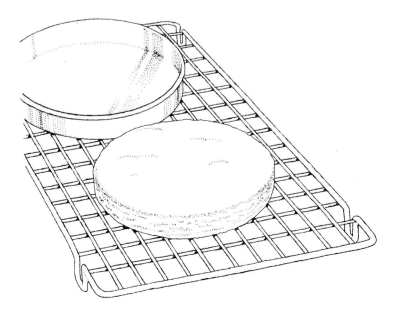

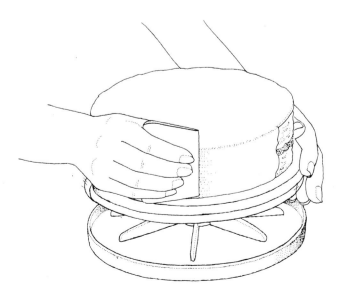

counsel of perfection on the eve of the party or wedding, but allow enough time, in time, to decorate carefully and well, and therefore enjoyably.

In later chapters you will learn how to pipe all sorts of trimmings, such as those using petal and leaf tubes, for items to apply or on the cake itself. Direct piping on the iced surface does not give a bold raised effect unless a very large tube is used. But even the lines produced by fine writing tubes can be built up by overpiping in the same or a contrasting colour to catch the eye.

Any of the icings recommended for modelling, or almond paste, produce fantastic results, and are so easy to tint with food colourings. Here your artistic talent gets full rein. Delicate pastels and shapes or rich colours and bold figures may be your choice. Examples of both are shown.

Once you have discovered how easy it is to strip away non-stick paper from piped shapes, go on to run-outs. Trace off any pattern, direct from the pages of this book or a greetings card. Fix securely to a board using the directions given on page 48, cover with greaseproof paper (U.S. waxed paper) fixed with dabs of icing. Pipe the outline and main details over the guide you have traced, let it dry and fill in with plain or tinted icing. If the shape is simple, such as a diamond or heart, and you need more than one run-out, trace the guide several times, moving your tracing paper to a fresh area each time, and fill in as many outlines as you require.

If you wish to try something really dainty, basket and lace work flow easily from the piping tube, but the shapes are delicate to handle. Make plenty and do not be discouraged if some of them break during the course of application. The amount of icing wasted is infinitesimal. Ribbon work, too, is fascinating. It looks so complicated, but the instructions soon disclose how easy it is to carry out.

Perhaps the most fun of all is to colour the icing with a paintbrush and palette of food colourings. Even if you restrict yourself to tipping daisy petals with pink, and dabbing in a yellow centre to the flower, it is a delight. Those who have won more confidence will enjoy recreating a scene from an original picture. See how it's done on page 50.

Confidence is the keyword to success in cake decorating. It soon comes with practice, but do study the line drawings as well as the gorgeous colour photographs which show you how to carry out each step, as well as the finished cakes.

If you feel you are just a beginner, start with an uncomplicated design which is bound to succeed. With the necessary tools and helpful advice at hand, you may be surprised to find you've uncovered a genuine talent so far undreamed of. It is my hope that you will. Many years ago, I did exactly that myself. I would like to add a word of thanks to a most experienced colleague in the field of cake decorating, Rosemary Wadey, who has contributed some lovely designs for very special cakes.

Audrey Ellis

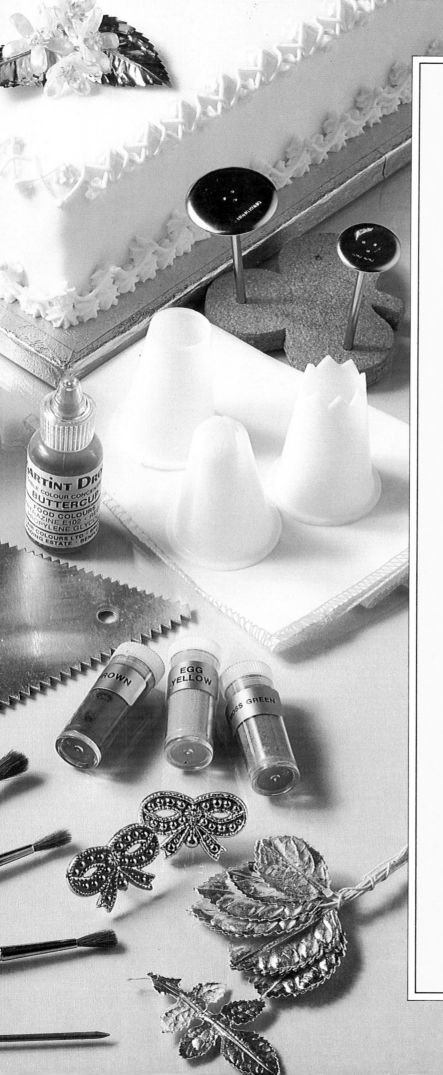

Choosing your Equipment

❦

You probably already have in your kitchen most of the items required. But some of the equipment needed for cake decorating consists of very small items which are delicate and could be damaged unless carefully handled and stored. Of these, by far the most important are your piping tubes or nozzles, as they are sometimes called. The best way to identify different tubes is by the number stamped on each one. But not all manufacturers use the same numbering so I have used only those most easily recognizable in my designs. Begin with plain writing tubes, so often needed, that may be as fine as 00, although most work can be achieved with tubes between the numbers 1 and 4. Good quality tubes are made of metal that wears well and gives the best definition, but there are many plastic tubes quite suitable for simple work. Check when buying to ensure that the tip of the tube is not damaged and that the seam is smooth. Especially in the case of star tubes, check that the claws are evenly separated, otherwise lop-sided shapes may result.

Mixing bowls Ovenproof glass such as Pyrex cannot be bettered. You can place it over boiling water, in the oven at moderate heat and best of all, you can always see at a glance what it contains. Cling film stretched over the top protects icings from forming a crust. You can mould a sheet down into it, touching the surface of the contents before sealing over the rim. Earthenware or stainless steel bowls can be used if you have not enough glass ones of the right size.

Linked rosette cake (see page 109).

Mixers and beaters An electric hand mixer is useful, although a rotary beater, to which you apply the energy, works as well if not as quickly. A balloon whisk is also good, especially for beating egg whites, which are needed for royal icing. A food processor helps to cream fats with sugar for cakes quickly, and to make smooth butter icings.

Knives and spatulas A round-bladed knife is a good tool for marking soft icings. A palette knife (U.S. spatula) is essential, preferably a long one with a flexible blade, and another similar but much smaller one. These are both needed to spread icings on the cake with a sweeping action that eliminates air bubbles. The tips can also be used for marking finishes. Either a shaped plastic or rubber-ended spatula (U.S. scraper) is the right tool to use for cleaning all the icing or cake mixture out of a bowl, to avoid costly waste of the ingredients.

Spoons One usually needs several sizes and types of spoon; wooden ones of two or three sizes, metal teaspoons and tablespoons, and a set of measuring spoons.

Brushes Tiny cleaning brushes are made specially to free icing tubes of stubborn dried icing. A plump larger brush helps get an even distribution of apricot glaze to make almond paste adhere to the surface of a cake. Delicate paint brushes are invaluable for touching in food colourings on icing.

Rulers A transparent plastic ruler marked in inches and centimetres is needed for measuring and, if very firm, can also do duty for scraping icing flat. Another kind of ruler, also described as an icing comb, has a serrated edge or edges giving interesting patterns when swept or dragged across the top of a cake or round the sides with the help of a turntable (see page 85).

Sieve Icing sugar (U.S. confectioners' sugar) should always be sifted through a fine mesh to ensure that no lumps form in the icing. One of the easiest cake decorations is to place an elaborate paper doily on top of a sponge layer cake and sift sugar over it. If the doily is carefully lifted off, the pattern will show up clearly.

Turntable This is a great aid in decorating with a professional touch. It consists of a heavy base with a flat rotating top. Cheaper ones tend to be made of plastic and to be low compared with the more expensive models made of metal 15 cm/6 inches high. To improvise, place a mixing bowl upside down on the work surface and mount an inverted dinner plate on it. You may possibly have some difficulty in turning the plate smoothly.

Paper icing bags For small quantities of icing or melted chocolate, a greaseproof paper (U.S. waxed paper) bag is most convenient. See below how to make them. If you do a lot of decorating work, it is a good idea to make up a number of these bags when you have time to spare, securing the centre seal at the back with transparent adhesive tape. For line work, snip off just the tip of the bag after it has been filled, but do not over-fill as icing may squeeze out of the top unless there is sufficient paper to fold down several times. To use with a fancy tube, snip off the end of the bag before putting in the tube and then fill. It is possible to add more icing to refill these bags but be prepared that they may split, so have plenty of spares ready.

Making a paper icing bag.

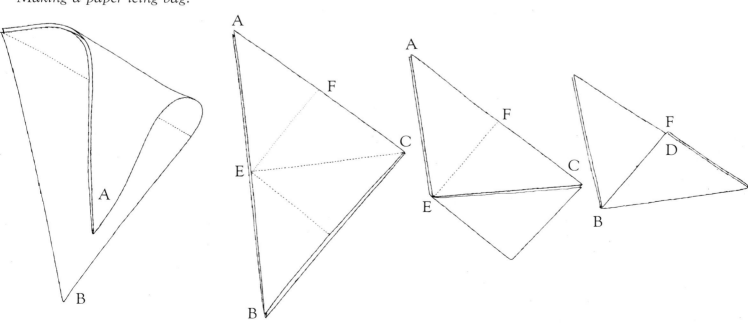

12

Nylon or plastic icing bags These have largely superseded the old linen bags which had to be boiled and dried thoroughly after each use. If your tubes do not have a screw thread, you will require a screw fitting to place inside the bag and a collar which is pressed up over the tube on the outside to screw into the connector and hold it in place. If your tubes are of the type which have a screw thread designed to fit an icing syringe, you will need a connector which you insert into the piping bag so that it protrudes from the end but is firmly held. Some bags have the ends already cut and firmly stitched round the edge which may make the aperture too large to be used in this way. The bags come in small, medium and large sizes. Choose small for delicate piping jobs in royal icing and medium for piping butter icings. The large size is best reserved for piping whipped cream or meringue.

Icing syringe The great advantage of this tool is that you can change the tubes to produce different effects without emptying the syringe. To fill or refill it, spoon the icing down one side of the tube to avoid trapping more air than necessary, then gradually press the plunger at a slight angle to allow any remaining air to escape. Take care not to over-fill, otherwise the plunger cannot be inserted satisfactorily. All syringes and material bags are easier to fill if placed, tube downwards, into a container, turning the cuff of a bag outwards over the edge, the first time you do it.

Icing nails When making a quantity of piped flowers, you should have an icing nail which consists of a pointed metal spike with a flat mushroom-like top. It is used by placing a small dot of icing in the centre and attaching a square of greaseproof paper (U.S. waxed paper). Hold the nail in one hand and pipe out the flower petals with the other, gradually turning the nail. Remove the square of paper with the flower on top and replace with another square of paper. Spread the piped flowers out on a board to dry before removing them from the paper. Improvise nails by inserting a skewer into the cork from a wine bottle. Other nails come in various shapes for making lattice-work baskets. The surface should be very lightly oiled before piping so that the basket can be eased off when dry.

Cake markers These can often be used instead of templates, the paper patterns through which designs are pricked out on cake tops. There are two types, one being wedge-shaped with a hole at the pointed end, through which it can be fixed in the centre of the cake with a pin, so that it can be swung round to mark even segments on the cake. The other kind is a half round with a straight side marked in inches and centimetres, and slots through which concentric circles can be pricked out.

Paper and foil Non-stick baking parchment, ideal for lining cake tins, is also useful for tracing designs over which run-outs can be piped and finished plaques can very easily be removed. Greaseproof paper is handy for making small piping bags and also for lining tins. Waxed paper is suitable for any of the above purposes. Foil, either heavy duty or folded to make several layers, can be moulded to support decorations while they dry out in the required shape.

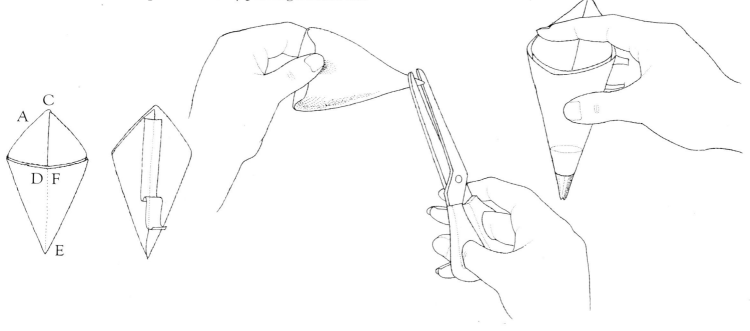

The Best of Basic Cakes

The greatest satisfaction comes from finding that under the decorative finish there is a cake of perfect texture and flavour. Bought cakes may look splendid, but the interior is often a disappointment. This chapter deals with the most useful recipes to guarantee success for your gâteaux, fancies and special occasion cakes.

If you cannot devote the time to baking a cake to be used as the foundation for an elaborately trimmed gâteau, and carry out the decorative scheme, bake the cake in advance and freeze.

Use non-stick tins, or carry out the instructions given for greasing and lining tins carefully. This makes such a difference to the finished result, so don't skip on preparing your tins. Either buy a number of liners for the bottom of the most frequently used round tins, or cut out several at a time. They take up so little storage space. Mixtures which require long cooking are better protected if you use double thickness greaseproof paper (U.S. waxed paper) inside the tin and tie two thicknesses of brown paper around the outside. Lighter mixtures need only single thickness paper.

To line a round tin, cut a circle for the base and a strip for the sides long enough to overlap and wide enough to come 2.5 cm/1 inch above the top of the tin. Fold up one long edge by this much and make slanting cuts along it about 2 cm/¾ inch apart. Grease the interior of the tin slightly, fit in the side strip, allowing the cuts to overlap on the base. Insert the bottom liner and press down evenly all over. The same method of lining is suitable for deep square, hexagonal or heart-shaped tins.

Whisked sponge

For either 2 (17.5-cm/7-inch) shallow cake tins or 1 deep tin, or 1 (20-cm/8-inch) deep shaped flan tin, or 1 rectangular tin (32.5 cm/13 inches by 22.5 cm/9 inches).

**3 large eggs
75 g/3 oz caster sugar (U.S. ⅓ cup granulated sugar)
75 g/3 oz plain flour (U.S. ¾ cup all-purpose flour)**

1. Heat the oven to 190°C/375°F, Gas Mark 5, grease the chosen tin or tins and sprinkle lightly with flour and caster sugar (U.S. granulated sugar).
2. Put the eggs and sugar in a large bowl and stand this over a pan of simmering water without allowing the base to touch the water. Whisk steadily, if possible using an electric mixer, until thick enough to fall back on itself in a firm ribbon when the beaters are lifted. Remove from the heat and whisk until cool. Sift half the flour over the whisked mixture and fold in lightly. Repeat with the remaining flour. Pour into the prepared tin or tins and tilt until the mixture makes an even layer.
3. Bake until just firm to the touch, allowing about 20–25 minutes for the shallow cake layers, 25–30 minutes for a deeper cake or flan and about 10 minutes for a rectangular cake. Turn out on a wire rack and leave to cool. If the rectangular cake is to be filled and rolled, turn out on to sugared paper and trim the edges. Roll up at once and cool before filling.

_____ VARIATIONS _____

Chocolate whisked sponge Replace 1 tablespoon of the flour with cocoa powder (U.S. unsweetened cocoa) and sift the two together before adding to the whisked mixture.
Coffee whisked sponge Add 1 tablespoon coffee essence (U.S. sweetened concentrated coffee flavoring) or 1½ teaspoons instant coffee dissolved in 1 teaspoon hot water. Whisk into the eggs and sugar when removed from the heat and before adding the dry ingredients.
Lemon or orange whisked sponge Add the finely grated rind of 1 small fruit to the eggs and sugar before whisking.
Vanilla or almond whisked sponge Add ¾ teaspoon vanilla or almond essence (U.S. vanilla or almond extract) to the whisked mixture when removed from the heat and before adding the dry ingredients.

Quantities to make Whisked sponge cakes of other sizes

For 2 (20-cm/8-inch) shallow cake tins or 1 deep tin, or 1 (17.5-cm/7-inch) square tin.

**4 large eggs
100 g/4 oz caster sugar (U.S. ½ cup granulated sugar)
100 g/4 oz plain flour (U.S. 1 cup all-purpose flour)**

Cook shallow cakes for about 25–30 minutes; deeper cakes for 30–35 minutes.

Fresh fruit sponge

(Illustrated opposite)

Make a 20-cm/8-inch Whisked sponge flan case. Cool on a wire rack and fill the centre with 1 quantity Crème Patissière (see page 132). Slice a selection of fresh fruit in contrasting colours, such as nectarines, bananas, kiwi fruit and black grapes (U.S. purple grapes). Sprinkle the fruit liberally with lemon juice to prevent discoloration. Quickly arrange the fruit in neat concentric rings on the pastry cream, then cover with glaze if liked.

Genoese sponge

For either 1 rectangular tin (27.5 cm/11 inches by 17.5 cm/7 inches and 4 cm/1½ inches deep), 2 (20-cm/8-inch) shallow cake tins or 1 deep loose-based tin, or 1 (17.5-cm/7-inch) square loose-based tin.

**40 g/1½ oz (U.S. 3 tablespoons) butter
75 g/3 oz plain flour (U.S. ¾ cup all-purpose flour)
3 large eggs
75 g/3 oz caster sugar (U.S. ⅓ cup granulated sugar)**

1. Heat the oven to 190°C/375°F, Gas Mark 5, grease the chosen tin or tins and line with greaseproof paper (U.S. waxed paper).
2. Melt the butter until it just flows then leave to cool but not solidify. Sift the flour twice. Put the eggs in a large bowl and whisk for a few minutes then whisk in the sugar lightly. Stand the bowl over a pan of simmering water without allowing the base to touch the water. Whisk, if possible with an electric mixer, until thick enough to fall back on itself in a firm ribbon when the beaters are lifted. Remove from the heat and whisk until cool. Carefully fold in half the flour, then the melted

Fresh fruit sponge.

butter and finally the remaining flour. Transfer the mixture to the prepared tin or tins and level the top lightly.

3. Bake until just firm to the touch, allowing about 20–25 minutes for the slab cake, 15–20 minutes for shallow cake layers or 25–30 minutes for a deeper cake. Turn out carefully on a wire rack and leave to cool before removing the lining paper.

_____ VARIATIONS _____

Lemon or orange Genoese sponge Add the finely grated rind of 1 small fruit to the eggs and sugar before whisking.

Almond or vanilla Genoese sponge Add 1 teaspoon almond or vanilla essence (U.S. almond or vanilla extract) to the whisked mixture before folding in the flour.

Chocolate Genoese sponge Measure the flour then remove 2 tablespoons (U.S. 3 tablespoons) and replace with an equal quantity of cocoa powder (U.S. unsweetened cocoa). Sift the cocoa with the flour before adding to the whisked mixture.

Coffee Genoese sponge Dissolve 2 teaspoons instant coffee in 1 teaspoon hot water. Whisk into the eggs and sugar when removed from the heat and before adding the dry ingredients.

Quantities to make Genoese sponge cakes of other sizes

For 2 (22.5-cm/9-inch) shallow cake tins or 1 deep tin, or 1 (20-cm/8-inch) square tin.

50 g/2 oz (U.S. $\frac{1}{4}$ cup) butter
100 g/4 oz plain flour (U.S. 1 cup all-purpose flour)
4 large eggs
100 g/4 oz caster sugar (U.S. $\frac{1}{2}$ cup granulated sugar)

Cook shallow cake layers for about 20–25 minutes; deeper cakes for 30–35 minutes.

For 2 (25-cm/10-inch) shallow cake tins or 1 deep tin, or 1 (22.5-cm/9-inch) square tin.

65 g/2$\frac{1}{2}$ oz (U.S. generous $\frac{1}{4}$ cup) butter
150 g/5 oz plain flour (U.S. 1$\frac{1}{4}$ cups all-purpose flour)
5 large eggs
150 g/5 oz caster sugar (U.S. $\frac{2}{3}$ cup granulated sugar)

Cook shallow cake layers for about 25–30 minutes; deeper cakes for 35–40 minutes.

French satin fancies.

18

French satin fancies

(Illustrated below left and cover)

Bake a 20-cm/8-inch square Genoese sponge cake (see opposite). Make up 2 quantities Satin icing paste (see page 34) and tint with 2 drops yellow and 2 drops red food colouring, kneading the paste well so that the colour is even. Make up 2 quantities raspberry Butter icing (see page 28).

To cut up the cake, mark off 5-cm/2-inch sections all round the top edge. Mark a diagonal across the centre of the cake to make two large triangles. Join up the marked points with lines parallel with the diagonal then join up marked points on two opposite sides of the cake, to give twelve diamond shapes and eight triangles.

Coat each piece of cake thinly with butter icing. Divide the icing paste into even sized balls, roll out each individually as thinly as possible and mould over the diamond shapes. Gather up the trimmings and re-roll to cover the triangles. Put the remaining butter icing into two paper icing bags fitted with a small star tube and a No. 2 writing tube and decorate the cakes with various designs.

Makes 12 diamond-shaped cakes and 8 triangular cakes

Easy doily decoration

(Illustrated below)

To give an unusual effect, bake a 20-cm/8-inch square cake, invert on a wire rack and decorate the flat base. When the cake is cold, place a round doily of the same size on top using several doilys together as this helps to keep the pattern distinct. Sift icing sugar (U.S. confectioners' sugar) evenly all over the top, if necessary fixing the doily in the centre with a pin. Remove the pin and lift off the doily carefully. Pipe the centre, and all round the square edge, or merely the corners, with pastel coloured butter icing of your choice appropriately flavoured. If desired, slice the cake through horizontally and fill with more butter icing before replacing the top and decorating.

Easy doily decoration.

Feather sponge cakes

For 2 (17.5-cm/7-inch) shallow cake tins or 1 deep tin, or 12 paper cake cases, or 1 (20-cm/8-inch) ring tin.

150 g/5 oz plain flour (U.S. 1¼ cups all-purpose flour)
25 g/1 oz cornflour (U.S. ¼ cup cornstarch)
2 teaspoons (U.S. 1 tablespoon) baking powder
½ teaspoon salt
150 g/5 oz caster sugar (U.S. ⅔ cup granulated sugar)
2 eggs, separated
90 ml/3½ fl oz (U.S. scant ½ cup) corn oil
90 ml/3½ fl oz (U.S. scant ½ cup) water

1. Heat the oven to 190°C/375°F, Gas Mark 5, grease the chosen tin or tins, line with greaseproof paper (U.S. waxed paper) and lightly grease the paper. Stand paper cake cases in bun tins (U.S. muffin pans) if possible, or arrange on a baking sheet (U.S. cookie sheet). Generously grease a ring tin.
2. Sift the flour, cornflour, baking powder and salt into a bowl and add the sugar. Put the egg whites into a separate clean bowl. Add the egg yolks, oil and water to the dry ingredients and beat well to form a smooth batter. Whisk the egg whites until stiff and fold in lightly and evenly. Transfer the mixture to the prepared tins.
3. Bake until firm to the touch, allowing about 25–30 minutes for the shallow cakes, 35–40 minutes for a deeper cake or ring tin or 15–20 minutes for small cakes. Turn out on a wire rack, remove the lining paper and leave to cool.

─────────── VARIATIONS ───────────

Coconut Feather sponge cakes Fold 2 tablespoons desiccated coconut (U.S. 3 tablespoons shredded coconut) into the cake mix before transferring to the tins for baking. If wished, ½ teaspoon coconut essence (U.S. coconut extract) can be added with the egg yolks.
Chocolate Feather sponge cakes Blend 2 tablespoons cocoa powder (U.S. 3 tablespoons unsweetened cocoa) with the oil and water to a smooth mixture before adding to the dry ingredients.

Quantities to make Feather sponge cakes of other sizes

For 2 (22.5-cm/9-inch) shallow cake tins or 1 deep tin, or 1 (20-cm/8-inch) square tin.

215 g/7½ oz plain flour (U.S. 1¾ cups all-purpose flour)
40 g/1½ oz cornflour (U.S. ⅓ cup cornstarch)
1 tablespoon (U.S. generous 1 tablespoon) baking powder
¾ teaspoon salt
215 g/7½ oz caster sugar (U.S. scant 1 cup granulated sugar)
3 eggs, separated
175 ml/6 fl oz (U.S. ¾ cup) corn oil
175 ml/6 fl oz (U.S. ¾ cup) water

Cook shallow cake layers at 190°C/375°F, Gas Mark 5 for about 35–40 minutes; deeper cakes at 180°C/350°F, Gas Mark 4 allowing about 1 hour.

Victoria sandwich cakes

For either 2 (17.5-cm/7-inch) shallow tins or 1 deep tin, 1 (15-cm/6-inch) square tin or 12 paper cake cases.

100 g/4 oz self-raising flour (U.S. 1 cup all-purpose flour sifted with 1 teaspoon baking powder)
pinch of salt
100 g/4 oz (U.S. ½ cup) butter or margarine
100 g/4 oz caster sugar (U.S. ½ cup granulated sugar)
2 eggs

1. Heat the oven to 180°C/350°F, Gas Mark 4, generously grease the chosen tin or tins and line the base with greaseproof paper (U.S. waxed paper). Stand cake cases in bun tins (U.S. muffin pans) if possible or on baking sheets (U.S. cookie sheets).
2. Sift the flour with the salt. Cream the butter and sugar together in a bowl until light and fluffy. Beat in the eggs, one at a time, then fold in the dry ingredients. Transfer the mixture to the prepared tin or tins or the paper cases.
3. Bake until just firm to the touch, allowing about 20–25 minutes for shallow cakes, 25–30 minutes for a deeper cake and 15–20 minutes for small cakes. Leave to stand in the tins for 1 minute then turn out on a wire rack, remove the lining paper from the large cakes and leave to cool.

Chocolate Victoria sandwich cake Replace 25 g/1 oz (U.S. ¼ cup) of the flour with an equal quantity of cocoa powder (U.S. unsweetened cocoa).

Lemon or orange Victoria sandwich cake Add the finely grated rind from 1 fruit to the butter and sugar during beating.

Coffee Victoria sandwich cake Add 1 tablespoon coffee essence (U.S. sweetened concentrated coffee flavoring) or dissolve 2 teaspoons instant coffee powder in 1 teaspoon hot water. Beat into the creamed mixture with the eggs.

Almond or vanilla Victoria sandwich cake Add 1 teaspoon almond or vanilla essence (U.S. almond or vanilla extract) to the creamed mixture before adding the eggs.

Walnut Victoria sandwich cake Fold 50 g/2 oz (U.S. ½ cup) finely chopped walnuts into the cake mixture before putting it in the tin or tins.

Quantities to make Victoria sandwich cakes of other sizes

For 2 (20-cm/8-inch) shallow tins or 1 deep tin, 1 (17.5-cm/7-inch) square tin or 1 rectangular tin about 27.5 cm/11 inches by 17.5 cm/7 inches and 4 cm/1½ inches deep.

175 g/6 oz self-raising flour (U.S. 1½ cups all-purpose flour sifted with 1½ teaspoons baking powder)
large pinch of salt
175 g/6 oz (U.S. ¾ cup) butter or margarine
175 g/6 oz caster sugar (U.S. ¾ cup granulated sugar)
3 eggs

Cook shallow cake layers at 180°C/350°F, Gas Mark 4 for about 25–30 minutes; deeper cakes at 160°C/325°F, Gas Mark 3 for about 45–50 minutes; the rectangular cake for about 35–40 minutes.

For 2 (22.5-cm/9-inch) shallow tins or 1 deep tin, or 1 (20-cm/8-inch) square tin.

225 g/8 oz self-raising flour (U.S. 2 cups all-purpose flour sifted with 2 teaspoons baking powder)
¼ teaspoon salt
225 g/8 oz (U.S. 1 cup) butter or margarine
225 g/8 oz caster sugar (U.S. 1 cup granulated sugar)
4 eggs

Cook shallow cake layers at 180°C/350°F, Gas Mark 4 for about 30–35 minutes; deeper cakes at 160°C/325°F, Gas Mark 3 for about 55–60 minutes.

QUICK-MIX VICTORIA SANDWICH CAKES
Use soft margarine instead of butter and add 1 teaspoon baking powder for each 100 g/4 oz (U.S. 1 cup) flour in basic recipe. Put all ingredients in a bowl and beat for 2 minutes or until well blended. Bake as in main recipe.

Superhint *For a quick decoration, hold cup cakes baked in paper cake cases by the base and dip the tops in Glacé icing (see page 31).*

Glacé fruit cakes

(Illustrated below)

This is an excellent last-minute mixture which produces a rich-tasting fruit cake that does not take long to mature. It is ideal for those miniature cakes which make acceptable gifts, particularly at Christmas. Make it more attractive by covering the top quite simply with rows of glacé cherries (U.S. candied cherries) and walnut halves coated with melted redcurrant jelly. For those who prefer a classic finish, cover the cakes with almond paste and royal icing or fondant moulding paste.

For 1 (20-cm/8-inch) round tin, 1 (17.5-cm/7-inch) square tin or 4 (10-cm/4-inch) tins.

100 g/4 oz (U.S. ½ cup) butter
175 g/6 oz soft brown sugar (U.S. ¾ cup light brown sugar)
1 teaspoon ground mixed spice
½ teaspoon bicarbonate of soda (U.S. baking soda)
300 ml/½ pint (U.S. 1¼ cups) milk
175 g/6 oz glacé pineapple, chopped (U.S. 1 cup chopped candied pineapple)

175 g/6 oz sultanas (U.S. 1 cup seedless white raisins)
50 g/2 oz (U.S. ⅓ cup) chopped angelica
100 g/4 oz glacé cherries (U.S. ½ cup candied cherries)
50 g/2 oz (U.S. ⅓ cup) chopped candied peel
50 g/2 oz (U.S. ½ cup) chopped walnuts or pecans
2 eggs
350 g/12 oz self-raising flour, sifted (U.S. 3 cups all-purpose flour sifted with 3 teaspoons baking powder)
2 tablespoons (U.S. 3 tablespoons) brandy

1. Heat the oven to 140°C/275°F, Gas Mark 1, grease the chosen tin or tins, line with a double thickness of greaseproof paper (U.S. waxed paper) and grease the paper. Tie a double thickness of brown paper around the outside of large tins. (If making the small cakes, use four clean empty 822-g/1-lb 13-oz fruit cans.)
2. Put the butter, sugar, spice, bicarbonate of soda, milk, fruit, peel and nuts into a large pan and heat gently, stirring, until the butter has melted. Bring to the boil and simmer 5 minutes. Leave to cool.
3. Add the eggs to the pan of fruit and sift in the flour. Mix well. Transfer the mixture to the prepared tin or tins.

4. Bake, allowing about 3 hours for a large cake and about $1\frac{1}{2}$ hours for the smaller cakes. Test frequently by inserting a fine skewer or wooden cocktail stick (U.S. toothpick). When the cakes are ready, the skewer should come out clean with no uncooked mixture clinging to it. Cool the cakes in the tin for 15 minutes, then turn out on a wire rack and remove the lining paper.

5. When cold, prick the cake or cakes with a needle or fine skewer and sprinkle with the brandy. Wrap and store for anything from 3 days to 1 month before decorating.

Dark rich fruit cakes

See on the chart overleaf quantities of ingredients and cooking times for round and square cakes.

1. Rinse the cherries, halve them and dry on absorbent kitchen towel. Mix with the dried fruit, candied peel, chopped almonds, grated lemon rind and spices in a bowl. Spoon over the brandy and stir lightly. Cover and leave to stand for 1 hour.

2. Heat the oven to 140°C/275°F, Gas Mark 1. Grease the chosen tin, line with two thicknesses of greaseproof paper (U.S. waxed paper) and tie a double-thickness of brown paper around the outside.

3. Sift the flour. Cream the butter and sugar together in a bowl until light and fluffy. Beat in the eggs, one at a time, adding a tablespoon of flour with each. Beat in the treacle then fold in the ground almonds and remaining flour. Finally, stir in the fruit mixture.

Creating heart-shaped and horseshoe cakes from basic round cakes.

4. Transfer the mixture to the prepared tin, level the surface then hollow out the centre slightly so that the baked cake will be flat.

5. Using the chart only as a rough guide, bake the cake until firm to the touch and a fine skewer or wooden cocktail stick (U.S. toothpick) inserted in the centre comes out clean, with no uncooked mixture clinging to it. Check three-quarters through the cooking time and cover lightly with a sheet of foil if the cake is becoming too brown.

6. Leave to cool in the tin, then remove and strip off the lining paper.

7. Prick the surface of the cake lightly with a needle or thin skewer and spoon over the brandy.

8. Wrap the cake in greaseproof paper (U.S. waxed paper), then enclose in foil or a plastic bag to make an airtight parcel. Leave to mature for at least 2 months before decorating.

USING FANCY CAKE TINS

Hexagonal and Heart-shaped tins Measure across widest diameter and use ingredients for equivalent round tin.

Horse-shoe-shaped tin Measure across widest diameter and use ingredients for a round tin 5 cm/2 inches less in diameter than this measurement.

SLAB CAKES

Measure the length and width of the chosen tin, add these measurements together and halve the total. Choose ingredients to fill a square tin of this size.

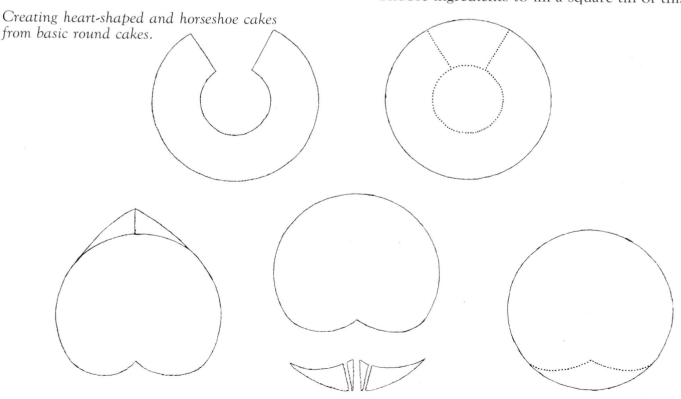

DARK RICH FRUIT CAKES – quantities of ingredients required

	Round 12.5 cm/5 inch Square 10 cm/4 inch	Round 15 cm/6 inch Square 12.5 cm/5 inch	Round 17.5 cm/7 inch Square 15 cm/6 inch	Round 20 cm/8 inch Square 17.5 cm/7 inch
butter or margarine	75 g/3 oz (U.S. $\frac{1}{3}$ cup)	90 g/3$\frac{1}{2}$ oz (U.S. scant $\frac{1}{2}$ cup)	150 g/5 oz (U.S. $\frac{2}{3}$ cup)	175 g/6 oz (U.S. $\frac{3}{4}$ cup)
soft brown sugar (U.S. light brown sugar)	75 g/3 oz (U.S. $\frac{1}{3}$ cup)	90 g/3$\frac{1}{2}$ oz (U.S. scant $\frac{1}{2}$ cup)	150 g/5 oz (U.S. $\frac{2}{3}$ cup)	175 g/6 oz (U.S. $\frac{3}{4}$ cup)
plain flour (U.S. all-purpose flour)	75 g/3 oz (U.S. $\frac{3}{4}$ cup)	100 g/4 oz (U.S. 1 cup)	175 g/6 oz (U.S. 1$\frac{1}{2}$ cups)	200 g/7 oz (U.S. 1$\frac{3}{4}$ cups)
ground nutmeg	$\frac{1}{4}$ teaspoon	$\frac{1}{4}$ teaspoon	$\frac{1}{2}$ teaspoon	$\frac{1}{2}$ teaspoon
ground mixed spices	$\frac{1}{2}$ teaspoon	$\frac{1}{2}$ teaspoon	$\frac{3}{4}$ teaspoon	$\frac{3}{4}$ teaspoon
ground cloves	small pinch	small pinch	large pinch	large pinch
glacé cherries (U.S. candied cherries), halved	4	6	50 g/2 oz (U.S. $\frac{1}{4}$ cup)	65 g/2$\frac{1}{2}$ oz (U.S. scant $\frac{1}{3}$ cup)
mixed dried fruit – currants, seedless raisins and sultanas (U.S. seedless white raisins)	250 g/9 oz (U.S. 1$\frac{1}{2}$ cups)	350 g/12 oz (U.S. 2 cups)	450 g/1 lb	625 g/1 lb 6 oz (U.S. 3$\frac{2}{3}$ cups)
chopped almonds	25 g/1 oz (U.S. $\frac{1}{4}$ cup)	40 g/1$\frac{1}{2}$ oz (U.S. $\frac{1}{3}$ cup)	50 g/2 oz (U.S. $\frac{1}{2}$ cup)	65 g/2$\frac{1}{2}$ oz (U.S. $\frac{2}{3}$ cup)
chopped candied peel	25 g/1 oz (U.S. scant $\frac{1}{4}$ cup)	40 g/1$\frac{1}{2}$ oz (U.S. $\frac{1}{4}$ cup)	50 g/2 oz (U.S. $\frac{1}{3}$ cup)	65 g/2$\frac{1}{2}$ oz (U.S. scant $\frac{1}{2}$ cup)
grated rind	$\frac{1}{2}$ lemon	$\frac{1}{2}$ lemon	1 lemon	1 lemon
ground almonds	25 g/1 oz (U.S. $\frac{1}{4}$ cup)	40 g/1$\frac{1}{2}$ oz (U.S. $\frac{1}{3}$ cup)	50 g/2 oz (U.S. $\frac{1}{2}$ cup)	65 g/2$\frac{1}{2}$ oz (U.S. $\frac{2}{3}$ cup)
large eggs	2 (size 3)	2 (size 2)	3 (size 2)	4 (size 2)
black treacle (U.S. molasses)	1 teaspoon	1$\frac{1}{2}$ teaspoons	1 tablespoon	1 tablespoon
brandy or sherry	2 teaspoons	1 tablespoon	4 teaspoons (U.S. 2 tablespoons)	2 tablespoons (U.S. 3 tablespoons)
approximate guide to cooking time	1$\frac{3}{4}$ hours	2 hours	2$\frac{1}{2}$ hours	3 hours
approximate weight of baked cake	675 g/1$\frac{1}{2}$ lb	900 g/2 lb	1.2 kg/2$\frac{3}{4}$ lb	1.7 kg/3$\frac{3}{4}$ lb
spirit for adding to baked cake	1 teaspoon	1$\frac{1}{2}$ teaspoons	2 teaspoons (U.S. 1 tablespoon)	1 tablespoon

Round 22.5 cm/9 inch Square 20 cm/8 inch	Round 25 cm/10 inch Square 22.5 cm/9 inch	Round 27.5 cm/11 inch Square 25 cm/10 inch	Round 30 cm/12 inch Square 27.5 cm/11 inch	Square 30 cm/12 inch
225 g/8 oz (U.S. 1 cup)	275 g/10 oz (U.S. $1\frac{1}{4}$ cups)	350 g/12 oz (U.S. $1\frac{1}{2}$ cups)	400 g/14 oz (U.S. $1\frac{3}{4}$ cups)	450 g/1 lb
225 g/8 oz (U.S. 1 cup)	275 g/10 oz (U.S. $1\frac{1}{4}$ cups)	350 g/12 oz (U.S. $1\frac{1}{2}$ cups)	400 g/14 oz (U.S. $1\frac{3}{4}$ cups)	450 g/1 lb
250 g/9 oz (U.S. $2\frac{1}{4}$ cups)	300 g/11 oz (U.S. $2\frac{3}{4}$ cups)	400 g/14 oz (U.S. $3\frac{1}{2}$ cups)	450 g/1 lb (U.S. 4 cups)	525 g/1 lb 3 oz (U.S. $4\frac{3}{4}$ cups)
$\frac{3}{4}$ teaspoon	$\frac{3}{4}$ teaspoon	1 teaspoon	$1\frac{1}{4}$ teaspoons	$1\frac{1}{2}$ teaspoons
1 teaspoon	1 teaspoon	$1\frac{1}{4}$ teaspoons	$1\frac{1}{4}$ teaspoons	$1\frac{1}{2}$ teaspoons
large pinch	$\frac{1}{4}$ teaspoon	$\frac{1}{4}$ teaspoon	$\frac{1}{4}$ teaspoon	$\frac{1}{2}$ teaspoon
75 g/3 oz (U.S. $\frac{1}{3}$ cup)	90 g/$3\frac{1}{2}$ oz (U.S. scant $\frac{1}{2}$ cup)	100 g/4 oz (U.S. $\frac{1}{2}$ cup)	150 g/5 oz (U.S. $\frac{2}{3}$ cup)	175 g/6 oz (U.S. $\frac{3}{4}$ cup)
800 g/$1\frac{3}{4}$ lb (U.S. $4\frac{2}{3}$ cups)	1 kg/2 lb 2 oz (U.S. $5\frac{2}{3}$ cups)	1.2 kg/$2\frac{3}{4}$ lb (U.S. $7\frac{1}{3}$ cups)	1.5 kg/$3\frac{1}{4}$ lb (U.S. $8\frac{2}{3}$ cups)	1.7 kg/$3\frac{3}{4}$ lb (U.S. 10 cups)
90 g/$3\frac{1}{2}$ oz (U.S. scant 1 cup)	100 g/4 oz (U.S. 1 cup)	150 g/5 oz (U.S. $1\frac{1}{4}$ cups)	175 g/6 oz (U.S. $1\frac{1}{2}$ cups)	200 g/7 oz (U.S. $1\frac{3}{4}$ cups)
90 g/$3\frac{1}{2}$ oz (U.S. generous $\frac{1}{2}$ cup)	100 g/4 oz (U.S. $\frac{2}{3}$ cup)	150 g/5 oz (U.S. scant 1 cup)	175 g/6 oz (U.S. 1 cup)	200 g/7 oz (U.S. generous 1 cup)
1 lemon	$1\frac{1}{2}$ lemons	2 lemons	$2\frac{1}{2}$ lemons	3 lemons
90 g/$3\frac{1}{2}$ oz (U.S. scant 1 cup)	100 g/4 oz (U.S. 1 cup)	150 g/5 oz (U.S. $1\frac{1}{4}$ cups)	175 g/6 oz (U.S. $1\frac{1}{2}$ cups)	200 g/7 oz (U.S. $1\frac{3}{4}$ cups)
5 (size 2)	6 (size 2)	7 (size 2)	8 (size 2)	9 (size 2)
1 tablespoon	4 teaspoons (U.S. 2 tablespoons)	2 tablespoons (U.S. 3 tablespoons)	2 tablespoons (U.S. 3 tablespoons)	scant 3 tablespoons (U.S. 4 tablespoons)
2 tablespoons (U.S. 3 tablespoons)	3 tablespoons (U.S. 4 tablespoons)	3 tablespoons (U.S. 4 tablespoons)	4 tablespoons (U.S. 6 tablespoons)	4 tablespoons (U.S. 6 tablespoons)
$3\frac{1}{4}$ hours	$3\frac{1}{2}$ hours	$3\frac{3}{4}$ hours	4 hours	$4\frac{1}{2}$ hours
2.2 kg/$4\frac{3}{4}$ lb	2.6 kg/$5\frac{3}{4}$ lb	3.2 kg/7 lb	3.9 kg/$8\frac{1}{2}$ lb	4.5 kg/10 lb
1 tablespoon	2 tablespoons (U.S. 3 tablespoons)	2 tablespoons (U.S. 3 tablespoons)	2 tablespoons (U.S. 3 tablespoons)	2 tablespoons (U.S. 3 tablespoons)

Icings and Frosting

Whether you choose a soft, creamy butter icing or one that sets firmly and will support elaborate decorations, this coating transforms a good basic cake into an exciting confection.

Delicate glacé icings and all the variations on French Crème au beurre are meant to be made up and eaten within a few days. Therefore, they are the ideal partners for delicate sponge cakes of the whisked, fatless, feather, Genoese and Victoria sandwich varieties. You can often afford to make fillings softer and more exciting than the icing for coating and piping by adding a flavourful touch of liqueur or fruit juice, reserving the amount you require for finishing the cake.

To achieve a smooth surface on such cakes, it may be necessary not only to brush the cake lightly to remove loose crumbs, but to cover it thinly with a first coat, called the 'crumb coat' and allow this to set for about 1 hour before applying a thicker second coat. Icings intended to set hard and keep for a considerable period of time, are those made with egg white and icing sugar (U.S. confectioners' sugar), with the possible addition of other ingredients such as gelatine or liquid glucose, which give the icing a pliable consistency, making it easy to work with.

Take the advice given about allowing each stage of the work to set and harden before continuing, really to heart. Run-out decorations, for instance, can be handled safely, even if very delicate, provided they are quite dry. Don't be impatient, and err on the side of caution by making extras to allow for breakages, especially when transporting an elaborate cake.

Butter icing

100 g/4 oz (U.S. ½ cup) butter
225 g/8 oz icing sugar, sifted (U.S. 1¾ cups sifted confectioners' sugar)
about 1 tablespoon warm milk

1. Put the butter into a bowl and beat until creamy. Gradually beat in the sugar and add enough milk to give a smooth icing that holds its shape well.
2. Leave plain or flavour and colour as desired.
Makes about 350 g/12 oz

--- VARIATIONS ---

Vanilla or raspberry butter icing Beat in ¼ teaspoon vanilla or raspberry essence (U.S. extract). Tint raspberry icing pink with food colouring.
Coffee butter icing Omit the milk and beat in 1 tablespoon coffee essence (U.S. sweetened concentrated coffee flavoring) or 2 teaspoons instant coffee dissolved in 2 teaspoons hot milk or water.
Chocolate butter icing Omit the milk. Melt 25 g/1 oz plain chocolate (U.S. scant ¼ cup semi-sweet chocolate pieces) in a bowl over a pan of hot water and beat into the icing. Alternatively, blend 1 tablespoon cocoa powder (U.S. unsweetened cocoa) with just enough hot milk to make a thick cream and beat this into the icing with 2 drops vanilla essence (U.S. vanilla extract).
Orange or lemon butter icing Omit the milk and use instead 1 tablespoon orange or lemon juice and the finely grated rind from 1 orange or 1 lemon.
Nutty butter cream Beat 50 g/2 oz (U.S. ½ cup) finely chopped nuts such as walnuts, pecans, roasted peanuts or cashews, toasted hazelnuts (U.S. filberts) or almonds into the icing before spreading. If the butter icing is to be piped, grind the nuts very finely before adding them.
Mint butter icing Omit the milk and beat 1 tablespoon crème de menthe into the icing. Reinforce the green tint with a drop or two of green food colouring if wished.

Crème au beurre

75 g/3 oz caster sugar (U.S. ⅓ cup granulated sugar)
4 tablespoons (U.S. 6 tablespoons) water
2 egg yolks
100–175 g/4–6 oz (U.S. ½–¾ cup) butter, preferably unsalted

1. Put the sugar and water into a heavy pan and stir over gentle heat until the sugar has completely dissolved. Then boil to 110°C/225°F. To test the syrup without using a thermometer, take two teaspoons, holding them back to back. Dip the bowls into the syrup then draw sharply apart. If a thread forms between the two spoons the syrup has reached the correct stage.
2. Put the egg yolks into a bowl and whisk well. Gradually pour the syrup, in a thin stream, into the egg yolks, whisking constantly. Continue whisking until cold and thick.
3. Put the butter in a separate bowl and beat until creamy. Add the whisked mixture, a little at a time, beating constantly.
Makes enough to fill and cover top of (17.5–20-cm/7–8-inch 2-layer) cake

--- VARIATIONS ---

Chocolate crème au beurre Melt 50 g/2 oz plain chocolate (U.S. ⅓ cup semi-sweet chocolate pieces) with 1 tablespoon water in a bowl over a pan of hot water. Cool slightly then beat into the crème as soon as the egg mousse has been incorporated.
Coffee crème au beurre Add 1–2 tablespoons coffee essence (U.S. 2–3 tablespoons sweetened concentrated coffee flavoring) or cold strong black coffee when the basic crème has just been made.
Orange or lemon crème au beurre Add the finely grated rind of 1 orange or 1 lemon to the butter before beating in the egg mousse.

Custard crème au beurre

2 egg yolks
150 ml/¼ pint (U.S. ⅔ cup) milk
50 g/2 oz caster sugar (U.S. ¼ cup granulated sugar)
175–225 g/6–8 oz (U.S. ¾–1 cup) butter, preferably unsalted

1. Put the egg yolks in a bowl. Bring the milk just to the boil in a pan. Remove from the heat and stir in the sugar until dissolved. Pour gradually into the beaten egg yolks, whisking constantly. Stand the bowl over a pan of simmering water or transfer to the top of a double boiler. Cook, stirring all the time, until the mixture thickens. Remove from the heat, cover the bowl and leave until cold.
2. Beat the butter in a bowl until light and fluffy. Beat in the custard, a little at a time, until the crème au beurre is smooth and thick. This buttercream can be flavoured in the same way as classic Crème au beurre (see above).
Makes enough to fill and cover top of 1 (20–27.5-cm/8–9-inch 2-layer) cake

Coffee crunch gâteau (see page 80).

Seven minute frosting

(Illustrated above)

1 egg white
175 g/6 oz caster sugar (U.S. ¾ cup granulated sugar)
pinch of cream of tartar
pinch of salt
2 tablespoons (U.S. 3 tablespoons) water

1. Put all the ingredients into a bowl and whisk until foamy.
2. Stand the bowl over a pan of simmering water and continue whisking steadily until the icing stands in peaks. This usually takes about 7 minutes.
3. Use the frosting immediately.
Makes enough to cover top and sides of 1 (17.5–20-cm/7–8-inch) cake

Cloud cake

(Illustrated above)

Bake a 20-cm/8-inch ring Feather sponge cake (see page 20) flavoured with raspberry essence. Make up 1 quantity Seven minute frosting (see above) and tint it very pale pink with food colouring. Put the cake on a serving plate and immediately swirl the warm frosting over it to cover completely. Mark the surface decoratively with a knife blade and, just before the icing sets, sprinkle with coloured silver balls.

1–3 : Stages in making Seven-minute frosting.
4 : Cloud cake.

American frosting

450 g/1 lb (U.S. 2 cups) granulated sugar
150 ml/¼ pint (U.S. ⅔ cup) water
pinch of cream of tartar
2 egg whites
few drops vanilla essence (U.S. vanilla extract)

1. Place the sugar, water and cream of tartar in a heavy pan and heat gently, stirring, until the sugar has completely dissolved. Then boil steadily to 120°C/240°F, or until a little syrup dropped into cold water forms a ball which does not lose its shape on removal from the water.
2. Just before the syrup reaches the correct temperature, put the egg whites in a clean bowl and whisk until stiff. Remove the syrup from the heat and, as soon as the bubbles have subsided, pour it in a thin stream into the egg whites, whisking constantly, until the frosting is thick, opaque and stands in soft peaks. Whisk in the vanilla and use immediately.
Makes sufficient to coat 1 (17.5-cm/7-inch) tube cake, or 1 (20–22.5-cm/8–9-inch) cake

VARIATIONS FOR SEVEN MINUTE AND
AMERICAN FROSTINGS

Caramel frosting Use demerara sugar (U.S. brown sugar) in place of the white sugar and boil the syrup to 130°C/250°F. Omit the vanilla.
Ginger frosting Fold 75 g/3 oz (U.S. ½ cup) chopped preserved ginger into the frosting just before spreading.
Lemon frosting Omit the vanilla and whisk 2 tablespoons (U.S. 3 tablespoons) lemon juice into the frosting before it thickens. When ready to use, stir in the finely grated rind of 1 lemon.
Raspberry frosting Beat a few drops of raspberry food flavouring and pink food colouring into the frosting in place of the vanilla.

Toffee icing

100 g/4 oz (U.S. ½ cup) butter or margarine
100 g/4 oz soft brown sugar (U.S. ½ cup light brown sugar)
2 tablespoons golden syrup (U.S. 3 tablespoons light corn syrup)
1 (198-g/7-oz) can sweetened condensed milk (or half a 396-g/14-oz can)
50 g/2 oz plain chocolate, broken up (U.S. ⅓ cup semi-sweet chocolate pieces)

1. Put the butter, sugar, syrup and condensed milk in a medium-sized heavy-based pan. Heat gently, stirring constantly, until the sugar has dissolved. Bring slowly to the boil and simmer for 3 minutes, stirring rapidly all the time. The toffee should be pale golden brown.
2. Remove from the heat, add the chocolate and beat for 2–3 minutes.
3. Use this icing immediately it is made, spreading it over the cake while still warm. Leave to set.
Makes sufficient to coat top and sides of 1 (20-cm/8-inch) cake

Chocolate fudge frosting

115 g/4½ oz plain chocolate (U.S. ⅔ cup semi-sweet chocolate pieces)
75 g/3 oz (U.S. ⅓ cup) butter
150 g/5 oz soft brown sugar (U.S. ⅔ cup light brown sugar)
3 tablespoons single cream (U.S. 4 tablespoons light cream)
275 g/10 oz icing sugar, sifted (U.S. 2¼ cups sifted confectioners' sugar)

1. Put the chocolate in a bowl and stand this over a pan of hot water until the chocolate softens.
2. Put the butter, brown sugar and cream in a pan. Heat gently, stirring, until the sugar has dissolved. Add the chocolate and mix well. When well blended, boil for 3 minutes. Remove from the heat and gradually add the icing sugar. Beat constantly until the frosting is thick enough to spread. Use while still warm and spread with a palette knife (U.S. spatula) dipped in hot water and dried.
Makes enough to fill and cover 1 (20–22.5-cm/ 8–9-inch 2-layer) cake

Glacé icing

225 g/8 oz icing sugar, sifted (U.S. 1¾ cups sifted confectioners' sugar)
2–3 tablespoons hot water or fruit juice

1. Put the sugar into a bowl and add the liquid very gradually, mixing to a consistency that will coat the back of a spoon fairly thickly. Add a few drops of food colouring if required.
2. Use the icing quickly or keep the bowl closely covered to prevent a crust forming.
Makes enough to coat top of 1 (17.5–20-cm/ 7–8-inch) cake

VARIATIONS

Coffee glacé icing Replace 1–2 teaspoons of the chosen liquid with coffee essence (U.S. 2–3 teaspoons sweetened concentrated coffee flavoring) or very strong black coffee.

Chocolate glacé icing Sift 1 tablespoon cocoa powder (U.S. unsweetened cocoa) with the sugar before adding the liquid.

Orange glacé icing Use orange juice as the liquid when making up the icing and add a drop or two of orange food colouring to reinforce the colour.

Lemon glacé icing Use lemon juice in place of some or all of the liquid in the icing. Tint with yellow food colouring if wished.

Almond paste

225 g/8 oz (U.S. 2 cups) ground almonds
100 g/4 oz icing sugar, sifted (U.S. scant 1 cup sifted confectioners' sugar)
100 g/4 oz caster sugar (U.S. ½ cup granulated sugar)
1 egg or 2 egg yolks
¼ teaspoon almond essence (U.S. almond extract)
½ teaspoon lemon juice

1. Put the almonds and sugars into a bowl and mix thoroughly. Beat the egg with the almond essence and lemon juice and mix sufficient into the almond mixture to give a firm paste.
2. Wrap the almond paste in foil or in a plastic bag to prevent it drying out.
Makes about 450 g/1 lb

—————————— VARIATIONS ——————————

Economical almond paste Use 150 g/5 oz (U.S. 1¼ cups) ground almonds, 150 g/5 oz sifted icing sugar (U.S. 1¼ cups sifted confectioners' sugar) and 150 g/5 oz caster sugar (U.S. ⅔ cup granulated sugar). Make up as above, increasing the almond flavouring to ½ teaspoon.

White almond paste Use 2 egg whites in place of the egg or egg yolks. Break up with a fork until foamy but do not whisk before using.

Approximate quantity of Almond paste needed to cover cakes

Round cake	Square cake	Almond paste
12.5 cm/5 inch	10 cm/4 inch	225 g/8 oz
15 cm/6 inch	12.5 cm/5 inch	350 g/12 oz
17.5 cm/7 inch	15 cm/6 inch	450 g/1 lb
20 cm/8 inch	17.5 cm/7 inch	550 g/1¼ lb
22.5 cm/9 inch	20 cm/8 inch	800 g/1¾ lb
25 cm/10 inch	22.5 cm/9 inch	900 g/2 lb
27.5 cm/11 inch	25 cm/10 inch	1 kg/2¼ lb
30 cm/12 inch	27.5 cm/11 inch	1.1 kg/2½ lb
	30 cm/12 inch	1.4 kg/3 lb

Covering cakes with a professional touch

To coat cakes with Almond paste
A fruit cake should have a level top, but if it has sunk slightly, turn it over and use the bottom as the top. Either brush the top and sides with lightly beaten egg white or with warm sieved apricot jam. You will need half the almond paste for the top, the remainder for the sides. Keep the working surface, rolling pin and hands dusted with icing sugar (U.S. confectioners' sugar). Measure the circumference and height of the cake exactly with string, and use this as a guide to roll out and cut a strip to fit round the side. Stand the cake on a turntable, which will allow you to run the rolling pin round the sides and eliminate all signs of a join. Roll the strip up lightly, place one end against the cake and unroll round it, pressing it in place as you go. Roll out the remaining paste into a circle slightly larger than the circumference of the cake. Invert the cake on to it and press down lightly. (If the cake is more than 25 cm/10 inches, it may be easier to lift the paste on the rolling pin and let it unroll across the top of the cake.) Roll over gently with your pin to remove trapped air or level any bumps, drawing excess paste with a palette knife (U.S. spatula) up firmly against the side of the cake and return it to the original position. The paste-covered surface will now be on top.

The same method using very thin white almond paste, bought ready-to-roll icing or Fondant moulding paste (see page 35) can be used over Madeira or Genoese mixtures for decorated gâteaux intended for formal piping. This gives a good undercoat for glacé icing, which does not cover well enough to give a really smooth surface, and tastes delicious. Be sure to let almond paste dry out for at least 24 hours before icing. If a fruit cake is for long storage, allow almond paste to dry for 7 days, otherwise the oil in the almonds will eventually seep through and discolour the white icing. (In the case of gâteaux, this precaution is not necessary, as the cakes are intended to be eaten within a few days of decorating.)

An alternative is to brush the almond paste coat with lightly beaten egg white. Let this dry, which takes only 15 minutes, then ice immediately. The almond paste layer stays moist, without discolouring the outer coat of icing.

Leftover almond paste can be moulded into tiny fruit shapes, such as bananas, oranges and apples, then painted with food colourings.

Coating a fruit cake with Almond paste.

33

Royal icing

2 large egg whites
about 450 g/1 lb icing sugar, sifted (U.S. 3½ cups
sifted confectioners' sugar)
2 teaspoons lemon juice
about 1 teaspoon glycerine (optional)

1. Put the egg whites in a large clean bowl and whisk until foamy.
2. Sift the sugar a second time and start adding it to the bowl, a tablespoon at a time at first, beating constantly with a wooden spoon or with an electric mixer on medium speed. Add the lemon juice and the remaining sugar, beating steadily until the icing will just stand in peaks.
3. If glycerine is being added, put it in at this stage and beat for a further 1 minute.
4. Cover the bowl with a damp cloth and leave to stand for at least 2 hours before using so that as many air bubbles as possible will disperse.
Makes about 500 g/1 lb 2 oz

Royal icing using powdered egg white

about 450 g/1 lb icing sugar, sifted (U.S. 3½ cups
sifted confectioners' sugar)
15 g/½ oz (U.S. 2 tablespoons) powdered egg
white (albumen)
75 ml/3 fl oz (U.S. ⅓ cup) cold water

1. Sift half the sugar into a bowl. Stir the egg white into the water until completely dissolved. Pour into the sugar and beat until smooth. Gradually sift in as much of the remaining sugar as is necessary to give an icing that will just stand in peaks.
2. Cover and leave before using as above.
Makes about 500 g/1 lb 2 oz

Approximate quantity of Royal icing needed to flat ice cakes with two thin coats plus decoration.

Round cake	Square cake	Royal icing with
12.5 cm/5 inch	10 cm/4 inch	450 g/1 lb sugar
15 cm/6 inch	12.5 cm/5 inch	675 g/1½ lb sugar
17.5 cm/7 inch	15 cm/6 inch	900 g/2 lb sugar
20 cm/8 inch	17.5 cm/7 inch	1.1 kg/2½ lb sugar
22.5 cm/9 inch	20 cm/8 inch	1.4 kg/3 lb sugar
25 cm/10 inch	22.5 cm/9 inch	1.6 kg/3½ lb sugar
27.5 cm/11 inch	25 cm/10 inch	1.8 kg/4 lb sugar
30 cm/12 inch	27.5 cm/11 inch	2 kg/4½ lb sugar
	30 cm/12 inch	2.2 kg/5 lb sugar

Gelatine icing

If you prefer to make a quick-setting icing without white of egg, try this alternative. It covers well and can be thickened with additional icing sugar (U.S. confectioners' sugar) for piping. If you require to store it overnight in a sealed container, warm slightly before using, placing the bowl over hot water and beating until the right consistency is obtained. Do not overheat or the icing may crystallize.

1 teaspoon powdered gelatine (U.S. gelatin)
150 ml/¼ pint (U.S. ⅔ cup) hot water
450 g/1 lb icing sugar, sifted (U.S. 3½ cups sifted
confectioners' sugar)

1. Sprinkle the gelatine over the water and allow to stand for 2 minutes then stir well until completely dissolved. Leave to cool.
2. Place the sugar in a bowl and add about 2 tablespoons (U.S. 3 tablespoons) of the gelatine liquid. Beat well until it forms a thick icing similar in consistency to Royal icing.

Note Gauge quantities required by referring to the Royal icing chart opposite. Both these icings will be the correct consistency for flat icing cakes. If required for piping, extra sugar will be needed so that the icing will hold its shape well.

Satin icing paste

25 g/1 oz (U.S. 2 tablespoons) margarine
2 tablespoons (U.S. 3 tablespoons) lemon juice
350 g/12 oz icing sugar, sifted (U.S. 2⅔ cups
sifted confectioners' sugar)
extra sifted icing sugar (U.S. confectioners'
sugar) for sprinkling

1. Put the margarine in a medium-sized pan with the lemon juice. Heat gently until the margarine just melts but do not allow it to become more than just warm. Remove from the heat and stir in about a third of the sugar. Return the pan to low heat and stir until the sugar has dissolved and bubbles begin to form at the sides of the pan. Continue cooking for 2 minutes exactly.
2. Remove from the heat again and gradually add the remaining sugar, stirring until well combined, then beat with a wooden spoon until cooled. Turn out on a board sifted with more sugar and knead the paste well until smooth and pliable.
3. Use immediately or seal in a plastic bag and refrigerate until required. Allow to come up to room temperature and knead well before using.
Makes about 400 g/14 oz

Fondant moulding paste

450 g/1 lb icing sugar, sifted (U.S. 3½ cups sifted
confectioners' sugar)
50 ml/2 fl oz (U.S. ¼ cup) liquid glucose
1 egg white
1 teaspoon vanilla essence (U.S. vanilla extract)
sifted icing sugar (U.S. confectioners' sugar) for
dusting
sifted cornflour (U.S. cornstarch) for moulding

1. Place the sugar in a bowl, make a hollow in the
centre and put in the glucose, egg white and
flavouring. Working with a wooden spoon at first
and then with your hand, gradually mix, drawing in
the sugar as you go, until the paste is smooth.
2. Turn out on a surface lightly dusted with more
sugar and knead until smooth and satiny. Keep the
paste covered until required, to prevent it from
drying out.
3. When ready for use, knead the paste on a surface
dusted with sugar until it is again pliable and
smooth, using sifted sugar on the rolling pin. When
moulding icing over a cake or making separate
moulded decorations, dip fingers in sifted cornflour to keep icing free and 'polish' the surface of a
fondant-covered cake by smoothing with fingertips
again coated with cornflour.
Makes about 500 g/1 lb 2 oz

Coloured moulding paste Add food colouring to
the paste at the end of step 1, kneading constantly
until the colour is even with no streaks.

To coat cakes with Fondant moulding paste
Follow the general rules for almond paste; however
there are a few differences. The paste should be
rolled rather thickly, as if it is to be applied to the
cake without an undercoat of almond paste – the
surface would not otherwise be very smooth. Dust
rolling pin, hands and the surface on which you
work liberally with a mixture of one third cornflour
(U.S. cornstarch) and two-thirds icing sugar (U.S.
confectioners' sugar) – don't be afraid that this
might affect the flavour of the icing, it will be quite
undetectable.

It is very important to brush every part of the
surface of the cake with a glaze to make the icing
adhere, otherwise you may find large trapped air
bubbles. You will not need to cut a separate top and
side strip unless you are coating a square cake,
when you may feel you will get a better defined edge
by working as with almond paste. Generally, if you
lift the rolled paste on the rolling pin over the top of

*Stages in covering a square cake with ready-to-roll
icing or Fondant moulding paste,
Simple holly Christmas cake.*

the cake and drape it as you lower it, you will find no trouble in moulding the icing to the shape of the cake, although it is important to avoid the weight of surplus icing dragging a hole in the side. Smooth excess icing upwards rather than downwards, quickly trim off most of the surplus and keep smoothing with your palms and closed fingers rather than fingertips – perhaps rolling the top gently with your pin – until it is satiny.

Removing excess fondant paste

You will find, if you use the above method, that at each corner of a square cake, there is a small square of superfluous icing. Have ready a pair of scissors and snip away most of this icing, bringing two edges neatly together down each corner. Other cake shapes also have their differences, for example a hexagonal cake. Here you will need to snip away six smaller corners, more like elongated triangles. The secret is to remove equal quantities of icing at every point, do not bring it all together at one place.

When coating a heart-shaped cake, most of the surplus icing is at the top inner curve of the heart, with a little on either side of the point. Remember, unlike the edge of royal icing, tiny slivers can be pared away with a sharp knife until you have a good junction with the cake board.

Note Bought Ready-to-roll icing can be treated in exactly the same way as home-made Fondant moulding paste. It is sold in convenient 227-g/8-oz packs, each equal to $\frac{1}{2}$ quantity of the basic recipe.

To cover cakes with Royal icing

For good results, a turntable is really essential. First ice the sides, covering them with plenty of icing, working with a swirling motion to eliminate air pockets.

Round cakes Place a ruler upright against the side at the back with one hand, turn the table with the

To cover a cake with Royal icing.

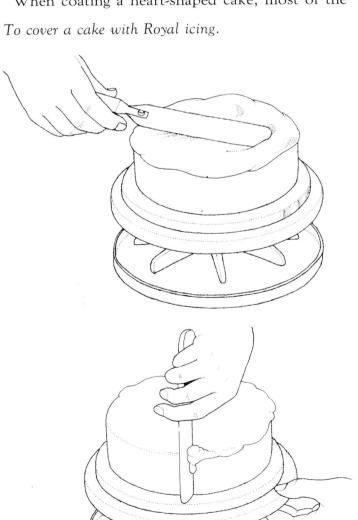

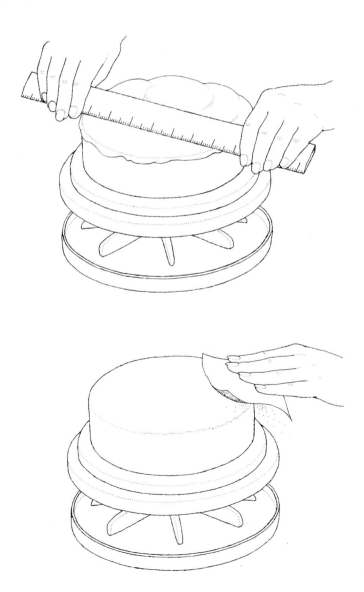

other, sweeping right round the cake as it turns without stopping. Be sure you place the ruler so that it will not clean away all the icing, but will leave a generous coating. Draw off the ruler at a slight angle to disguise the join. An icing scraper may be easier to use, because it is only about 15 cm/6 inches along the straight side and shaped for convenient holding on the other. Do not move the ruler or scraper, keep it still against the cake and move only the turntable. Cover the remaining icing with a damp cloth or with cling film to prevent a crust forming and wait at least 2 hours for the sides to harden before icing the top. Spoon out sufficient icing on the centre and swirl it out to the edges with a palette knife (U.S. spatula), as before. Holding the ruler well out to the ends, so that your fingertips will not touch the surface by mistake, run it across the top from back to front in one movement. The angle of the ruler must not be more than 45 degrees. Remove surplus icing from the side by rotating the turntable while holding a palette knife upright against the side. This is why you must let the icing on the sides dry first, or it will 'drag' when you clear surplus from the top. Allow to dry for at least 24 hours, longer if possible, before decorating. Any tiny irregularities may be smoothed off with very fine sandpaper and the powdery residue carefully brushed away.

Square cakes The method is similar, but first ice two opposite sides. Allow to dry for at least 2 hours before icing the other 2 opposite sides. To make right-angled corners, draw two palette knives upright against adjacent sides together.

Before decorating, position the cake on a silver or gold-coloured board. For heavy cakes the thick boards are essential, although thin ones will do for gâteaux or upper tiers.

Simple holly Christmas cake

(Illustrated below)

If you have no time in the busy days before Christmas to carry out a fancy piping design, just flat ice your cake with Royal icing or Fondant moulding paste. Pipe shells of royal icing round the top edge, scatter with multi-coloured sprinkles and place a sprig of holly leaves with red berries in the centre, as shown here, with leaves moulded from green tinted almond paste and glacé cherries (U.S. candied cherries) to represent the berries.

Stages in covering a heart-shaped cake
with ready-to-roll icing or
Fondant moulding paste.

Layered cake coverings

Sometimes a filling or soft icing is coated with another layer of a different texture and consistency. Here are some examples which produce particularly luscious results.

Double icing

Glacé icing does not always cover a bumpy cake surface well. To give a smooth result, it is better to cover large cakes or small fancies first with a thin layer of butter icing or even of fondant moulding paste or bought ready-to-roll icing. In the latter case, this will not adhere to the cake surface unless the crumb is first brushed with boiled and sieved apricot jam. Be liberal with the quantity of glacé icing used, and pour it over the 'undercoated' cake in the usual way.

Fancy raised surfaces

Small cakes can be made much more interesting by piping with a soft butter icing or crème au beurre before pouring on glacé icing. For instance, pipe a thick rope shape across the centre of each individual fancy so that the finished cake will have a raised ridge in the middle. Or pipe the shape of a pear cut in half and lying flat on the centre. When the glacé icing has been applied and is quite dry, you can paint in the shape of the pear with food colourings, ranging from greenish yellow to blush pink for the riper side of the fruit.

Note Chill piped shapes until quite firm before proceeding.

Contrasting decorations

Using butter icing tinted in a toning or contrasting colour, pipe the surface with rosettes or lattice-work, topped if liked with silver balls or fragments of crystallized flower petals. Do not be tempted to use any heavy decorations as glacé icing will not support the weight.

Chocolate accents

Drizzle melted chocolate from a paper icing bag in a fine zig-zag pattern, or in a spiral ending in the centre. Or, cover the top of a round cake with a layer of coffee butter icing, chill until very firm then pour over a layer of melted and slightly cooled cake covering from a pack which sets quickly giving a nice glossy finish.

Superhint *Don't be niggardly with glacé icing. Turn it almost all at once on to the centre of the cake and just help it with a palette knife (U.S. spatula) to spread evenly, including down the sides of the cake if this is desired. It is much less successful to use very little glacé icing, and then to add an overcoating.*

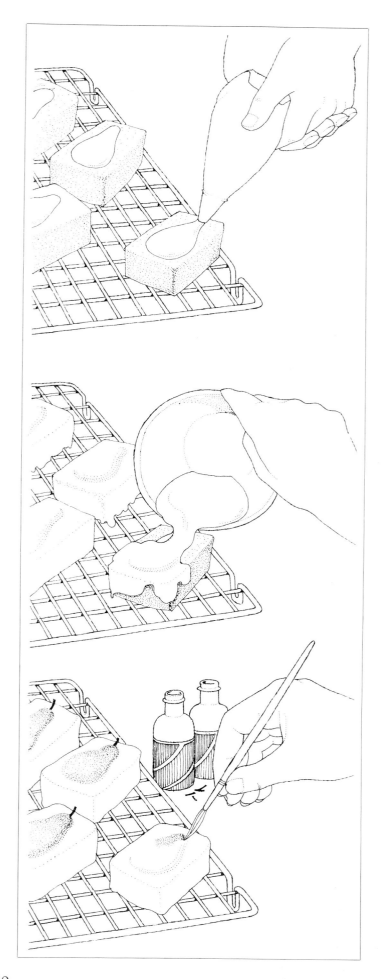

Drawing your own templates

It is comparatively easy to transform your inspiration for a design into a workable pattern. Make a rough sketch first of the complete scheme.

1. Cut a piece of greaseproof paper (U.S. waxed paper) exactly to fit the top of your cake, whatever its shape. Fold the paper into four or into eight if the design is elaborate and intended for a large cake. The edge may be star-shaped, formed by convex curves or concave curves like the ones shown here. Copy a section of the edge on to the folded paper and prick through this. Unfold and complete the edge design in pencil. Fold again and cut along the outline. Try out the template on your cake. If it is satisfactory, proceed to the next stage.

2. Refold the template. Copy any details of the design nearer the centre on it and prick through all the folds so that it is reproduced four or eight times. Open up the paper, complete the design in pencil, and lay it on the cake. Prick out the whole design, including the edge, holding the paper steady by fixing a pin in the centre or, if this is to be left clear, at four points round the edge. Remember your piping must cover all the pin pricks. You may

prefer to cut a shape out of thin card for the edge of the pattern and prick round this instead.

3. If the sides are to be covered with a ribbon, or left plain, you will not need a template for them. If they are part of the design, cut a strip exactly to fit the circumference and height of the iced cake and fold in four or eight as required. (For a square cake, fold in four sections only.) Copy the design for one section or side on one end of the paper strip, fold and mark the design with pin pricks. Unfold, and draw in. Fix the paper with pins where the marks will not show, and prick out the design.

4. You are now ready to begin piping, but don't discard the templates. Keep in a transparent plastic bag, labelled with the name and details of the design. For example, 'Template – 3 tier wedding cake, 15-cm/6-inch, 20-cm/8-inch and 25-cm/10-inch tiers'. You may need it again, or you can save time by slightly adjusting the pattern for future cakes.

5. Use a plastic cake marker when possible, as for concentric circles and flourishes, or refer to basic geometric patterns illustrated here, rather than drawing these free-hand. Accurate matching of each section of the design goes far to produce a professional-looking result.

40

Star template

Petal template

Curved

Heart

Square scallop

Turret

Piping and Modelling Techniques

It is easy to buy all sorts of decorations to dress up a flat iced cake, but once you have mastered the various arts described in this chapter, you will experience the glow of achievement which comes from the knowledge that 'it is all your own work'.

As you progress, you will probably find that you prefer to use a syringe or material bag for piping jobs which require large quantities of icing, and small paper piping bags (see page 12) for the finishing touches. Try out the techniques of making dots, pearls, teardrops, rosettes, shells, scrolls and so on, on a clean laminated working surface until you gain confidence.

Even if you are not economical enough to scrape up the pipings and return them to the bag for re-use, it requires only 1 egg white and 225 g/8 oz (U.S. 1¾ cups) sugar to give yourself a quantity large enough to make many experiments. Sometimes you may feel inspired to pipe a greeting or name free-hand, and find yourself disappointed with the result. It is well worth while to trace the letters and prick them out through the tracing so that the words are evenly spaced and the letters of the same height.

Modelling items from the smallest flower to quite large figures is something very different from piping, and it is so easy with Fondant moulding paste (see page 35) or bought Ready-to-roll icing. On the whole, the best results come from tinting the icing the required colour rather than painting the moulded shapes after forming them.

How to fill and use piping bags

Using a cloth piping bag Hold in one hand with the tube downwards and the top half of the bag turned back in a cuff over your hand. With the other hand, spoon in icing, shaking it down until it settles, and continue until the bag is half full. Support the tube, so that icing does not fall out, and twist the bag just above the level of icing. Support the weight of the bag with one hand, pressing out and controlling the flow of icing with your fingers. Steady and direct the tube near the bottom of the bag with the other hand, cupping it in your palm.

Using a paper icing bag This will be too small and the material too stiff to turn down. Just fill it halfway, and close the bag by folding in the two corners at the top to the middle, then the top over the folded corners, very gently pressing the icing into the tube. Support the hand that holds the bag in the palm of your other hand, which may rest on the table to steady both hands. Press out icing with your thumb. Or support the bag with both hands together, bringing the thumbs together to push out icing. Test on a board, or table top, until the flow is smooth and regular.

Line work and borders

By changing piping tubes you can produce innumerable different effects with royal icing. Some tubes can be used to give more than one result, according to the amount of pressure you exert. Opposite are some examples of a variety of finishes using a small collection of popular tubes.

If you are using paper icing bags (see page 12), make up a quantity of them. If the bag splits and begins to ooze icing, you should not have to abandon the work while you make up another bag. Have several always at the ready!

Although there are literally dozens of different tubes to choose from, most designs require only a few tubes. For example, a star tube produces shells, rosettes, coiled ropes and scrolls. By pressing longer and slightly harder without raising the tube, a larger shape is produced. Shells can be elongated by pulling the tube gradually away to a point, which makes an impressive border (see Noel Cake, page 149).

Lattice and lace work

A trellis (diagonal) or lattice (square) design requires a steady hand to keep the lines straight, but provides excellent coverage for large areas, or to disguise parts of the icing that are not quite smooth and regular. Begin with one set of parallel lines, using a No. 1 or 2 tube, spaced about 6 mm/¼ inch apart. If the measured length of the first line is 7.5 cm/3 inches, continue until the distance across the parallel lines is 7.5 cm/3 inches. Pipe a straight line from the left-hand top corner to the right-hand

lower corner. Fill in parallel lines on either side, joining each time to the tip of a piped upright. This method helps you to keep the trellis work even.

With lattice, it helps you to achieve a good square shape if you pipe in one parallel line about four 'boxes' down the lattice first, and then fill in the intermediary lines. After that, continue, watching always that the end of each crossing line straggles neither upwards nor downwards. Surround the trellis or lattice with a fine line to give it a definite edge. To add importance, when the trellis or lattice is dry, overpipe with a second set of lines in the same colour or a contrasting colour.

Maze or random lace pattern

Fill in the edge of the cake board with a thin layer of icing covered with a maze, or use a maze pattern on the cake to give interest to areas not otherwise decoratively piped. Use a writing tube, either very small in size or larger to complement the rest of the scheme. Pipe a continuous line as long as possible, moving the tube around in random swirls and working always sideways or towards yourself. Use a turntable to help you move constantly on to uncovered areas. Maze pattern needs a fine border line, or small rosettes, to give it a finish.

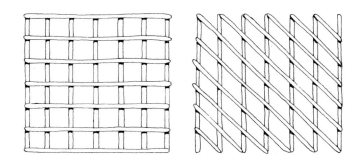

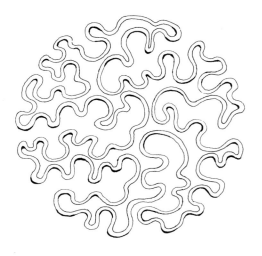

Lattice, trellis and random lace.

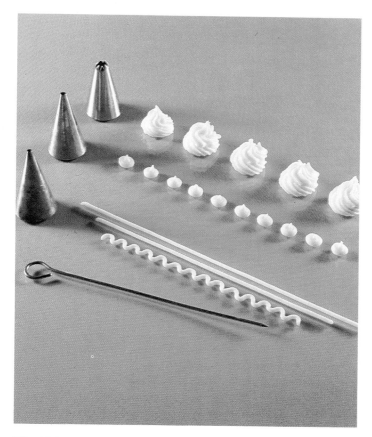

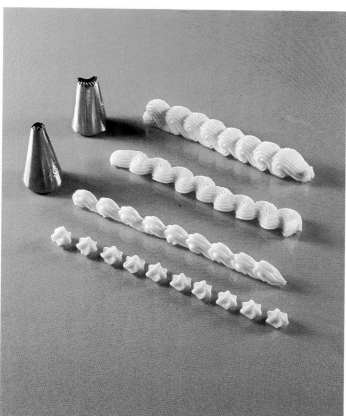

Before carrying out a design on a cake, plan the finished effect by experimenting with tubes in different ways. For example, you can produce large, dramatic flower shapes or small delicate flower heads from royal icing with the same tube, as shown above. To become expert in the design of your choice, pipe a number of the shapes you will be using on a board first to develop fluency and confidence.

Piped flowers and leaves

Royal icing is essential to make these successfully. When dry, the shapes become very hard and durable, can be handled if sufficient care is used, and stored in boxes for months. The colours do not change or fade, but they can be pearlized when mounted on a cake with blusher powder. As they remain rather brittle, store between sheets of lightly crumpled tissue paper and do not compress the layers as you pack them.

To make flat piped flowers Have plenty of 5-cm/2-inch squares of non-stick baking parchment (U.S. waxed paper) ready, and your piping bag fitted with a petal tube and filled with the right shade and consistency of icing. Attach one piece of paper to an icing nail with a dab of icing. Hold the nail upright with one hand and press the thick side of the tube to the centre of the paper. Press out a petal, pivoting the tube around the central point. Release pressure and withdraw the tube. Twirl the nail towards you clockwise and pipe another petal anti-clockwise, slightly overlapping the first. Match the shape of petals to the natural flower, giving it the correct number of petals and rounded, ragged or elongated edge. For instance, the sweet pea is made with an almost oval single petal and then a smaller, tighter one on top. Pipe in centres, stamens and sepals, then paint in further details when the flower is dry.

To make leaves Use a leaf tube, press on to the centre of the paper and pull away steadily to form a point of the desired length. Move the tube lightly forwards and back to form veins in the leaf. To make leaves variegated in colour, fill first one side of the bag and then the other, using two shades of icing. As for writing and forming fine linework, a paper bag can be used without a tube, merely by snipping off the end. For simple leaves, snip off at an angle and place the point first to the paper.

To make raised piped flowers Prepare the icing bag fitted with a large petal tube and papers as above. Fix one paper to the nail. Press the tube firmly against the paper, so that it dents the icing holding it to the nail. Begin with a small cone, coiling a ribbon of icing towards yourself and simultaneously turning the nail away from you. Finish off, so that you have a wider base than the curved top which should show a tight spiral. To make the first separate petal, pipe out a half circle against the cone, fanning out the centre to turn back the edge very slightly. Overlap the next 3–4 petals, forming a complete circle. This makes a small rose. Full-blown roses need 5–7 petals, each increasing in size. (To make a rosebud, add one small petal only, wrapped round the cone.)

Piping borders and flowers.

To make daises As an aid, draw in a circle the size of the finished flower on the paper. According to the size required, use a small or large writing tube, press it down firmly at the centre, drawing out the icing to finish in a point at the edge of the circle Turn the nail fractionally and pipe in another petal. As you complete the petals, turn the nail evenly so that each one radiates out correctly from the centre. Pipe a tiny dot in the centre and colour this yellow later. Or, have ready another bag of icing tinted yellow and use it to pipe in all the centres when you have made enough daisies. For a brighter effect, use a silver ball, pressed in before the icing sets, or mimosa balls for larger daisies.

To make two-toned flowers Either fill the bag with two different icings (for instance mauve and yellow or brown for pansies) so that the petals are variegated, or paint in the second colour later (see pages 48–49).

To pipe small flowers and leaves directly on to a cake

Use a small writing tube. To make forget-me-knots, pipe 5 pale blue dots in a circle, just touching, and one pale yellow dot in the centre. To make tiny daisies, pipe 7 teardrops, with the same tube using white icing, radiating out from one yellow dot. Very tiny flowers are best made without centres.

Leaves can be piped straight on to the cake, to fill out a design of applied flowers and to cover icing used to anchor flowers in place. Very small leaves can be made by piping teardrop shapes singly, joined or on either side of a thin line to represent a stem. They can also be made by piping teardrops of pale green icing between flower heads.

With all these free-hand piping techniques, practise first on a board.

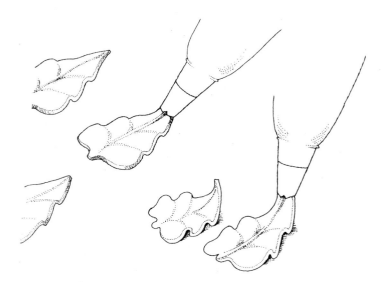

Making run-outs

This process is not difficult, if the shapes are allowed to 'rest' long enough to set really hard before being eased away from the paper. It is always advisable to make such decorations separately and fix them in place later, as it is quite tricky to pipe the outline and flood with softer icing on the cake.

1. Draw your design, such as a heart or a sporting motif, on a piece of thin card. Place under a sheet of non-stick baking parchment (U.S. waxed paper). Trace over it lightly with a pencil, move the paper and trace again as many times as necessary, making a few extra to allow for breakages. Or, if you are experienced enough, use a No. 1 or 2 writing tube and pipe a continuous outline on the parchment without tracing, keeping it weighted so that it does not move. Then continue as above, thus eliminating one stage of the work. Make the joins extra neat, to get a perfect outline.

2. Allow the outlines to dry while you thin down the icing with a few drops of water or egg white so that you can run it from a spoon into the centre of the shape. With a fine skewer, help the icing to fill the shape fully, but not to overflow the edge. If any air bubbles appear, prick them with a pin.

3. Allow the sheets to dry for at least 24 hours, then carefully slip a palette knife (U.S. spatula) under the edge of one shape. If it comes away still slightly damp underneath, leave at least 12 hours longer. Large run-outs are better detached by placing the paper on a board or thin book. Hold the paper firm with one hand and slide the book away, stripping the paper off as the underside is exposed.

Lace edgings

Small lace edgings can be piped out on non-stick baking parchment (U.S. waxed paper) and moved when dry, as they are usually attached sticking out at an angle from the side or top of the cake. Draw a line on waxed paper and, using the ruler again, mark points about 2.5-cm/1-inch apart, 1.25 cm/½ inch above this line. Using a No. 1 writing tube, pipe 1.25-cm/½-inch bases for the motifs, top with three half-circles, then two, then one, pyramid fashion, with its own centre on the mark above the base line. Pipe out about twice as many motifs as you think you will need, as some will break when being removed or may need replacing when the cake is moved. Allow to dry for several hours, then loosen with a palette knife (U.S. spatula) and fix with royal icing.

Making 'collars' to extend cake surfaces
Collars for square cakes You will need four, one to fit over each corner; or for large cakes eight, of which four will be centred on the straight sides. The

Making and finishing separate cake decorations.

48

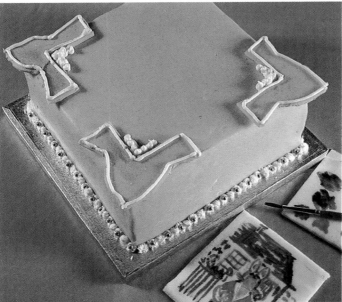

inner edge of a corner collar should be a right angle. The inner edge of a side collar should be straight. Trace off the template shape opposite, varying the size and curves of the outer design according to your own fancy, on to thin card. You can then either place traced templates under non-stick baking parchment (U.S. waxed paper) and outline them to make run-outs, moving the template as often as necessary to make the required number of run-outs and at least one extra for breakage. Fill in (see pages 48–49) and allow to set hard before moving the shapes. Or you can roll out some Fondant moulding paste fairly thinly and cut round your pattern. Move each shape on to non-stick baking parchment to dry and leave for several days if possible, when they will be quite hard.

Carry out the basic decoration, such as outlining with a writing tube. Fix the shapes in place with dabs of icing, remembering that not too much of the collar should protrude beyond the edge of the cake because it may tend to 'droop' or break. Add any further decoration such as the butterflies shown here, when the collars are firmly set. You can then decide whether to strengthen the outlines with further piping.

Collars for round cakes Follow the same instructions but make inner edges curved to follow the shape of the cake top. Again the size of the cake will determine how many collars are required evenly spaced out round the edge.

Easter egg cake

Make up 1½ quantities Fondant moulding paste (see page 35), reserve about one sixth and tint the rest a spring-like shade of green. Place a 17.5-cm/7-inch square Madeira cake (see page 116) on a 22.5-cm/9-inch square silver-coloured cake board and brush with apricot glaze as directed in Dreamy butterfly cake. Trace off the shape for the collar from page 51 and use this to make a template from thin card. Roll out a third of the green fondant and cut 4 collars. Gather up the trimmings, knead into the remaining green fondant and use to flat ice the cake (see page 35). Roll out the white fondant and trim to fit a piece of thin card measuring 12.5 cm/5 inches by 10 cm/4 inches. Brush the icing with a little egg white and stick it to the card. Leave the cake, collars and plaque to dry. Trace off an appropriate design from an Easter card and prick this out on the plaque. Using a fine paint brush and food colourings diluted with water, fill in the design, outlining details with an icing pen if desired. Make

Dreamy butterfly cake in preparation.
Easter egg cake in preparation.

up 1 quantity Royal icing (see page 34). Position the plaque in the centre of the cake and affix with dots of icing. Using a No. 2 tube, outline the collars, then make a decorative border around the cake. Pipe beads evenly all round the base and a second row above alternate beads. Top single beads with silver balls. Affix the collars 6 cm/¼ inch in from each corner with dabs of icing. Pipe tiny beads round the plaque and inner angle of each collar. Using royal icing and a medium-sized star tube, pipe out a 'nest' in the centre of each top side edge of the cake. When dry, fill each one with 5 sugar eggs. Remove the plaque before cutting the cake.

Dreamy butterfly cake

Tint 1¼ quantities Fondant moulding paste (see page 35) very pale pink. Copy the collar shape on pages 48–49, making the inner sides of the template 8 cm/3¼ inches. Roll out half the fondant and cut 4 collars using the template. Gather up the trimmings and knead them into the remaining fondant. Place a 17.5-cm/7-inch square Madeira cake (see page 116) on a 22.5-cm/9-inch square silver-coloured board, brush with 225 g/8 oz (U.S. ⅔ cup) apricot jam, boiled and sieved, then flat ice with the pink fondant (see page 35). Make up 1 quantity Royal icing (see page 34) and tint half of it a slightly deeper shade of pink. Make 8 pink butterfly 'wing' flooded plaques using the right and left wing designs. Pipe 30 pieces of lace edging in pink (see page 48). To make the butterfly 'bodies', mark a line 2.5 cm/1 inch long on a piece of parchment. With pink royal icing and a No. 2 tube, pipe along the line 3 times so that the lines of icing are side by side and touching. Using the same tube, pipe a tight looped zig-zag over the lines, to cover them, and finish one end with a small bead for the butterfly head. Make 3 more bodies. With the same tube, pipe dots as shown around the edge of the collars. Leave all to dry. To finish the cake, put the white royal icing in a piping bag fitted with a medium-sized star tube and pipe a row of rosettes all round the base. Pipe a second row immediately above the first row on the side of the cake. Pipe a small pink dot on alternate rosettes in the first row. Finish the top corners by affixing the collars 6 mm/¼ inch in from the edge, securing with dabs of icing. Pipe a double line of icing, long enough to affix a pair of butterfly wings at an angle close together. Place the 'body' over the central join. Decorate the remaining corners of the cake with butterflies in the same way. Fix 3 pieces of lace edging along the inner edge of the collars with dots of white icing, and place a single piece of edging at each base corner.

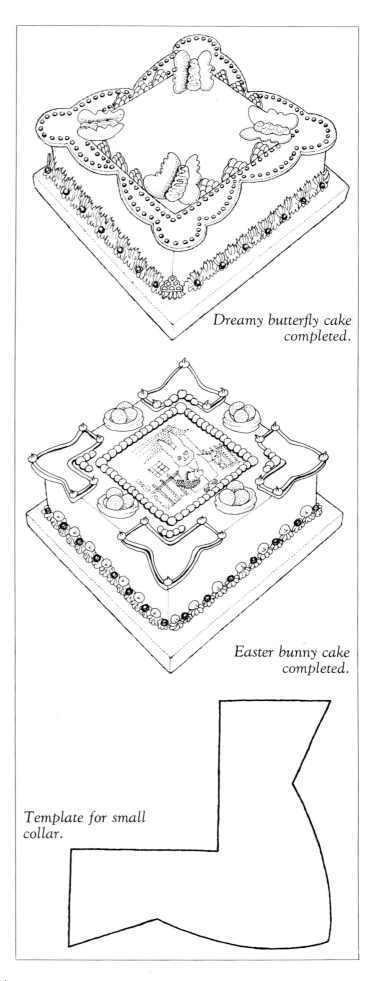

Dreamy butterfly cake completed.

Easter bunny cake completed.

Template for small collar.

How to make moulded decorations

Moulding paste and bought ready-to-roll icing have the advantage that suitably protected they can be kept for months and then kneaded again ready for use. Seal closely in cling film, then put the ball of covered icing in a plastic bag. Almond paste can also be coloured and moulded in exactly the same way as fondant moulding paste.

Any moulded decorations that require to be curved can be given the correct shape by drying off draped over the cups of an inverted bun tin, or resting against the sides of the bun shapes themselves. Larger curves, such as for a basket (see page 113), can be given by laying the flat icing over a rolling pin. For small curves, lay over the handle of a wooden spoon. Remove when quite firm.

To make holly leaves
Roll out tinted icing or almond paste between two sheets of non-stick baking parchment (U.S. waxed paper). Using a 5-cm/2-inch fluted cutter, cut out a circle. Move the cutter along the surface and stamp out an oval-shaped leaf from one side of the circle and a second one from the other side. Mark in the veins with a knife blade and pinch the points of the leaves with your fingers to make a good shape. Place over the handle of a wooden spoon and allow to dry off so that the leaves are slightly curved.

To mould Christmas roses
Make some cardboard drying rings, sufficient for all the roses you will need. Cut lengths of thin card about 11 cm/4½ inches long and 1.25 cm/½ inch wide, form them into rings and secure with tape. Arrange on a clean worktop. Each rose needs five petals, all the same size and shape.
Roll a piece of moulding paste into a ball the size of a pea. Press it out into a petal shape as for a rose. Place in a ring, base at bottom and edge of petal curling back over the ring. Make four more petals and place them overlapping to complete the circle and fill the base completely. Press down in the centre so that the petals stick together. Make up the total number of roses required in this way. When the flowers are quite firm, remove from the rings. Using a No. 1 writing tube and royal icing tinted pale yellow, pipe a circle of 'teardrops' in the centre of each rose for the stamens.

Stages in moulding holly leaves.

To mould primroses

Mould a number of elongated shapes from balls of yellow fondant, each the size of a small cherry. Make a cut across the top half-way down, but off centre. Snip into two petals on the small side, three on the large side. Bend out the petals, taking care not to snap them off, working them thin between thumb and forefinger. Cut out a tiny nick from the centre of each petal. When dry, paint in the centre with darker yellow or a spot of brown food colouring, and add a ring of pale green colouring if you wish.

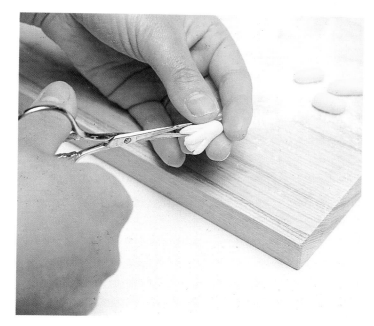

To mould simple white daisies

Make a ball of icing as for Primroses and snip into six sections. Fold back each section, pinching it into an elongated petal. Press a tiny ball of yellow icing into the centre of each flower.

To mould snowdrops

Each snowdrop requires five small oval white petals. Shape the first petal round a cocktail stick (U.S. toothpick) and the second petal overlapping this on both sides. Withdraw the stick and mould the other three petals round the 'heart' of the flower. Cover the base with a thin moulding of pale green paste and make a short stem. Dry off as for roses (see page 54).

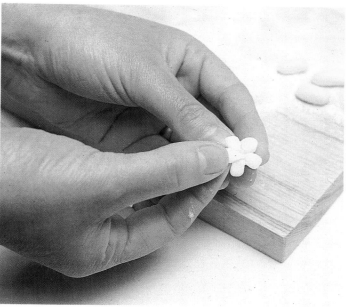

To mould bell-like flowers

For bluebells, take a small ball of icing about the size of a large pea and press the end of a paintbrush into it. Remove gently, snip out tiny triangles all round the edge and turn these points up until they curl back like petals. You will need a number of these flower heads to make up one complete bluebell.

Superhint *Moulding flowers and other shapes is easier than you might expect, but do work the icing well with your hands until it becomes soft and pliable. Cold icing does not mould well, and the warmth of your hands is an advantage here.*

Stages in moulding primroses.

To mould roses

These look more natural if different shades of icing are used (see Golden rose basket pages 106–107). To make simple yellow roses, tint the icing all the same colour. To make shaded roses, shape the buds of the darkest colour, the first three petals of the medium shade and the outer petals of the palest. Remember the flowers will dry a shade or two darker than when first made. Knead the icing until very smooth and evenly coloured, and keep in a plastic bag while not in use.

Take tiny amounts of the icing and press between the thumb and a finger (which should be dipped in cornflour (U.S. cornstarch) to prevent sticking) to make circles in graduated sizes 1.25 cm/$\frac{1}{2}$ inch up to 2.5 cm/1 inch. They must be paper thin especially at the edges. Twist a small circle round to form the centre of the flower, then gradually attach individual petals, each a little larger than the previous one and twist them round the flower, opening out the top of the petals to make a realistic rose. A large rose will need about 5–7 petals; a medium-sized rose 3–4 petals and a rosebud only the centre and one petal. Arrange the flowers on non-stick baking parchment (U.S. waxed paper) and leave to dry in a warm place for at least 24 hours and preferably longer. When completely dry, remove from the parchment and store in boxes with sheets of crumpled tissue between the layers. Do not compress the layers when packing.

To make sugar bells

You will require two or three small plastic bell decorations. Mix granulated sugar with egg white until the mixture resembles damp sand. Pack into the bells and leave for about 25 minutes. Knock each shape out of the bell and place carefully on non-stick baking parchment (U.S. waxed paper) until the outside is hard but the centre is still damp. Scrape out the damp inner centres to leave an even thickness bell-shaped 'shell'. Insert a short length of gift-tie ribbon, secure with a dot of fondant and shape a 'clanger' of fondant round the other end (see page 149).

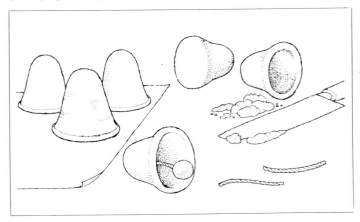

Stages in moulding roses.

LETTERS AND NUMERALS TO TRACE.

ABCDEFGHIJK
LMNOPQRSTU
VWXYZ
abcdefghijklm
nopqrstuvwxyz
1234567890

Merry Christmas

Happy Birthday

Chocolate decorations

Melted chocolate is very easy to work with and produces most attractive decorations. Always melt it in a bowl over a pan of hot water and do not allow the water to boil or it may spoil the texture of the chocolate. Melt-in-the-bag chocolate-flavour cake coverings are even easier to use as you need only pop the sealed bag in water until the chocolate is fully melted. If necessary, pour the melted chocolate into a paper icing bag (see page 12) and snip off the end. If using melt-in-the-bag, merely cut off a corner of the pack.

Piped numbers and letters Draw these on non-stick baking parchment (U.S. waxed paper) and overpipe with chocolate. Leave to set then peel the parchment away from the back of the shapes. Do not handle with your fingers as the warmth of your hand will melt them.

Chocolate leaves Choose unblemished rose or other leaves all of the same size and coat the undersides thinly with chocolate. Repeat the coating at least once to make a firm decoration. When set, peel off the leaves.

Cut-outs and curls Spread the melted chocolate evenly in a thin layer on a sheet of non-stick baking parchment (U.S. waxed paper) and allow to set. But before it becomes too hard, stamp out shapes such as hearts, crescent moons, etc. with fancy cutters. Curls are best made before the chocolate is too hard. Shave the surface into long curls using a sharp straight-bladed knife. Chill the decorations until needed.

Left: Spider's web cake (see page 89).
Below: Making chocolate decorations.

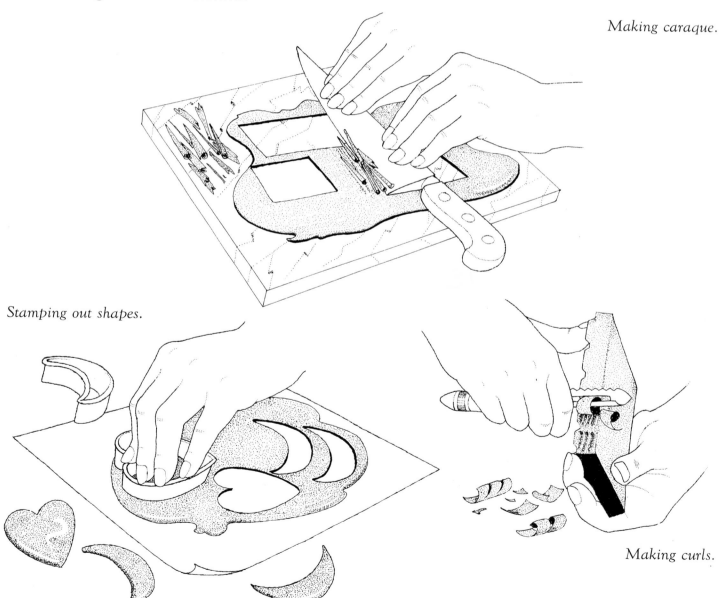

Making caraque.

Stamping out shapes.

Making curls.

57

Decorated Gâteaux

Many an expert started her career in cake decorating with simple gâteaux, rather than more formally iced cakes. Although the design for a gâteau should be definite and neatly carried out, it is far from rigid and does not require as much patient care and pre-planning to achieve.

There is no need to wait until you have mastered all the techniques of covering and piping. Begin with a plain two-layer sponge cake, put together with fresh jam, and whipped cream or butter icing. Lay a lace doily over the top, sprinkle icing sugar (U.S. confectioners' sugar) evenly over it through a fine sieve and lift off the doily upwards with one firm gesture for a simple, effective pattern.

Or try another way; spread butter icing thickly and as smoothly as you can over the top of the cake, using a flat blade dipped in hot water and well shaken dry. Make sure you keep the edge of the icing round; do not distort the circle so that it becomes lopsided.

Take an icing comb and draw it straight across the top from one side to the other. Don't hesitate in the middle, continue boldly right across. Now the edge of the circle may not be as neat as it was. Restore the shape by outlining with chocolate dots, buttons or walnut halves. With practice, you can go on to make such specialities as a Magyar Dobostorte.

You will find that most gâteaux are based on sponge cakes of the Victoria sandwich or Genoese variety. They are not intended for long keeping, unless well wrapped and frozen, but when coated and decorated will retain their freshness for at least a week.

Left: Crescent moon gâteau (see page 66)
Right: Ring-a-rosy gâteau (see page 67).

Lemon curd cheesecake

(Illustrated below)

BASE

50 g/2 oz (U.S. ¼ cup) butter or margarine
25 g/1 oz caster sugar (U.S. 2 tablespoons
granulated sugar)
40 g/1½ oz plain flour (U.S. scant ⅓ cup all-
purpose flour), sifted
40 g/1½ oz (U.S. scant ½ cup) rolled oats

FILLING AND DECORATION

225 g/8 oz curd cheese (U.S. ½ cup cream cheese
combined with ½ cup sieved cottage cheese)
finely grated rind of 1 lemon
1 tablespoon lemon juice
25 g/1 oz plain flour (U.S. ¼ cup all-purpose
flour)
75 g/3 oz caster sugar (U.S. ⅓ cup granulated
sugar)
2 eggs, separated
200 ml/7 fl oz double cream (U.S. scant 1 cup
heavy cream)
about 3 tablespoons (U.S. 4 tablespoons) lemon
curd

1. Heat the oven to 180°C/350°F, Gas Mark 4 and have ready a 17.5-cm/7-inch loose-based cake tin.
2. To make the base, cream the butter and sugar together in a bowl until light and fluffy. Stir in the flour and oats to form a stiff mixture. Press this into the base of the tin and level the surface. Bake for 10 minutes.
3. Meanwhile, beat together the cheese, lemon rind and juice then gradually add the flour, sugar, egg yolks and 150 ml/¼ pint (U.S. ⅔ cup) of the cream. Beat well. Whisk the egg whites in a clean bowl until stiff and fold in gently but thoroughly. Pour over the cooked base.
4. Reduce the oven temperature to 160°C/325°F, Gas Mark 3 and bake the cheesecake for 1 hour. Leave in the tin until cold.
5. Spread the lemon curd over the surface and mark wavy lines in the topping with a fork. Whip the remaining cream and place in a piping bag fitted with a small star tube. Pipe a continuous scroll of cream around the edge of the cheesecake.
Serves 6–8

Lemon curd cheesecake.

Feather-iced nut gâteau

(Illustrated below)

CAKE
ingredients for 2 (20-cm/8-inch) layers Orange
Victoria sandwich (see page 20)
50 g/2 oz flaked almonds (U.S. ½ cup slivered
almonds), toasted and chopped
FILLING AND DECORATION
about 2 tablespoons (U.S. 3 tablespoons) orange
juice
1 quantity coffee Butter icing (see page 28)
50 g/2 oz flaked almonds (U.S. ½ cup slivered
almonds), toasted and chopped
1 quantity coffee Glacé icing (see page 31)
40 g/1½ oz icing sugar, sifted (U.S. ⅓ cup sifted
confectioners' sugar)

1. Bake the cake layers, folding the nuts into the mixture before transferring it to the prepared tins. Turn out on a wire rack to cool and remove the lining paper.

2. Beat half the orange juice into the butter icing and use about two-thirds to sandwich the cakes together. Spread the remainder over the sides of the cake and coat in the nuts. Place the cake on a serving plate.

3. Make up the coffee glacé icing, pour over the top of the cake and spread quickly to make a neat round shape. While the icing is still wet, mix enough of the remaining orange juice into the icing sugar to make an icing the same consistency as the coffee glacé icing. Place in a paper piping bag (see page 12). Snip off the tip of the bag and pipe ten parallel lines of orange icing across the top of the cake. Feather the icing by drawing a fine skewer six times across the lines, three times in one direction and then three times in the other. Leave to set before serving.
Serves 8

Feather iced nut gâteau.

Diagonal piped fruit sponge

(Illustrated opposite)

CAKE
1 (22.5-cm/9-inch) square Genoese sponge (see
page 18)
FILLING AND DECORATION
1 tablespoon Kirsch or pineapple juice
100 ml/4 fl oz (U.S. ½ cup) apricot or pineapple
jam
2 (35-g/1¼-oz) sachets cream topping mix
225 ml/8 fl oz (U.S. 1 cup) cold milk
75 g/3 oz flaked almonds (U.S. ¾ cup slivered
almonds), toasted
about 225 g/8 oz black grapes (U.S. about ½ lb
purple grapes), halved

1. Split the cake into two layers. Stir the liqueur
into the jam and use to sandwich the cake layers
together. Place on a serving dish.
2. Make up the topping mixes with the specified
quantity of milk to give a stiff piping consistency.
Spread some on the top and sides of the cake, then
coat the sides with almonds. Place the remaining
topping mix in a piping bag fitted with a large star
tube.
3. Mark the top of the cake lightly in diagonal lines
with the tip of a knife blade. Using these marks as a
guide, pipe five lines of shells on the cake. Between
these lines, pipe straight lines of topping. Remove
any pips (U.S. pits) from the grapes and arrange the
halves neatly in rows on the straight lines of
topping.
Serves 9

Diagonal piped fruit sponge.

Marking in parallel lines.

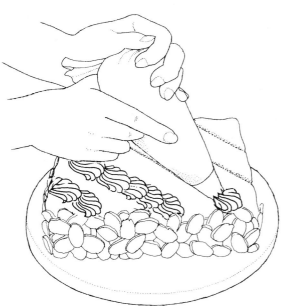

Piping in the shells.

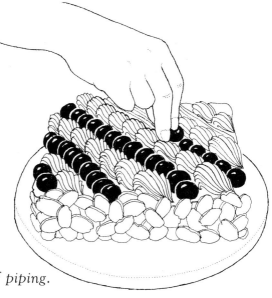

Placing grapes over straight line of piping.

Toffee walnut cake

(Illustrated opposite)

FILLING
75 g/3 oz (U.S. ⅓ cup) butter
175 g/6 oz icing sugar, sifted (U.S. 1⅓ cups sifted
confectioners' sugar)
25 g/1 oz (U.S. ¼ cup) finely chopped walnuts or
pecans
CAKE
2 (20-cm/8-inch) layers Victoria sandwich cake
(see page 20)
ICING AND DECORATION
1 quantity Toffee icing (see page 31)
50 g/2 oz (U.S. ½ cup) chopped walnuts or
pecans
fresh or silk flowers and butterfly decoration

1. To make the filling, beat the butter and sugar together and, when smooth, add the nuts. Use to sandwich the cake layers together and place on a serving dish.
2. Make up the Toffee icing, pour it over the cake and spread to cover the top and sides evenly. Leave to cool. Press the nuts around the sides of the cake. Decorate the top with flowers and the butterfly.
Serves 6–8

—————————— VARIATION ——————————

Toffee orange sandwich Make up 2 layers of Orange Victoria sandwich and flavour the filling with the finely grated rind of 1 orange and enough orange juice to give the icing a smooth piping consistency. Tint it pale orange with food colouring if wished. Omit the nuts in the filling and around the sides of the cake. Put the cake layers together with about a third of the icing and cover with toffee icing as in the main recipe. When cold, put the remaining orange icing in a piping bag fitted with a medium-sized star tube and pipe a shell border around the base of the cake and rosettes around the top edge. Use up remaining icing by piping more rosettes into the centre of the cake. Decorate with very well drained canned mandarin orange segments if wished, placing them in two concentric circles inside the rosette border.

Superhint *To pipe an even shell edging work towards you, pressing the tube down on the surface, moving away then up and over, drawing the pipe off to make a 'tail', which is covered by the next shell.*

Toffee walnut cake.

Cheesy lemon cake

(Illustrated below)

CAKE
1 bought Lemon spice bar cake (measuring
about 16 cm/6½ inches by 8 cm/3¼ inches by
5 cm/2 inches deep)
ICING
50 g/2 oz (U.S. ¼ cup) butter, softened
100 g/4 oz (U.S. ½ cup) cream cheese
225 g/8 oz icing sugar, sifted (U.S. 1¾ cups sifted
confectioners' sugar)
juice of 1 lemon
DECORATION
50 g/2 oz chopped hazelnuts (U.S. ½ cup chopped
filberts), toasted
2–3 crystallized orange slices (U.S. candied
orange slices), quartered

1. Split the cake into two layers.
2. Beat the icing ingredients together until soft.
3. Use a little icing to stick the two pieces of cake
together side by side on a serving plate. Spread the
remainder over the cakes to mask them completely.
Press nuts around the cake sides. Arrange the
orange pieces, overlapping, in a diagonal line.
Serves 6

Crescent moon gâteau

(Illustrated on pages 58–59)

CAKE
ingredients for 1 (20-cm/8-inch) deep Genoese
sponge (see page 16)
COVERING AND DECORATION
1 quantity Butter icing (see page 28)
150 ml/¼ pint (U.S. ⅔ cup) lemon curd
few drops green food colouring
1½ quantities Glacé icing (see page 31)
¼ quantity Almond paste (see page 33)
24 silver balls

1. Heat the oven to 190°C/375°F, Gas Mark 5,
grease and line a 20-cm/8-inch hexagonal tin or
round tin. Bake the cake for about 30 minutes, or
until firm to the touch. Leave in the tin for 10
minutes then turn out on a wire rack and cool
before removing the lining paper.
2. Split the cake into three layers. Make up the
butter icing and beat in half the lemon curd. Tint
pale green with food colouring. Sandwich the cake

Cheesy lemon cake.

layers together with the remaining lemon curd. Stand the cake on a wire rack over a tray and use about half the butter icing to cover the sides, making the surface as smooth as possible by spreading it with a palette knife (U.S. spatula) dipped in hot water and dried. Leave for at least 2 hours.

3. Make up the glacé icing and pour it carefully over the cake to cover it completely, using the knife dipped in hot water to get an even covering. Leave to set until firm.

4. Roll out the almond paste thinly. Cut six small crescent moon shapes and one larger crescent moon by using plain round cutters then stamping out a small segment from each with the same cutter.

5. Put the remaining butter icing in a piping bag fitted with a medium-sized star tube. Pipe a shell border round the top of the cake 1.25 cm/½ inch in from the edge, then lines of rosettes down the cake corners and a scroll edging around the base.

6. Fix the small crescent moons to the sides of the cake and the larger moon in the centre with dots of icing and pipe three small rosettes above each moon. Top each small rosette on the side of the cake with a silver ball and the rosettes on top of the cake with two silver balls, to represent the stars.

Serves 8–10

Ring-a-rosy gâteau

(Illustrated on pages 58–59)

CAKE
175 g/6 oz (U.S. ¾ cup) butter or margarine
175 g/6 oz caster sugar (U.S. ¾ cup granulated sugar)
3 eggs
few drops of red food colouring
175 g/6 oz self-raising flour, sifted (U.S. 1½ cups all-purpose flour sifted with 1½ teaspoons baking powder)
75 g/3 oz plain flour (U.S. ¾ cup all-purpose flour), sifted
1 tablespoon milk
SYRUP
50 g/2 oz (U.S. ¼ cup) granulated sugar
50 ml/2 fl oz (U.S. ¼ cup) water
2 tablespoons (U.S. 3 tablespoons) triple distilled rose water
COATING AND DECORATION
1 quantity Glacé icing (see page 31)
100 g/4 oz (U.S. ½ cup) butter or margarine
225 g/8 oz icing sugar, sifted (U.S. 1¾ cups sifted confectioners' sugar)
2 tablespoons (U.S. 3 tablespoons) triple distilled rose water
few drops of red food colouring
6 pink jelly diamond-shaped cake decorations

1. Heat the oven to 160°C/325°F, Gas Mark 3, grease a 15-cm/6-inch hexagonal or round cake tin and line with greaseproof paper (U.S. waxed paper).

2. Cream the butter and sugar together in a bowl until light and fluffy. Add the eggs, one at a time, beating well after each addition. Tint deep pink with food colouring. Fold in the flour and the milk. Transfer the mixture to the prepared tin and level the surface.

3. Bake for about 1 hour and 5 minutes, or until firm to the touch. Leave to stand in the tin for 5 minutes.

4. Meanwhile, make the syrup. Dissolve the sugar in the water in a pan, then bring to the boil. Simmer for 3 minutes, stir in the rose water and remove from the heat.

5. Turn out the cake on a wire rack and remove the lining paper. Trim off the top to make it level and turn the cake upside-down on the rack. Spoon the hot syrup over the warm cake. Leave until cold.

6. Make up the glacé icing and pour it carefully over the cake, spreading it with a palette knife (U.S. spatula) dipped in hot water, to give an even covering. Leave to set until firm.

7. Make up the butter icing by beating the butter with the sugar and rose water until fluffy. Tint pale pink with food colouring. Take two thirds of the butter icing and tint a deeper pink. Put a little of the darker icing into a paper icing bag (see page 12) fitted with a small star tube.

8. Mark the top of the cake lightly with two circles, one 5 cm/2 inches in diameter and one 10 cm/4 inches in diameter using plain cutters.

9. Beginning with the small circle and the paper bag of darker icing, pipe tiny rosettes around the circle. Put all the remaining darker icing into a piping bag fitted with a medium-sized star tube and the pale icing into a paper icing bag fitted with the small star tube. Pipe tiny rosettes of pale icing around the larger circle on top of the cake. Pipe a scroll border of darker icing using the larger tube, alternating the scrolls from left and right and spacing them out to give an even number on each side of the cake. Pipe a scroll border round the base. Prick out three semi-circles on each side of the cake above the scrolls and pipe five tiny rosettes of pale icing to make each semi-circle. Finish by pressing a diamond-shaped cake decoration on each corner of the cake.

Serves 6–8

Fudge slice

(Illustrated opposite)

175 g/6 oz (U.S. ¾ cup) butter
3 tablespoons golden syrup (U.S. 4 tablespoons light corn syrup)
350 g/12 oz sweet biscuits, crushed (U.S. 4 cups sweet cookie crumbs)
50 g/2 oz (U.S. ⅓ cup) seedless raisins
100 g/4 oz glacé cherries, quartered (U.S. ½ cup candied cherries, quartered)
100 g/4 oz plain chocolate (U.S. ⅔ cup semi-sweet chocolate pieces), chopped
ICING
50 g/2 oz plain chocolate (U.S. ⅓ cup semi-sweet chocolate pieces)
25 g/1 oz (U.S. 2 tablespoons) butter
2 tablespoons (U.S. 3 tablespoons) water
175 g/6 oz icing sugar, sifted (U.S. 1⅓ cups sifted confectioners' sugar)
DECORATION
5 glacé cherry halves (U.S. candied cherry halves)
10 angelica 'leaves'

1. Grease a 450-g/1-lb loaf-shaped tin and line the base with greaseproof paper (U.S. waxed paper).
2. Melt the butter and syrup in a pan. Stir in the biscuit crumbs, fruit and chocolate. Press firmly into the prepared tin and chill until set.
3. Turn out of the tin and cut into three layers.
4. To make the icing, put the chocolate, butter and water in a pan. Place over gentle heat, stirring occasionally, until the chocolate has melted. Remove from the heat, then stir in the sugar. Beat until cool and thick.
5. Sandwich the fruity slice layers together with the icing and spread a layer over the top, lifting the surface into peaks with a knife blade. Decorate the top with a line of cherries and angelica 'leaves'.
Serves 6–8

Chunky chocolate cake

(Illustrated opposite)

CAKE
150 g/5 oz plain flour (U.S. 1¼ cups all-purpose flour)
65 g/2½ oz drinking chocolate powder (U.S. scant ⅓ cup sweetened cocoa)
1 teaspoon baking powder
100 g/4 oz milk chocolate (U.S. 4 squares sweet chocolate)
100 g/4 oz (U.S. ½ cup) butter
100 g/4 oz caster or soft brown sugar (U.S. ½ cup granulated or light brown sugar)
2 eggs, beaten
2 teaspoons coffee essence (U.S. 1 tablespoon sweetened concentrated coffee flavoring) or 2 teaspoons (U.S. 1 tablespoon) instant coffee moistened with a little hot water
25 g/1 oz (U.S. ¼ cup) ground almonds
50 g/2 oz (U.S. ½ cup) chopped walnuts
ICING
65 g/2½ oz milk chocolate (U.S. 2½ squares sweet chocolate)

1. Heat the oven to 180°C/350°F, Gas Mark 4, grease a 17.5-cm/7-inch cake tin and line the base with greaseproof paper (U.S. waxed paper).
2. Sift the flour with the drinking chocolate powder and baking powder. Quarter each square of chocolate (U.S. quarter each square of chocolate then quarter each smaller piece). Beat the butter and sugar together in a bowl until light and fluffy. Gradually beat in the eggs then fold in the coffee essence, nuts and dry ingredients to give a dropping consistency. Fold in the chocolate pieces. Transfer the mixture to the prepared tin and hollow out the centre slightly.
3. Bake for 50 minutes. Turn out on a wire rack, remove the lining paper and leave to cool.
4. Melt the chocolate in a bowl over a pan of hot water but do not stir it. When soft, spread over the cake and mark the top into lines with a knife blade. Serve when the chocolate topping is set.
Serves 8

Above: Chunky chocolate cake. Below: Fudge slice.

Meringue gâteau

MERINGUE
2 teaspoons (U.S. 1 tablespoon) instant coffee
powder
50 g/2 oz ground roasted hazelnuts (U.S. ½ cup
ground roasted filberts)
1½ quantities Basic meringue (see page 141)
using equal quantities of caster and icing sugar
(U.S. granulated and confectioners' sugar)
FILLING
2 quantities chocolate Crème au beurre (see
page 28)
DECORATION
50 g/2 oz plain chocolate (U.S. ⅓ cup semi-sweet
chocolate pieces)

1. Heat the oven to 110°C/225°F, Gas Mark ¼, line
two baking sheets (U.S. cookie sheets) with non-
stick baking parchment (U.S. waxed paper) and
draw a 17.5-cm/7-inch circle on each.
2. Beat the coffee powder and nuts into the
meringue mixture and spread inside the circles on
the lined sheets.
3. Dry out in the oven for 2–4 hours, or until the
parchment peels away cleanly from the meringue.
Cool on a wire rack.
4. Make up the filling and cool.
5. To make chocolate curls see page 57. Chill.
6. To assemble the gâteau, place one meringue
round on a serving dish and spread with half the
chocolate filling. Top with the second meringue
round and the rest of the chocolate filling. Arrange
the chocolate curls over the surface.
Serves 8

_____ VARIATION _____

Peach dacquoise Omit the coffee and hazelnuts
(U.S. filberts) in the meringue layers and substitute
50 g/2 oz (U.S. ½ cup) ground almonds and ½
teaspoon almond essence (U.S. almond extract).
Instead of the chocolate filling and decoration, use
300 ml/½ pint double cream (U.S. 1¼ cups heavy
cream), whipped with 1 tablespoon sifted icing
sugar (U.S. confectioners' sugar). Drain a 425-g/15-
oz can of peach slices really well on absorbent
kitchen towel, patting the slices with more paper
until the syrup is absorbed. Spread half the cream
on a meringue layer on a serving plate. Reserve 16
peach slices and arrange the remainder on the
cream. Cover with the second meringue layer and
the rest of the cream. Put the reserved peach slices
together in pairs in the shape of petals radiating out
from the centre of the gâteau and finish with a glacé
cherry (U.S. candied cherry) in the middle.

Malakoff gâteau

2 teaspoons instant coffee
2 teaspoons boiling water
100 g/4 oz (U.S. ½ cup) butter
100 g/4 oz caster sugar (U.S. ½ cup granulated
sugar)
3 egg yolks
100 g/4 oz chopped hazelnuts (U.S. 1 cup
chopped filberts)
5 tablespoons (U.S. 6 tablespoons) rum
1 (198-g/7-oz) can sweetened condensed milk
(or half a 397-g/14-oz can)
75 ml/3 fl oz (U.S. ⅓ cup) cold water
about 30 sponge fingers (U.S. ladyfingers)
DECORATION
300 ml/½ pint double cream (U.S. 1¼ cups heavy
cream), whipped
16 whole hazelnuts (U.S. filberts)
8 glacé cherries (U.S. candied cherries), halved

1. Line a 1-kg/2-lb loaf-shaped tin with foil.
Moisten the coffee with the hot water. Cream the
butter and sugar together in a bowl until light and
fluffy. Beat in the egg yolks, one at a time, then add
the coffee, nuts, 3 tablespoons (U.S. 4 tablespoons)
each of the rum and condensed milk. In a separate
bowl, combine the remaining rum, condensed milk
and the cold water.
2. Arrange a layer of sponge fingers in the base of
the tin, spoon a little of the rum and milk mixture
over them then spread with some of the coffee
mixture. Repeat these layers until all the ingredients are used up, ending with a layer of sponge
fingers trimmed to fit.
3. Cover the top with foil and weight down evenly
all over. Chill for 2–3 hours.
4. To serve the gâteau, remove the weights and foil
top, turn the cake out on a serving dish and peel off
the lining foil. Mask completely with about half the
cream. Place the remaining cream in a piping bag
fitted with a large star tube and pipe rosettes around
the top edge and shells around the base. Decorate
by spiking the rosettes alternately with hazelnuts
and cherry halves.
Serves 8

Cointreau and cream gâteau.

Cointreau and cream gâteau

(Illustrated below)

CAKE
150 g/5 oz plain flour (U.S. 1¼ cups all-purpose flour)

2½ teaspoons (U.S. 1 tablespoon) baking powder

25 g/1 oz cocoa powder (U.S. ¼ cup unsweetened cocoa)

175 g/6 oz (U.S. ¾ cup) softened butter or soft margarine

175 g/6 oz dark soft brown sugar (U.S. ¾ cup brown sugar)

3 eggs

50 g/2 oz (U.S. ½ cup) finely chopped mixed nuts

FILLING AND DECORATION
2 tablespoons (U.S. 3 tablespoons) Cointreau or sweet sherry

3 tablespoons (U.S. 4 tablespoons) apricot jam

300 ml/½ pint double cream (U.S. 1¼ cups heavy cream)

2 large chocolate flakes

18 whole blanched hazelnuts (U.S. whole blanched filberts), toasted

1. Heat the oven to 160°C/325°F, Gas Mark 3, grease a 17.5-cm/7-inch square cake tin, line the base with greaseproof paper (U.S. waxed paper) and grease the paper.
2. Sift the flour, baking powder and cocoa into a bowl, add the remaining cake ingredients and beat for 2 minutes, or until creamy. Transfer the mixture to the prepared tin and level the surface.
3. Bake for about 45 minutes, or until firm to the touch. Turn out on a wire rack, remove the lining paper and leave to cool.
4. To assemble the gâteau, split the cake into two layers and sprinkle half the liqueur over both. Place the base on a serving dish and spread with the jam. Whip the cream with the remaining liqueur until just stiff and swirl about one third over the jam. Top with the second layer of cake and use another third of the cream to coat the sides.
5. Split one flake in half lengthways and cut each half into three pieces. Crumble the second flake and press on to the sides of the cake. Cover the top with the remaining cream and mark into lines with a knife blade. Arrange three groups of hazelnuts down the centre of the cake, with a row of pieces of flake on either side.

Serves 9

Chocolate and ginger cheesecake

(Illustrated opposite)

BASE
75 g/3 oz (U.S. ⅓ cup) butter
175 g/6 oz gingernut biscuits, crushed (U.S. 2 cups crushed gingersnap cookies)
50 g/2 oz demerara sugar (U.S. ¼ cup brown sugar)

FILLING
100 ml/4 fl oz (U.S. ½ cup) water
15 g/½ oz powdered gelatine (U.S. 1 envelope gelatin)
150 g/5 oz plain chocolate (U.S. scant 1 cup semi-sweet chocolate pieces)
225 g/8 oz (U.S. 1 cup) cream cheese
50 g/2 oz soft brown sugar (U.S. ¼ cup light brown sugar)
2 eggs, separated
150 ml/¼ pint (U.S. ⅔ cup) natural yogurt
2 pieces preserved ginger, finely chopped
1 tablespoon ginger syrup from jar
50 g/2 oz caster sugar (U.S. ¼ cup granulated sugar)

DECORATION
50 g/2 oz plain chocolate (U.S. 2 squares semi-sweet chocolate)
2 pieces preserved ginger, sliced

1. Have ready a 20-cm/8-inch loose-based cake tin. Melt the butter in a pan then mix in the biscuit crumbs and demerara sugar. Press into the tin and level the surface.

2. Put the water in a small bowl, sprinkle on the gelatine and leave to stand for 5 minutes. Then place the bowl over a pan of hot water until the gelatine has completely dissolved. Melt the chocolate in a bowl over a pan of hot water in the same way.

3. Put the cheese in a bowl and beat until smooth. Gradually beat in the soft brown sugar and egg yolks, then add the yogurt, dissolved gelatine and melted chocolate. Mix well. Leave until the mixture is beginning to set. Fold in the ginger and ginger syrup.

4. Whisk the egg whites in a clean bowl until stiff. Gradually add the caster sugar, a tablespoon at a time, whisking well after each addition until the meringue is firm and glossy. Fold into the chocolate mixture. Pour over the crumb base and tilt the tin to give an even layer. Chill until set.

5. Remove the tin and transfer the cheesecake, still on the metal base, to a serving plate. Using a potato peeler, make eight good curls from the chocolate. Reserve these for the top of the cheesecake and grate the remaining chocolate coarsely. Cover the sides of the cheesecake with grated chocolate and sprinkle the remainder in the centre. Arrange eight slices of ginger evenly round the edge of the cheesecake and top each with a chocolate curl.
Serves 8

--- VARIATIONS ---

Chocolate and cherry cheesecake Use 175 g/6 oz digestive biscuits, crushed (U.S. 2 cups Graham cracker crumbs) instead of the gingernuts (U.S. gingersnap cookies). Omit the ginger and ginger syrup in the filling and substitute 8 drained maraschino cherries (U.S. cocktail cherries), roughly chopped, and 1 tablespoon syrup from the jar. While the cheesecake is setting, make 16 chocolate leaves (see page 57). Decorate the top of the dessert with eight cherry halves, each flanked by a pair of chocolate leaves.

Pineapple and ginger cheesecake Make the cheesecake as in the main recipe but serve decorated with cream and pineapple pieces. Whip 150 ml/¼ pint double cream (U.S. ⅔ cup heavy cream) and place in a piping bag fitted with a large star tube. Pipe a shell border of cream around the cheesecake, working out the placing of the shells so that there are 16. Drain two canned pineapple rings really well and divide each into eight pieces. Arrange these evenly around the cream border, tucking each one into the 'tail' of a shell where it is overlapped by the large curved shape of the following shell.

Chocolate and ginger cheesecake.

Satin cake

(Illustrated opposite)

CAKE
75 g/3 oz plain flour (U.S. $\frac{3}{4}$ cup all-purpose flour)
25 g/1 oz cocoa powder (U.S. $\frac{1}{4}$ cup unsweetened cocoa)
$\frac{1}{2}$ teaspoon baking powder
4 eggs, separated
1 tablespoon orange juice
2 tablespoons (U.S. 3 tablespoons) cold water
50 g/2 oz (U.S. $\frac{1}{4}$ cup) butter, melted
150 g/5 oz caster sugar (U.S. $\frac{2}{3}$ cup granulated sugar)
FILLING AND DECORATION
150 ml/$\frac{1}{4}$ pint double cream (U.S. $\frac{2}{3}$ cup heavy cream), whipped
100 g/4 oz (U.S. $\frac{1}{2}$ cup) cream cheese
5 teaspoons (U.S. 2 tablespoons) orange juice
350 g/12 oz icing sugar, sifted (U.S. $2\frac{2}{3}$ cups sifted confectioners' sugar)
5 yellow glacé cherries (U.S. candied cherries)
5 small 'leaves' of angelica

1. Heat the oven to 190°C/375°F, Gas Mark 5, grease a 17.5-cm/7-inch cake tin and line with greaseproof paper (U.S. waxed paper).
2. Sift the flour with the cocoa and baking powder and set aside. Beat the egg yolks with the orange juice, water and melted butter in a large bowl. Put the egg whites and sugar into a separate bowl and whisk until thick. Fold the meringue into the butter mixture. Add the dry ingredients and fold in lightly but thoroughly. Transfer the mixture to the prepared tin.
3. Bake for about 40 minutes, or until firm to the touch. If necessary, protect the top of the cake with a sheet of greaseproof paper (U.S. waxed paper) to prevent overbrowning. Turn out on a wire rack, remove the lining paper and leave to cool.
4. Split the cake into two layers and sandwich together with cream. Place on a serving dish.
5. To make the frosting, beat the cheese until smooth, gradually adding the orange juice and then the sugar to form a fudgy consistency. Spread over the cake and lift the surface into small peaks with the tip of a knife. Decorate with the cherries and angelica 'leaves'.
Serves 8

Almond delight

(Illustrated opposite)

CAKE
65 g/$2\frac{1}{2}$ oz (U.S. scant $\frac{1}{3}$ cup) butter
2 tablespoons (U.S. 3 tablespoons) dried breadcrumbs
100 g/4 oz self-raising flour, sifted (U.S. 1 cup all-purpose flour sifted with 1 teaspoon baking powder)
1 tablespoon cocoa powder (U.S. unsweetened cocoa)
2 eggs
100 g/4 oz caster sugar (U.S. $\frac{1}{2}$ cup granulated sugar)
2 tablespoons single cream (U.S. 3 tablespoons light cream)
TOPPING
50 g/2 oz (U.S. $\frac{1}{4}$ cup) butter
50 g/2 oz caster sugar (U.S. $\frac{1}{4}$ cup granulated sugar)
1 tablespoon plain flour (U.S. all-purpose flour)
50 g/2 oz flaked almonds (U.S. $\frac{1}{2}$ cup slivered almonds)
2 teaspoons (U.S. 1 tablespoon) milk

1. Heat the oven to 180°C/350°F, Gas Mark 4, grease a 17.5-cm/7-inch loose-based cake tin using 15 g/$\frac{1}{2}$ oz (U.S. 1 tablespoon) of the butter then sprinkle with the breadcrumbs.
2. Sift the flour with the cocoa and set aside. Melt the remaining butter until just soft enough to pour and leave to cool. Put the eggs and sugar in a large bowl over a pan of simmering water and whisk steadily, if possible using an electric mixer, until the mixture falls back on itself in a thick ribbon when the beaters are lifted. Remove from the heat, fold in the dry ingredients with the butter and cream. Transfer the mixture to the prepared tin.
3. Bake for 30 minutes. Have the topping ready to put on the cake at this stage.
4. Melt the butter in a pan and stir in the sugar, flour, almonds and milk. Cook for 1 minute, stirring gently all the time.
5. Pull out the oven rack slightly so that you can spread the topping on the cake. Bake for a further 15–20 minutes, or until the topping is a rich golden brown and the cake is cooked through. A wooden cocktail stick (U.S. toothpick) inserted in the centre should come out clean if the cake is ready. Cool in the tin for 20 minutes then transfer to a wire rack to finish cooling.
Serves 8

Above: Almond delight.
Centre right: Tipsy cake (see page 76)
Below: Satin cake.

Tipsy cake

(Illustrated on page 75)

CAKE
100 g/4 oz plain chocolate (U.S. ⅔ cup semi-sweet chocolate pieces)
175 g/6 oz (U.S. ¾ cup) margarine
175 g/6 oz caster sugar (U.S. ¾ cup granulated)
3 eggs
175 g/6 oz self-raising flour, sifted (U.S. 1½ cups all-purpose flour sifted with 1½ teaspoons baking powder)
pinch of salt
few drops vanilla essence (U.S. vanilla extract)
SYRUP
100 g/4 oz (U.S. ½ cup) granulated sugar
6 tablespoons (U.S. 9 tablespoons) water
2 tablespoons (U.S. 3 tablespoons) brandy, rum or sherry
FILLING AND DECORATION
300 ml/½ pint (U.S. 1¼ cups) whipping cream
1 tablespoon caster sugar (U.S. granulated)

1. Melt the chocolate over a pan of hot water, then spread half of it quite thickly on a sheet of non-stick baking parchment (U.S. waxed paper) and leave to set. Keep the remaining chocolate melted.
2. Heat oven to 190°C/375°F, Gas Mark 5, grease two 20-cm/8-inch shallow cake tins and line bases with greaseproof paper (U.S. waxed paper).
3. Cream the margarine and sugar together in a bowl until light and fluffy. Add the eggs, one at a time, beating well after each addition. Fold in the flour and salt.
4. Take half the mixture to another bowl. Add vanilla to one portion and the melted chocolate to the other. Place alternate spoons of the vanilla and chocolate mixtures in the prepared tins, ensuring that they are evenly filled. Swirl the colours together lightly then smooth over the tops, hollowing out the centres slightly.
5. Bake for about 25 minutes, or until firm to the touch. Turn on to a rack, remove paper and cool.
6. To make the syrup, heat the sugar and water on a pan, stirring, until dissolved. Boil rapidly for 3 minutes. Cool slightly before adding the brandy. Spoon over the cake layers just before assembling.
7. With a sharp knife, cut the set chocolate into four good 4-cm/1½-inch squares. Cut each into two triangles.
8. Whip the cream until it will hold its shape then fold in the sugar. Place in a piping bag fitted with a large star tube. Invert one cake so that the marbled pattern shows and pipe a circle of rosettes round the edge. Sandwich the cakes together with the remaining cream. Use seven chocolate triangles to spike rosettes evenly round the cake.
Serves 8

Tipsy cake stages.

Cranberry orange gâteau

(Illustrated below)

CAKE
2 large eggs
100 g/4 oz caster sugar (U.S. ½ cup granulated sugar)
100 g/4 oz plain flour (U.S. 1 cup all-purpose flour)
finely grated rind of ½ orange
FILLING AND DECORATION
225 g/8 oz (U.S. ½ lb) fresh or frozen cranberries
150 ml/¼ pint (U.S. ⅔ cup) orange juice
about 75 g/3 oz caster sugar (U.S. ⅓ cup granulated sugar)
300 ml/½ pint double cream (U.S. 1¼ cups heavy cream)
2 tablespoons (U.S. 3 tablespoons) milk
3–4 tablespoons (U.S. 4–6 tablespoons) Grand Marnier or Cointreau
50 g/2 oz flaked almonds (U.S. ½ cup slivered almonds), toasted
16 jellied orange slices (U.S. sugared orange candy slices)

1. Heat the oven to 180°C/350°F, Gas Mark 4, grease a 20-cm/8-inch loose-based cake tin and line with greaseproof paper (U.S. waxed paper).
2. Make the whisked sponge following the basic method (see page 16), folding in the orange rind with the flour. Transfer the mixture to the tin.
3. Bake for about 25 minutes, or until just firm to the touch. Turn out on a wire rack, remove the lining paper and leave to cool.
4. To make the filling, put the cranberries and orange juice into a pan, cover and cook gently for about 10 minutes, or until all the berries have 'popped' and are tender. The mixture should be thick and pulpy. If necessary, remove the lid and boil for a few minutes to get the right consistency. Sweeten to taste and leave until cold. Whip the cream with the milk until holding its shape well.
5. To assemble the gâteau, split the cake into two layers and sprinkle both with liqueur. Put the base on a serving plate and spread with about three-quarters of the cranberry mixture and a quarter of the cream. Top with the second layer of cake. Put about one third of the remaining cream into a piping bag fitted with a large star tube. Use the rest to mask the whole cake, marking the top with a knife. Press almonds round the sides.
6. Pipe a 5-cm/2-inch circle of small rosettes of cream in the centre of the cake, then pipe eight large rosettes around the edge of the cake. Spoon the remaining cranberry filling into the central cream ring and spike each large rosette with a pair of orange slices. Chill for at least 2 hours.
Serves 8

Apple and almond flan

(Illustrated opposite)

PASTRY
225 g/8 oz plain flour (U.S. 2 cups all-purpose flour)
pinch of salt
50 g/2 oz (U.S. $\frac{1}{4}$ cup) butter or margarine
50 g/2 oz (U.S. $\frac{1}{4}$ cup) lard or white fat
about 2 tablespoons (U.S. 3 tablespoons) water
FILLING
3–4 tablespoons raspberry jam
50 g/2 oz (U.S. $\frac{1}{4}$ cup) butter or margarine
50 g/2 oz caster sugar (U.S. $\frac{1}{4}$ cup granulated sugar)
1 large egg
few drops almond essence (U.S. extract)
40 g/1$\frac{1}{2}$ oz self-raising flour, sifted (U.S. generous $\frac{1}{3}$ cup all-purpose flour sifted with $\frac{1}{2}$ teaspoon baking powder)
25 g/1 oz (U.S. $\frac{1}{4}$ cup) ground almonds
350 g/12 oz Bramley apples (U.S. $\frac{3}{4}$ lb cooking apples), peeled, cored and thinly sliced
ICING
75 g/3 oz (U.S. $\frac{1}{3}$ cup) butter
175 g/6 oz icing sugar, sifted (U.S. 1$\frac{1}{3}$ cups sifted confectioners' sugar)
about 1 teaspoon lemon juice
few drops green food colouring

1. To make the pastry, sift the flour and salt into a bowl and rub or cut in the fats until the mixture resembles breadcrumbs. Add enough water to make a firm dough and knead lightly until smooth.
2. Heat the oven to 180°C/350°F, Gas Mark 4 and have ready 20-cm/8-inch flan tin or dish. Roll out the pastry to line the dish and spread with jam.
3. To make the filling, cream the butter and sugar together in a bowl until light and fluffy. Beat in the egg and essence then fold in the flour and almonds.
4. Arrange the apple slices evenly over the jam. Cover with the almond mixture, spreading it so that it covers the apples and touches the pastry edges.
5. Bake for about 45 minutes, or until golden brown and firm to the touch. Leave to cool.
6. To make the icing, cream the butter and sugar together, then beat in enough lemon juice to make a smooth piping consistency. Tint pale green with food colouring. Place about one third of the icing in a paper piping bag fitted with a medium-sized star tube and spread the remainder over the flan. Pipe a continuous scroll of icing around the edge and a row of rosettes about 2.5 cm/1 inch inside this.
Serves 6–8

Above right: Coffee crunch gâteau (see page 80).
Centre left: Pear and coconut tart (see page 80).
Below right: Apple and almond flan.

78

Coffee crunch gâteau

(Illustrated on pages 29 and 78–79)

CAKE
50 g/2 oz plain flour (U.S. ½ cup all-purpose flour)
1 teaspoon baking powder
50 g/2 oz caster sugar (U.S. ¼ cup granulated sugar)
50 g/2 oz (U.S. ¼ cup) soft margarine
1 large egg
1 teaspoon coffee essence (U.S. sweetened concentrated coffee flavoring)
BASE
100 g/4 oz (U.S. ½ cup) butter or margarine
50 g/2 oz soft brown sugar (U.S. ¼ cup light brown sugar)
25 g/1 oz (U.S. ¼ cup) chopped walnuts or pecans
100 g/4 oz (U.S. 5 cups) wheat flakes
FILLING AND DECORATION
100 g/4 oz (U.S. ½ cup) butter or margarine
about 225 g/8 oz icing sugar, sifted (U.S. 1¾ cups sifted confectioners' sugar)
1 tablespoon coffee essence (U.S. sweetened concentrated coffee flavoring)
25 g/1 oz (U.S. ¼ cup) chopped walnuts or pecans

1. Heat the oven to 180°C/350°F, Gas Mark 4, grease a 17.5-cm/7-inch shallow cake tin and line the base with greaseproof paper (U.S. waxed paper). Have ready also a 17.5-cm/7-inch flan ring standing on a serving plate.
2. Sift the flour and baking powder into a bowl, add all the other ingredients for the cake and beat for 2 minutes, until smooth and creamy. Transfer the mixture to the prepared tin and level the surface.
3. Bake for about 20 minutes, or until firm to the touch. Turn out on a wire rack, remove the lining paper and leave to cool.
4. To make the base, melt the butter with the sugar in a pan then add the nuts and flakes and mix well. Press into the flan ring, level the surface and chill until firm.
5. To make the filling, cream the butter and sugar together in a bowl until light and fluffy. Gradually beat in the coffee essence. Take about one third and mix in the walnuts.
6. To assemble the gâteau, remove the flan ring and spread the walnut icing on the crunch base. Top with the cake layer and use just over half the remaining icing to cover the surface. Mark the icing in lines with a knife blade. Put the rest of the icing in a piping bag fitted with a large star tube and pipe a twisted circle around the top of the cake, about 2.5 cm/1 inch in from the edge.
Serves 6–8

Pear and coconut tart

(Illustrated on pages 78–79)

PASTRY
225 g/8 oz plain flour (U.S. 2 cups all-purpose flour)
50 g/2 oz (U.S. ¼ cup) lard or white fat
50 g/2 oz (U.S. ¼ cup) butter or margarine
about 2 tablespoons (U.S. 3 tablespoons) water
FILLING
4 tablespoons (U.S. 6 tablespoons) apricot jam
40 g/1½ oz plain flour (U.S. generous ⅓ cup all-purpose flour)
¾ teaspoon baking powder
50 g/2 oz (U.S. ¼ cup) butter or margarine
50 g/2 oz caster sugar (U.S. ¼ cup granulated sugar)
1 large egg
25 g/1 oz desiccated or shredded coconut (U.S. ⅓ cup shredded coconut)
TOPPING
2 ripe but firm Conference pears (U.S. ripe but firm eating pears)
50 g/2 oz caster sugar (U.S. ¼ cup granulated sugar)
75 g/3 oz plain chocolate (U.S. ½ cup semi-sweet chocolate pieces)
2 tablespoons (U.S. 3 tablespoons) wheat flakes
2 tablespoons (U.S. 3 tablespoons) shredded coconut

1. To make the pastry, sift the flour into a bowl and rub or cut in the fats until the mixture resembles breadcrumbs. Add enough water to make a firm dough and knead lightly until smooth.
2. Heat the oven to 190°C/375°F, Gas Mark 5 and have ready a 20-cm/8-inch flan tin or shallow cake tin. Roll out the pastry to line the chosen tin and spread the jam in the base.
3. To make the filling, sift the flour and baking powder. Cream the butter and sugar together in a bowl until light and fluffy. Beat in the egg then fold in the dry ingredients and coconut. Spread over the jam in the pastry case.
4. Bake for about 40 minutes, or until well risen, golden brown and firm to the touch. Leave to cool.
5. Meanwhile, peel the pears, quarter them and remove the cores. Place the pear quarters in a pan with the sugar and just enough water to cover. Bring to the boil, cover and simmer for 5 minutes. Allow to stand in the liquid for 5 minutes then drain and cool. (Reserve the left-over syrup for use in a fruit salad or sweet sauce.)
6. Melt the chocolate in a bowl over a pan of hot water and put about a quarter into a paper piping bag (see page 12). Snip off the tip of the bag and pipe a zig-zag line backwards and forwards over the best 6 pear quarters. Leave to set. Stir the wheat flakes

and shredded coconut into the remaining chocolate.

7. Transfer the flan to a serving dish and arrange the pears on top. Spoon the chocolate mixture in small heaps between the pears.
Serves 6

Gâteau Paris-Brest

PASTRY
1 quantity Choux pastry (see page 139)
1 egg, beaten
15 g/½ oz flaked almonds (U.S. 1 tablespoon slivered almonds)
icing sugar (U.S. confectioners' sugar) for sprinkling
FILLING
50 g/2 oz (U.S. ½ cup) unblanched almonds
50 g/2 oz caster sugar (U.S. ¼ cup granulated sugar)
300 ml/½ pint double cream (U.S. 1¼ cups heavy cream), whipped

1. Heat the oven to 200°C/400°F, Gas Mark 6 and grease and lightly flour a baking sheet (U.S. cookie sheet). Mark a 20-cm/8-inch circle on the sheet.
2. Put the choux pastry into a piping bag fitted with a 2.5-cm/1-inch plain tube and pipe a ring of paste out on the prepared sheet into the marked circle. Brush the ring with egg, sprinkle with the almonds and sift evenly with sugar.
3. Bake for about 30 minutes, or until the ring is golden brown. Remove from the oven and split through the centre so that the bottom ring is slightly larger than the top ring. Cool both, cut surface upwards, on a wire rack.
4. While the ring is baking, make the praline. Have ready a greased baking sheet (U.S. cookie sheet). Put the almonds and sugar in a heavy-based pan and stir over moderate heat until the sugar turns to liquid. Cook until the caramel is golden brown and the nuts well toasted. Pour immediately on to the prepared sheet and leave to cool.
5. Break up the praline when cold and grind to a coarse powder in a food processor or blender; alternatively, pound with a rolling pin.
6. Whip the cream and fold in the praline powder. At serving time, put the base of the ring on a plate and fill with the praline cream. Lay the lid lightly on top and sprinkle with more sugar. This gâteau is best eaten within 2 hours of finishing.
Serves 6–8

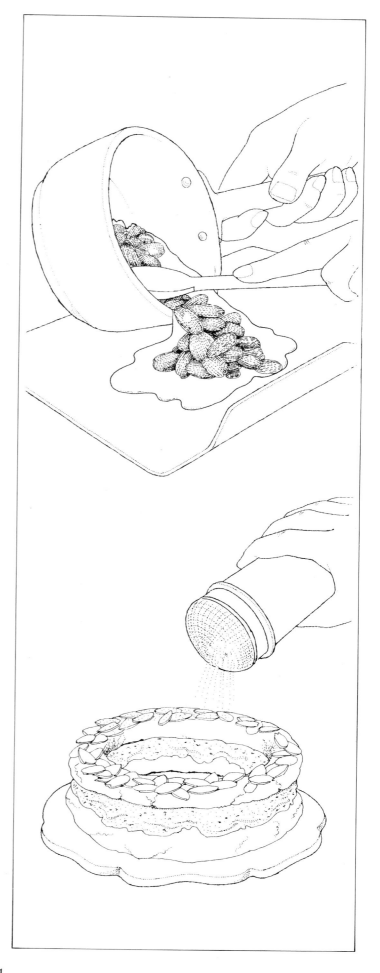

Schwarzwald Kirschtorte

CAKE
40 g/1½ oz (U.S. 3 tablespoons) butter
65 g/2½ oz plain flour (U.S. scant ⅔ cup all-purpose flour)
15 g/½ oz cocoa powder (U.S. 2 tablespoons unsweetened cocoa)
3 large eggs
75 g/3 oz caster sugar (U.S. ⅓ cup granulated sugar)
FILLING AND DECORATION
100 g/4 oz plain chocolate (U.S. ⅔ cup semi-sweet chocolate pieces)
1 (425-g/15-oz) can black cherries
2 teaspoons (U.S. 1 tablespoon) arrowroot
300 ml/½ pint double cream (U.S. 1¼ cups heavy cream)
1 tablespoon creamy milk
2 tablespoons (U.S. 3 tablespoons) Kirsch

1. Heat the oven to 190°C/375°F, Gas Mark 5, grease a 20-cm/8-inch loose-based cake tin and line with greaseproof paper (U.S. waxed paper).
2. Make up the Genoese mixture using the basic method (see page 16), sifting the flour with the cocoa twice. Transfer the mixture to the tin.
3. Bake for 20–25 minutes, or until well risen and firm to the touch. Turn out on a wire rack, remove the lining paper and leave to cool.
4. Make large chocolate curls (see page 57).
5. Drain the cherries and make the syrup up to 150 ml/¼ pint (U.S. ⅔ cup) with water if necessary. Put the arrowroot in a small pan and gradually blend in the measured syrup. Heat, stirring constantly, until thickened and clear. Reserve eight cherries for the decoration, halve the remainder, discarding the stones (U.S. pits) and stir the fruit into the sauce. Transfer to a bowl and cool.
6. Whip the cream and milk together until holding its shape firmly but not stiff.
7. To assemble the torte, split the cake into three layers. Place the bottom layer on a serving dish and sprinkle with half the liqueur. Spread over half the cherry filling and a little of the cream, then cover with the second cake layer. Repeat this once, positioning the top layer of cake carefully.
8. Mask the cake completely using most of the remaining cream and make a decorative pattern on the top with the tip of a knife. Cover the sides with chocolate curls. Put the rest of the cream in a piping bag fitted with a large star tube, pipe eight rosettes on top of the cake and top each with a reserved cherry. Leave the gâteau to stand for 2 hours.
Serves 8

Above right: Hungarian moka gâteau (see page 84).
Centre left: Schwartzwald kirschtorte.
Below right: Magyar Dobostorte.

Magyar Dobostorte

CAKE
150 g/5 oz plain flour (U.S. 1¼ cups all-purpose flour)
4 eggs
175 g/6 oz caster sugar (U.S. ¾ cup granulated sugar)
½ teaspoon vanilla essence (U.S. vanilla extract)
CARAMEL
100 g/4 oz caster sugar (U.S. ½ cup granulated sugar)
1 tablespoon water
FILLING AND DECORATION
12 green grapes
little whisked egg white
caster sugar (U.S. granulated sugar) for sprinkling
2 quantities chocolate Crème au beurre (see page 28)
50 g/2 oz plain chocolate (U.S. 2 squares semi-sweet chocolate), coarsely grated

1. Heat the oven to 180°C/350°F, Gas Mark 4, line five baking sheets (U.S. cookie sheets) with non-stick baking parchment and draw a rectangle 25 cm/10 inches by 11.5 cm/4½ inches on each sheet. Or you can grease and flour the sheets, marking the rectangles with the handle of a spoon.
2. Make up the Whisked sponge mixture using the basic method (see page 16), adding the vanilla essence when the bowl is removed from the heat.
3. Spread evenly among the marked rectangles.
4. Bake for about 10 minutes, or until pale golden brown and just firm to the touch. Trim the cake edges to the original size, transfer to racks and cool.
5. Select the most even layer for the top of the gâteau and place it on a lightly greased wire rack over a baking sheet (U.S. cookie sheet). To make the caramel, put the sugar and water in a pan and heat gently until the sugar has completely dissolved. Then boil steadily until the caramel is golden brown. Remove from the heat and pour immediately over the sponge layer on the rack to cover it completely. As it sets, mark into 8.
6. To frost the grapes, brush them with egg white then dip in sugar until coated all over. Leave to dry on non-stick paper (U.S. waxed paper).
7. Take half the crème au beurre and fold in the grated chocolate. Use to sandwich the sponge layers together, putting the caramelled layer on top.
8. Use half the remaining crème au beurre to mask the sides of the cake. Put the rest into a piping bag fitted with a large star tube and pipe two rosettes on each section of cake. Decorate alternate sections with three frosted grapes or an extra rosette.
Serves 8

Hungarian moka gâteau

(Illustrated on page 82)

CAKE
50 g/2 oz (U.S. ¼ cup) butter
100 g/4 oz plain flour (U.S. 1 cup all-purpose flour)
4 large eggs
100 g/4 oz caster sugar (U.S. ½ cup granulated sugar)
FILLING AND DECORATION
40 g/1½ oz plain chocolate (U.S. ¼ cup semi-sweet chocolate pieces)
1½ quantities coffee Crème au beurre (see page 28)
50 g/2 oz flaked almonds (U.S. ½ cup slivered almonds), toasted
1 quantity coffee Glacé icing (see page 31)

1. Heat the oven to 190°C/375°F, Gas Mark 5 and grease and flour a 22.5-cm/9-inch moule-à-manqué tin or loose-based cake tin.
2. Make up the Genoese mixture using the basic method (see page 16). Transfer the mixture to the prepared tin.
3. Bake for 25–30 minutes, or until well risen and firm to the touch. Turn out on to a wire rack and leave to cool.
4. Melt the chocolate and use to make 7–10 small chocolate leaves (see page 57).
5. To assemble the gâteau, split the cake into three layers and sandwich them together with some of the crème au beurre. Place on a serving dish. Put half the remaining crème au beurre into a piping bag fitted with a large star tube and use the rest to coat the sides of the gâteau. Press on the almonds.
6. Pour the glacé icing over the top of the cake and, as it sets, pipe shells round the edge. When the glacé icing is completely set, use any remaining crème au beurre to pipe a few rosettes in the centre of the gâteau and complete the decoration with the chocolate leaves.
Serves 8–10

Tarta Sevilliana

PASTRY
1 quantity French flan pastry (see page 135)
FILLING
100 g/4 oz (U.S. ⅓ cup) apricot jam
100 g/4 oz caster sugar (U.S. ½ cup granulated sugar)
100 g/4 oz (U.S. 1 cup) ground almonds
2 tablespoons (U.S. 3 tablespoons) Kirsch
¼ teaspoon almond essence (U.S. almond extract)
3 eggs
50 g/2 oz (U.S. ¼ cup) butter, melted
DECORATION
100 g/4 oz (U.S. 1 cup) ground almonds
100 g/4 oz caster sugar (U.S. ½ cup granulated sugar)
about 1 egg white
100 g/4 oz (U.S. ⅓ cup) apricot jam, sieved

1. Heat the oven to 190°C/375°F, Gas Mark 5 and have ready a 20-cm/8-inch moule-à-manque or shallow cake tin.
2. Roll out the pastry, use to line the chosen tin but trim the edge a little above the rim of the tin. Spread the jam in the base.
3. To make the filling, reserve 1 tablespoon of the sugar and put the rest in a food processor or blender with the almonds, liqueur, almond flavouring and one of the eggs. Alternatively, pound the ingredients by hand. Process until thick and almost white. Separate the other eggs, add the yolks to the mixture, then the butter. Whisk the egg whites in a clean bowl until stiff then add the reserved sugar and whisk until firm and glossy. Fold in the almond mixture and spoon into the pastry case.
4. Bake for 45 minutes, or until filling is firm and brown. Cool in the tin for 15 minutes then turn upside-down on a wire rack and leave until cold.
5. To make the topping, process the nuts and sugar in a food processor or pound as above, gradually adding small quantities of egg white until the mixture is soft enough to pipe, but firm enough to hold its shape.
6. Reduce the oven temperature to 180°C/350°F, Gas Mark 4, place the tart on a heatproof plate and protect edges with foil. Put the topping in a piping bag fitted with a 6-mm/¼-inch plain tube and pipe a lattice over the tart.
7. Bake for 10 minutes, or until the decoration starts to take colour.
8. Boil the jam gently until thick then leave until warm and place in a paper icing bag (see page 12). Snip off the end and flood the spaces between the lines of topping with glaze. Serve chilled.
Serves 8

Crème de menthe gâteau

(Illustrated below)

CAKE
ingredients for 1 (20-cm/8-inch) deep chocolate Victoria sandwich cake (see page 20)
FILLING AND DECORATION
175 g/6 oz (U.S. ¾ cup) butter or margarine
225 g/8 oz icing sugar, sifted (U.S. 1¾ cups sifted confectioners' sugar)
3 tablespoons (U.S. 4 tablespoons) crème de menthe
1–2 drops green food colouring (optional)
few crystallized rose petals (U.S. few candied rose petals)

1. Make up the cake mixture and bake in a loose-based cake tin. Leave to cool on the base of the tin.
2. To make the icing, cream the butter until soft then add the sugar and beat until light and fluffy. Reserve 3 tablespoons (U.S. 4 tablespoons) of the icing and beat the liqueur into the remainder. Add a drop or two of green food colouring to give the icing a good green tint.
3. Split the cake into two layers and sandwich together with some of the green butter icing. Keep the cake on the metal cake tin base and spread the remaining green icing on the top and sides. Stand the cake on an icing turntable. Hold a serrated icing comb against the side of the cake and rotate the turntable with one hand, keeping the comb still with the other. Transfer the cake, still on the base, to a serving plate. Using an icing ruler with serrated edge longer than the diameter of the cake, and starting at the side furthest away from you, draw the ruler across the top of the cake to make wavy lines in the icing. Begin with small waves, increase the movement to give larger waves in the centre and return to small waves at the side nearest to you.
4. Put the reserved white icing in a paper icing bag (see page 12) fitted with a medium-sized star tube. Pipe a continuous open coil of icing around the edge of the cake to make a border. Spike the border with a few rose petals at five points, spacing these out evenly.
Serves 8

Crème de menthe gâteau.

85

Kiwi cream gâteau

(Illustrated opposite)

CREAM TOPPING
100 ml/4 fl oz (U.S. ½ cup) milk
150 g/5 oz (U.S. ⅔ cup) unsalted butter, cut into small pieces
1 tablespoon icing sugar (U.S. confectioners' sugar), sifted
½ teaspoon vanilla essence (U.S. vanilla extract)
CAKE
1 (20-cm/8-inch) square chocolate Victoria sandwich cake (see page 20)
DECORATION
16 glacé cherries (U.S. candied cherries)
2 kiwi fruit, peeled and sliced

1. Make the cream topping the day before you intend to complete the cake. Put the milk and butter into a small pan and heat very gently, stirring, until the butter melts. Do not allow to boil. Pour the warm mixture into a liquidizer and blend on medium speed for 10 seconds. Switch off and leave to stand for 10 seconds. Repeat the blending and resting twice more. Pour into a jug, cover and leave to stand for 30 minutes, then stir gently. Chill for at least 8 hours.
2. Bake the cake and leave to cool. Transfer to a board or serving plate.
3. Whip the home-made cream. Chill the bowl and beaters first as cool equipment improves the texture. If using an electric mixer, begin at slow speed. When the cream thickens, add the sugar and vanilla and continue whipping until firm enough to hold its shape.
4. Mask the cake with about half the cream, smoothing the sides with a palette knife (U.S. spatula) and marking the top in diagonal lines with the tip of the knife. Put the remaining cream into a piping bag fitted with a large star tube.
5. Mark the centre of the cake and pipe in a large rosette of cream. Then pipe two facing 'S' shapes out from the centre almost to one corner of the cake. Repeat the same decoration from the centre to the other three corners in turn. Arrange groups of three cherries half-way along each side, and single cherries where the swirls come together at the centre. Arrange two overlapping slices of kiwi fruit in each corner and spike the central rosette with four upright slices between the 'S' shapes. Chill for at least 30 minutes before serving.
Serves 9

Stages in making Kiwi cream gâteau.

Vacherin de framboises

MERINGUE
1½ quantities Meringue cuite (see page 141)
FILLING
350 g/12 oz (U.S. ¾ lb) raspberries
2 tablespoons caster sugar (U.S. 3 tablespoons
granulated sugar)
1 quantity cream topping (see opposite)
whipped
1 tablespoon Grand Marnier or Cointreau

1. Heat the oven to 140°C/275°F, Gas Mark 1, line two baking sheets (U.S. cookie sheets) with non-stick baking parchment (U.S. waxed paper) and draw a 17.5-cm/7-inch circle on each.
2. Spread most of the meringue inside the circles. Place the remaining meringue in a piping bag fitted with a 2-cm/¾-inch star tube. Pipe out seven large rosettes of meringue on the edges of the parchment, well away from the meringue circles.
3. Dry out in the oven for about 50 minutes. Cool on a wire rack.
4. Meanwhile, spread the raspberries on a plate and sprinkle with the sugar. Leave to stand for 1 hour, or until the juice runs freely.
5. When ready to assemble the gâteau, whip the cream topping with the liqueur and add the syrup from the raspberries. Place one meringue round on a serving dish, spread with half the raspberry cream and spoon over half the raspberries. Cover with the remaining meringue round and the rest of the raspberry cream. Spoon the last of the raspberries into the centre and arrange the meringue rosettes round the edge. Best eaten within 1 hour of finishing.
Serves 8

_____ VARIATIONS _____

Crown meringue gâteau Make and bake the meringue layers and rosettes as above. Omit the raspberries, sugar and liqueur. Grate 75 g/3 oz plain chocolate (U.S. 3 squares semi-sweet chocolate) and fold into the whipped cream. Place one meringue layer on a serving dish and spread over half the chocolate cream. Top with the remaining meringue layer and the rest of the chocolate cream. Arrange the meringue rosettes around the edge and fill the centres with strawberries.

Tropical Pavlova When the meringue has thickened, whisk in 1 teaspoon vinegar and 1 teaspoon cornflour (U.S. cornstarch). Spread immediately into a 22.5-cm/9-inch circle on a baking sheet lined with non-stick baking parchment (U.S. cookie sheet lined with waxed paper) and hollow out the centre slightly with the back of a spoon. Bake as in the main recipe for about 1 hour, or until firm. A Pavlova is not a dry meringue. Leave to cool then carefully transfer to a serving plate. Spread half the cream topping lightly in the hollow of the Pavlova and arrange a layer of well-drained canned lychees on top. Pipe large rosettes of the remaining cream topping using a star tube and spike these with halved slices of Kiwi fruit. Sprinkle the lychees with toasted shredded coconut.

Covering and decorating cakes with cream
Since so many people prefer not to eat cakes covered with a traditional sugar icing, there is quite a vogue for carrying out elaborate designs of covering and piping cakes with cream. Fresh whipped cream will not keep as long as butter icing, although the decorated cake can be open frozen, then covered to protect it, and stored in the freezer for several weeks. But cream which is made by the method shown below keeps twice as long as fresh dairy cream bought in a carton, and costs considerably less. It also has the advantage that, provided you have milk and unsalted butter available, you can make it whenever you like.

Storing meringues
Unfilled dry meringue shapes can be kept in an airtight container for up to a month, or in the freezer for six months. Pack in a rigid container as even when frozen they remain very fragile.

Chocolate layer gâteau

CAKE
3 tablespoons cocoa powder (U.S. 4 tablespoons unsweetened cocoa)

2 tablespoons (U.S. 3 tablespoons) hot water

175 g/6 oz (U.S. ¾ cup) butter or margarine

175 g/6 oz light soft brown sugar (U.S. ¾ cup light brown sugar)

3 large eggs

175 g/6 oz self-raising flour, sifted (U.S. 1½ cups all-purpose flour sifted with 1½ teaspoons baking powder)

FILLING AND DECORATION
about 100 g/4 oz plain chocolate (U.S. ⅔ cup semi-sweet chocolate pieces)

25 g/1 oz cocoa powder (U.S. ¼ cup unsweetened cocoa), sifted

little hot water

175 g/6 oz (U.S. ¾ cup) butter

350 g/12 oz icing sugar, sifted (U.S. 2⅔ cups sifted confectioners' sugar)

about 50 g/2 oz chocolate vermicelli (U.S. about ½ cup chocolate-flavored sprinkles or grated chocolate)

1. Heat the oven to 190°C/375°F, Gas Mark 5, grease two 20-cm/8-inch shallow cake tins and line with non-stick baking parchment (U.S. waxed paper).

2. Blend the cocoa with the water and leave to cool. Cream the butter and sugar together in a bowl until pale and fluffy. Beat in the eggs, one at a time, adding a tablespoon of flour with each. Beat in the cocoa mixture then fold in the remaining flour. Divide between the prepared tins and level the surface.

3. Bake for about 25 minutes or until just firm to the touch. Turn out the cakes on a wire rack, remove the lining paper and leave to cool.

4. Meanwhile, make the chocolate lace fans. On a sheet of non-stick baking parchment draw 14 elongated triangles, each having a base of 2.5 cm/1 inch and the long sides measuring 7.5 cm/3 inches. Melt the chocolate and place in a paper icing bag (see page 12). Snip off the end of the bag and pipe around the outside of each triangle. Then fill in with lines of chocolate in a random lace pattern, joining the two long sides of the triangles. Chill until set then carefully peel away the parchment and keep the fans chilled until required. You will need 12 good ones for the decoration.

5. To make the icing, blend the cocoa with just enough hot water to make a thick smooth cream. Put the butter in a bowl and beat until soft. Gradually add the sugar, alternately with the cocoa mixture, beating well until the icing is fluffy. Add a few extra drops of water if the icing is too stiff.

6. To assemble the gâteau, sandwich the cakes together with about a quarter of the icing. Coat the sides with a further quarter of the icing. Sprinkle the vermicelli on a sheet of non-stick baking parchment and roll the sides of the cake in this to coat evenly. Place on a serving dish. Spread more icing on the top of the cake and put the rest into a piping bag fitted with a medium-sized star tube. Pipe 12 rosettes of icing evenly round the top of the cake, about 1.25 cm/½ inch in from the edge. Set one chocolate fan on each rosette with the point into the centre. Pipe any remaining icing in a large whirl in the centre of the gâteau.
Serves 8–10

Chocolate lace fans.

Spider's web cake

(Illustrated on page 56)

CAKE
2 (17.5-cm/7-inch) layers Whisked sponge (see page 16)
FILLING AND DECORATION
2 (100-g/3½-oz) packs melt-in-the-bag chocolate cake covering
300 ml/½ pint double cream (U.S. 1¼ cups heavy cream)
½ quantity Glacé icing (see page 31)

1. Bake the cake layers and leave to cool. Meanwhile, make the chocolate shapes. Have ready a sheet of non-stick baking parchment (U.S. waxed paper). Melt the packs of cake covering in hot water as directed. Reserve about half one pack in a bowl and spread the rest of the cake covering over the parchment to make an even layer. Leave to set, then stamp out 5-cm/2-inch shapes with fancy cutters, hearts, diamonds etc. You will need eight shapes. Chill until required. Chop the chocolate trimmings very finely.
2. Place one cake layer on a serving platter. Whip the cream, reserve about two-thirds and mix the chocolate chips into the remainder. Use to sandwich the cake layers together.
3. Melt the reserved chocolate again if necessary by standing the bowl over hot water. Place in a paper icing bag (see page 12). Spread the glacé icing over the top of the cake. While the icing is still wet, snip off the tip of the bag and pipe five circles of chocolate on the top of the cake. Feather the icing immediately by drawing a fine skewer eight times from the centre to the outside of the cake evenly all round. Then draw the skewer from the outside of the cake to the centre eight times, working between the first lines. Leave to set until firm.
4. Spread cream around the sides of the cake and stick on the chocolate shapes. Put the rest into a piping bag fitted with a medium-sized star tube and pipe rosettes around the top of the cake and between the chocolate shapes.
Serves 8

Frosted angel cake

CAKE
50 g/2 oz self-raising flour (U.S. ½ cup all-purpose flour sifted with ½ teaspoon baking powder)
100 g/4 oz caster sugar (U.S. ½ cup granulated sugar)
4 egg whites
½ teaspoon cream of tartar
½ teaspoon vanilla essence (U.S. vanilla extract)
FILLING AND DECORATION
1 quantity American frosting (see page 31)
40 g/1½ oz (U.S. ⅓ cup) chopped walnuts or pecans
8 walnut or pecan halves

1. Heat the oven to 150°C/300°F, Gas Mark 2 and have ready an ungreased 17.5-cm/7-inch tube tin.
2. Sift the flour with the sugar three times. Place the egg whites in a clean bowl, add the cream of tartar and whisk until stiff. Sprinkle in the vanilla then fold in the dry ingredients lightly. When evenly blended, transfer the mixture to the tin and run a knife blade through it to break any air bubbles.
3. Bake for about 40 minutes, or until just firm to the touch. Lay a sheet of greaseproof paper (U.S. waxed paper) lightly over the cake when it is pale golden to prevent over-browning.
4. Leave the cake in the tin until cold, if possible inverting the tin over a wire rack during cooling. Loosen the cake by running a knife blade around it, then turn out on a serving plate. Split the cake into two layers.
5. Make up the frosting. Immediately take 2 rounded tablespoons (U.S. 3 rounded tablespoons) frosting, mix quickly with the chopped nuts and use to sandwich the cake layers together.
6. Spread the remaining frosting over the cake to cover the top, sides and inside the hollow. Mark the surface into swirls with a palette knife (U.S. spatula). Press the walnut halves lightly around the top edge and leave to set.
Serves 8

Strawberry flake crunch

(Illustrated below)

100 g/4 oz plain chocolate (U.S. $\frac{2}{3}$ cup semi-
sweet chocolate pieces)
100 g/4 oz (U.S. $\frac{1}{2}$ cup) butter
3 tablespoons golden syrup (U.S. 4 tablespoons
light corn syrup)
100 g/4 oz icing sugar, sifted (U.S. scant 1 cup
sifted confectioners' sugar)
finely grated rind of 1 orange
175 g/6 oz (U.S. 6 cups) cornflakes
FILLING AND DECORATION
300 ml/$\frac{1}{2}$ pint (U.S. $1\frac{1}{4}$ cups) whipping cream
about 225 g/8 oz ($\frac{1}{2}$ lb) strawberries, halved
6 small milk chocolate flakes

1. Grease two 17.5-cm/7-inch shallow cake tins and line the bases with greaseproof paper (U.S. waxed paper).
2. Place the chocolate in a large pan with the butter and syrup and heat very gently until the chocolate has melted. Stir in the sugar, orange rind and cornflakes, mixing well.
3. Divide the mixture between the prepared tins and press lightly. Chill until firm.

4. To assemble the gâteau, turn one cornflake layer out on a serving dish. Place the cream in a piping bag fitted with a large star tube and pipe about half on the layer. Reserve six neat strawberry halves for the decoration and arrange the rest on the cream. Top with the second cornflake layer. Pipe a ring of cream around the edge and the remainder in a large rosette in the centre. Set the flakes on top like the spokes of a wheel and put strawberry halves between them. This gâteau is best eaten within 4 hours of making.
Serves 6

Strawberry flake crunch.

Caramel coffee gâteau

(Illustrated on page 2)

CAKE
3 large eggs
100 g/4 oz soft light brown sugar (U.S. ½ cup light brown sugar)
2 teaspoons (U.S. 1 tablespoon) instant coffee powder
1 teaspoon boiling water
75 g/3 oz plain flour (U.S. ¾ cup all-purpose flour), sifted
FILLING AND DECORATION
1½ quantities coffee Crème au beurre (page 28)
50 g/2 oz flaked almonds (U.S. ½ cup slivered almonds), toasted
50 g/2 oz (U.S. ¼ cup) butter
50 g/2 oz light soft brown sugar (U.S. ¼ cup light brown sugar)
pinch of salt
75 ml/3 fl oz evaporated milk or single cream (U.S. ⅓ cup evaporated milk or light cream)
about 175 g/6 oz icing sugar, sifted (U.S. 1⅓ cups sifted confectioners' sugar)
25 g/1 oz plain chocolate (U.S. 1 square semi-sweet chocolate)

1. Heat the oven to 190°C/375°F, Gas Mark 5, grease two 17.5-cm/7-inch shallow cake tins and line with non-stick parchment (U.S. waxed paper).
2. Make up the Whisked sponge mixture as in the basic method (see page 16). Dissolve the coffee in the water and whisk into the eggs and sugar before adding the flour.
3. Divide the mixture between the tins. Bake for about 20 minutes, or until just firm to the touch. Turn on to a rack, remove the paper and cool.
4. Split each sponge layer in half to make four layers in all. Sandwich them together using almost half the crème au beurre and place on a serving plate. Spread more around the sides and press on the almonds. Put the remaining crème au beurre into a piping bag fitted with a large star tube.
5. To make up the topping, put the butter, brown sugar, salt and milk into a pan and heat very gently, stirring, until the sugar has dissolved and the mixture is smooth. Remove from the heat and sift in half the icing sugar. Beat well then gradually add enough of the remaining sugar to give a glossy smooth icing which will coat the back of the spoon thickly. Pour on top of the cake and leave to set.
6. Pipe a scroll border of crème au beurre around the edge of the cake.
7. Melt the chocolate in a bowl over a pan of hot water and place in a paper icing bag (see page 12). Snip off the tip and pipe a zig-zag line of chocolate over the caramel icing. Leave to set before serving.
Serves 10

Tia Maria coffee nut gâteau

(Illustrated opposite)

CAKE
225 g/8 oz (U.S. 1 cup) butter
225 g/8 oz caster sugar (U.S. 1 cup granulated sugar)
4 eggs
225 g/8 oz self-raising flour, sifted (U.S. 2 cups all-purpose flour sifted with 2 teaspoons baking powder)
50 g/2 oz (U.S. ½ cup) chopped nuts
FILLING AND DECORATION
275 g/10 oz (U.S. 1¼ cups) butter
275 g/10 oz icing sugar, sifted (U.S. 2¼ cups sifted confectioners' sugar)
2 tablespoons (U.S. 3 tablespoons) strong black coffee
4 tablespoons (U.S. scant 6 tablespoons) Tia Maria
50 g/2 oz flaked almonds (U.S. ½ cup slivered almonds), toasted

1. Heat the oven to 190°C/375°F, Gas Mark 5, grease two 22.5-cm/9-inch shallow cake tins and line the bases with greaseproof paper (U.S. waxed paper).
2. Cream the butter in a bowl until soft, then add the sugar and beat until light and fluffy. Add the eggs, one at a time, beating well after each addition. Fold in the flour and nuts. Divide the mixture between the prepared tins and level the surface.
3. Bake for 20 minutes, or until golden brown. Turn out on a wire rack, remove the lining paper and leave to cool.
4. Beat the butter for the icing until creamy then gradually add the sugar, coffee and Tia Maria.
5. To assemble the gâteau, sandwich the cakes together with about a quarter of the icing. Spread another quarter around the sides and coat with the almonds. Stand the cake on a serving dish and spread about half the remaining icing over the top. Mark swirls in the surface with a knife blade. Put the rest of the icing in a piping bag fitted with a large star tube and pipe rosettes all round the edge of the cake and in the centre.
Serves 8

Tia Maria coffee nut gâteau.

Cherry liqueur cake Omit the nuts in the cake layers but add 1 tablespoon Cherry Marnier or cherry brandy to the cake mixture with the eggs. To make the filling, use 1 egg yolk instead of the coffee and cherry liqueur for the Tia Maria. Crush 100 g/4 oz (U.S. 2–3 large) almond macaroons and use the crumbs to coat the sides of the cake in place of the nuts.

Pearl gâteau Make the cake layers, omitting the nuts and flavouring the mixture with 1 teaspoon vanilla essence (U.S. vanilla extract). While the cakes are in the oven, make up ½ quantity of Meringue cuite (see page 141). Turn the cake layers out on a wire rack for 5 minutes, leaving the oven on, then choose the one with the best surface and place on a baking sheet (U.S. cookie sheet). Put the meringue in a piping bag fitted with a 6-mm/¼-inch plain tube and pipe 'pearls' all round the top edge of the cake. Then continue piping concentric circles of meringue pearls until the top is covered. Place in the oven for about 3 minutes, until the meringue just starts to take colour. Make up half the filling mixture and carefully sandwich the cakes together with some of it. Spread the rest around the sides and mark the surface with the prongs of a fork.

Swirling out curved lines from the centre.

Mayfair chocolate gâteau

(Illustrated below)

100 g/4 oz plain chocolate (U.S. ⅔ cup semi-sweet chocolate pieces)
3 tablespoons (U.S. 4 tablespoons) water
175 g/6 oz (U.S. ¾ cup) butter or margarine
175 g/6 oz (U.S. ¾ cup) soft brown sugar
1 teaspoon vanilla essence (U.S. vanilla extract)
4 large eggs, separated
150 g/5 oz self-raising flour (U.S. 1¼ cups all-purpose flour sifted with 1¼ teaspoons baking powder)
25 g/1 oz cocoa (U.S. ¼ cup unsweetened cocoa)
ICING AND DECORATION
40 g/1½ oz (U.S. 3 tablespoons) butter
2 tablespoons (U.S. 3 tablespoons) water
50 g/2 oz caster sugar (U.S. ¼ cup granulated sugar)
1 teaspoon vanilla essence (U.S. vanilla extract)
75 g/3 oz icing sugar, sifted (U.S. scant ¾ cup sifted confectioners' sugar)
25 g/1 oz cocoa (U.S. ¼ cup unsweetened cocoa)
300 ml/½ pint double cream (U.S. 1¼ cups heavy cream)

50 g/2 oz plain chocolate (U.S. 2 squares semi-sweet chocolate), grated
1 chocolate square, triangle or curl (page 57)

1. Heat the oven to 180°C/350°F, Gas Mark 4, grease two 20-cm/8-inch shallow cake tins and line the bases with greaseproof (U.S. waxed) paper.
2. Put the chocolate and water in a bowl and stand this over a pan of hot water until the chocolate has melted. Stir lightly to blend. Cream the butter with the sugar and essence in a bowl until light and fluffy. Beat in the egg yolks, one at a time, then the chocolate. Sift the flour with the cocoa and fold in. Whisk the egg whites in a clean bowl until stiff and gently but thoroughly combine with the cake mixture. Divide the mixture between the tins.
3. Bake for about 25 minutes, or until firm to the touch. Turn on to a rack, remove paper and cool.
4. To make the icing, put the butter, water, sugar and vanilla in a pan and heat gently, stirring, until the sugar has dissolved. Remove from the heat, add the icing sugar and cocoa and beat well. Cool. Whip the cream and fold ⅔ into the cold mixture.
5. To assemble the gâteau, sandwich the cakes together with some of the icing then place on a serving plate and mask it completely with the remainder. Press the grated chocolate on the sides of the cake and mark the top with a knife blade.

Using a large star tube pipe one rosette of cream in the centre of the cake and spike with the chocolate decoration. Pipe a border of rosettes round the edge.
Serves 8

Pineapple savarin

DOUGH
1 teaspoon caster sugar (U.S. granulated sugar)
175 ml/6 fl oz (U.S. ¾ cup) warm milk
(43°C/110°F)
1 tablespoon dried yeast (U.S. active dried yeast)
225 g/8 oz plain flour (U.S. 2 cups all-purpose flour), sifted
pinch of salt
3 eggs, beaten
100 g/4 oz (U.S. ½ cup) butter, melted
SYRUP
100 g/4 oz (U.S. ½ cup) granulated sugar
175 ml/6 fl oz (U.S. ¾ cup) pineapple juice
50 ml/2 fl oz (U.S. ¼ cup) water
3 tablespoons (U.S. 4 tablespoons) rum
GLAZE
50 ml/2 fl oz (U.S. ¼ cup) pineapple or apricot jam, sieved
1 tablespoon water
DECORATION
300 ml/½ pint (U.S. 1¼ cups) whipping cream, whipped
4 rings glacé pineapple (U.S. candied pineapple)
8 glacé cherries (U.S. candied cherries), halved

1. Dissolve the sugar in the milk and sprinkle on the yeast. Leave in a warm place for about 10 minutes, or until frothy. Meanwhile, grease a 22.5-cm/9-inch plain ring tin.
2. Sift the flour and salt into a bowl and make a well in the centre. Drop in the egg, yeast liquid and butter and beat until smooth. Pour into the prepared mould, cover with greased cling film and leave in a warm place for about 45 minutes, or until the dough has almost filled the tin. While rising, heat the oven to 200°C/400°F, Gas Mark 6.
3. Uncover and bake for 40 minutes, or until golden and firm to the touch. Turn on a rack and cool.
4. To make the syrup, place the sugar, pineapple juice and water in a pan and heat gently, stirring, until the sugar has dissolved. Boil for 4 minutes then remove from the heat and stir in the rum.
5. Transfer the savarin to a serving plate and prick all over with a fine skewer or cocktail stick (U.S.

Mayfair chocolate gâteau.

toothpick). Spoon the hot syrup slowly over the ring and leave it to stand for at least 1 hour.
6. Place the jam and water in a pan and heat, stirring all the time, until smooth. Brush over the ring.
7. Put the cream into a piping bag fitted with a large star tube. Pipe eight large rosettes evenly around the top of the ring then the rest in a continuous spiral to fill the centre. Divide each pineapple ring into eight pieces. Decorate every cream rosette with a cherry half on top and a pineapple piece on either side, pressed in to look like butterfly wings. Spike the cream filling with the remaining pineapple.
Serves 8

Pecan square dance cake

CAKE
190 g/6½ oz plain flour (U.S. 1⅔ cups all-purpose flour)
2 teaspoons (U.S. 1 tablespoon) baking powder
½ teaspoon salt
225 g/8 oz caster sugar (U.S. 1 cup granulated sugar)
100 g/4 oz (U.S. ½ cup) butter, softened
150 ml/¼ pint (U.S. ⅔ cup) milk
3 egg whites
finely grated rind of ½ orange
½ teaspoon vanilla essence (U.S. vanilla extract)
50 g/2 oz (U.S. ½ cup) chopped pecans
DECORATION
25 g/1 oz plain chocolate (U.S. 1 square semi-sweet chocolate)
4 teaspoons (U.S. 2 tablespoons) warm milk
100 g/4 oz (U.S. ½ cup) butter, softened
275 g/10 oz icing sugar, sifted (U.S. 2¼ cups sifted confectioners' sugar)
1 egg yolk
½ teaspoon vanilla essence (U.S. vanilla extract)
100 g/4 oz (U.S. 1 cup) finely chopped pecans
8 pecan halves

1. Heat the oven to 180°C/350°F, Gas Mark 4, grease a 20-cm/8-inch square tin and sprinkle with flour.
2. Sift the flour, baking powder and salt into a bowl then sprinkle on the sugar. Add the butter and milk and beat, if possible using an electric mixer on medium speed, for 1½ minutes. Add the unbeaten egg whites, orange rind and vanilla and beat again for a further 1½ minutes. Fold in the nuts, transfer to the prepared tin and level the surface.
3. Bake for about 45 minutes, or until just firm to the touch. Leave in the tin for 5 minutes then turn out and cool on a wire rack.
4. To make the icing, melt the chocolate with half the milk in a bowl over a pan of hot water. Stir to blend then leave to cool slightly. Put the butter,

sugar, egg yolk and vanilla into a bowl and beat well until smooth. Take just under half the icing and mix in the chocolate. Chill until firm enough to spread.
5. Divide the cake into four squares with a sharp knife and cover two opposite squares with vanilla icing and the remaining two with chocolate icing. Mark the surface of the icing on each square of cake diagonally in lines with a knife blade. Put the four squares of cake together on a serving plate so that they just adhere. Do not press hard enough to squeeze out the icing. Use the chopped nuts to cover the sides of the cake then decorate the top with a pecan half in each corner and four pecan halves in the centre, each one lying along a join line of chocolate and vanilla icing.
Serves 9

Strawberry cream shortbread

(Illustrated opposite)

SHORTBREAD
275 g/10 oz plain flour (U.S. 2½ cups all-purpose flour)
50 g/2 oz (U.S. ⅓ cup) ground rice
100 g/4 oz caster sugar (U.S. ½ cup granulated sugar)
225 g/8 oz (U.S. 1 cup) butter
FILLING AND DECORATION
300 ml/½ pint double cream (U.S. 1¼ cups heavy cream)
little sugar for sprinkling if wished
few even-sized strawberries

1. Heat the oven to 160°C/325°F, Gas Mark 3, grease two 17.5-cm/7-inch fluted shallow tins and line each base with a circle of non-stick baking parchment (U.S. waxed paper).
2. Sift the flour into a bowl and add the rice and sugar. Gradually rub or cut in the butter, then work with your fingertips until the mixture can be pressed into a ball. Knead thoroughly. Divide the mixture in half and press into the prepared tins.

3. Bake for about 45 minutes, or until pale golden. Leave in the tins until firm then turn out and cut one shortbread into eight wedges.
4. Place the whole shortbread layer on a serving dish. Whip the cream and spread half of it over the shortbread, keeping well clear of the edge. Arrange four wedges of shortbread from the second layer evenly on the cream and sprinkle with sugar if wished. Put the remaining cream into a piping bag fitted with a large star tube and pipe a large rosette in the centre of the cake and a large whirl of cream between each shortbread wedge. Top the cream decorations with strawberries. (Serve the remaining four shortbread wedges separately.)
Serves 6–8

_____ VARIATION _____

Individual strawberry shortbreads Serve wedges of shortbread decorated with cream and strawberry slices. Place whipped cream in a piping bag fitted with a medium-sized star tube and pipe a heart shape on each shortbread wedge. Take one large strawberry for each individual 'cake' and cut it into four neat slices. Lay these, overlapping, in the centre of the cream heart.

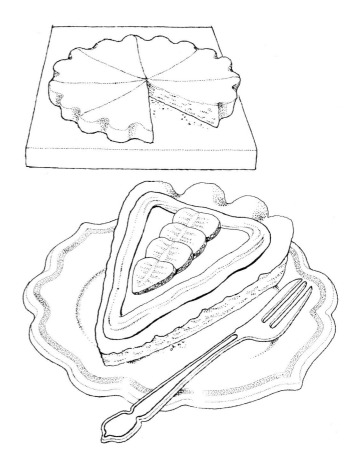

Strawberry cream shortbread.

Cakes for Grand Occasions

On very special occasions, the centrepiece of the catering plan is usually a very special cake. This is a long-standing tradition and, since such cakes are expensive to buy, well worth making yourself. It is a process to which you must devote plenty of time, as it is carried out in stages.

When deciding on the colour scheme, keep the whole décor of the table setting in mind. For instance, if the wedding theme is pale yellow for bridesmaids' dresses, flowers, table napkins – choose that as the colour to make up moulded or piped roses or other flowers and motifs. For a christening, once you know whether the baby is a boy or girl, that will dictate the colour scheme.

Single tier cakes do not present any special problem, but since a tiered wedding cake is made so rarely, here are some hints to achieve complete success. The pillars should be round or square, according to the shape of the cakes. The bottom tier board will have to carry considerable weight. Assemble the tiers for a 'trial run' beforehand, but thereafter keep them in separate boxes until the day of the occasion. Take no risks with the danger of upper tiers subsiding into the bottom layer by leaving it assembled overnight. When it comes to cutting the cake, direct the bride and groom to cut into the bottom tier in the least heavily decorated part, using just the tip of the knife at the centre and then pulling it down to the board at the part of the blade where it meets the handle.

American bridal cake (see pages 116–117)

Primrose valentine cake

(Illustrated opposite)

CAKE
ingredients for 1 (20-cm/8-inch) Dark rich fruit cake baked in a heart-shaped tin (see pages 23–25)
COVERING AND DECORATION
about 225 g/8 oz (U.S. ⅔ cup) apricot jam, boiled and sieved
1¼ quantities Almond paste (see page 33)
1 (25-cm/10-inch) wide heart-shaped or round silver-coloured cake board
½ quantity Royal icing (see page 34)
little whisked egg white
about 550 g/1¼ lb bought Ready-to-roll icing or 1½ quantities Fondant moulding paste (see page 35)
green food colouring
MOULDED FLOWERS
about 100 g/4 oz bought Ready-to-roll icing or ¼ quantity Fondant moulding paste (see page 35)
yellow, brown and green food colourings
DECORATION
1 metre/39 inches of 2.5 cm/1 inch wide pale green ribbon

1. Brush the cake with apricot jam and cover with almond paste (see page 33). Leave to dry for 24 hours.
2. Position the cake on the board, securing with a little royal icing. Brush the almond paste all over with egg white and cover with almost all the ready-to-roll icing or moulding paste (see page 35). Roll out the reserved icing thinly and cut six heart-shapes about 5 cm/2 inches high.
3. Use the 100 g/4 oz ready-to-roll icing or moulding paste to mould 8–10 snowdrops (see page 52) and 12–15 primroses (see page 52). Lay the flowers and heart-shapes on nonstick baking parchment (U.S. waxed paper) and leave them and the cake to dry for at least 24 hours.
4. To finish the cake, prick out the words 'Be my Valentine' on the top. Put most of the royal icing in a piping bag fitted with a medium-sized star tube and pipe a shell border around the base of the cake. Tint the remaining icing pale green and place in a piping bag fitted with a No. 2 writing tube. Pipe an outline 6 mm/¼ inch in from the edge around each heart-shaped plaque. Pipe the message on top of the cake and when dry overpipe. Tie the ribbon around the sides of the cake then attach the hearts over the ribbon with a little royal icing. Arrange the flowers in groups on the cake and attach with dots of royal icing.
Serves about 16

Madeira primrose valentine cake The decoration can also be carried out on a Madeira cake mixture baked in the heart-shaped tin. Use ingredients for the 20-cm/8-inch central tier of the American bridal cake (see page 116). Trim the baked cake flat and turn it upside down before coating. Omit the almond paste if wished and brush the cake with apricot jam before applying the icing.

Golden wedding cake

CAKE
1 (22.5-cm/9-inch) square Dark rich fruit cake (see pages 23–25)
COVERING AND DECORATION
225 g/8 oz (U.S. ⅔ cup) apricot jam, boiled and sieved
2 quantities Almond paste (see page 33)
2 quantities Fondant moulding paste (see page 35)
yellow food colouring
1 (27.5-cm/11-inch) square gold-coloured cake board
whisked egg white
¾ quantity Royal icing (see page 34)

1. Brush the cake with jam and cover with almond paste (see page 33). Leave to dry.
2. Roll out some of the fondant paste and use to cut ten heart-shaped plaques as in Primrose valentine cake (opposite). Tint all remaining paste golden yellow with food colouring, kneading it in well.
3. Position the cake on the board, brush with egg white and flat ice with the yellow fondant. Put the plaques on non-stick baking parchment (U.S. waxed paper) and leave them and the cake to dry for at least 24 hours.
4. Draw the initial of the first name of the wife in five of the plaques and the initial of the first name of the husband in the others.
5. Reserve about one third of the royal icing and tint the remainder golden yellow to match the fondant. Place in a piping bag fitted with a No. 2 plain tube. Pipe the initials on the plaques, leave to set briefly, then pipe tiny beads or dots all round the top edges of the plaques. Leave to dry thoroughly.
6. Mount a pair of plaques, centred, on each side of the cake, with the points of the hearts slightly inclined together. Secure them with dabs of icing.
7. Draw the word 'Congratulations', the full first names of the couple and the number '50' on a piece

Primrose valentine cake.

of greaseproof paper (U.S. waxed paper). Prick out diagonally on top of the cake with 'Congratulations' on one line, the names in a line below this, then space allowed to position the last pair of hearts before pricking out the number of years married underneath.

8. First position the plaques, fixing them once more with the points of the hearts inclined together. Put the reserved white royal icing in a piping bag fitted with a No. 2 tube and pipe in the greeting, names and number. If wished, leave to dry and overpipe with a No. 1 tube.

9. Mix together all the remaining royal icing and add more colouring if necessary to get the golden yellow shade again. Put in a piping bag fitted with a small star tube and pipe a shell border around the base of the cake where it touches the board, to neaten.

Serves about 20

_____ VARIATION _____

Silver wedding cake Use a silver-coloured board, make the plaques pale blue and cover the cake with white fondant. Pipe the plaques with white royal icing and top each other bead around the edge with a silver ball. Pipe the greeting, names and number '25' in pale blue and decorate the base corners of the cake with pairs of silver leaves or bells.

Congratulations cake

(Illustrated opposite)

This lovely design suits may different occasions as a name or names can be piped in under the word 'Congratulations' to celebrate an exam success, an engagement or a wedding anniversary.

CAKE
1 (20-cm/8-inch) square Dark rich fruit cake
(see pages 23–25)
COVERING AND DECORATION
175–225 g/6–8 oz (U.S. $\frac{1}{2}$–$\frac{2}{3}$ cup) apricot jam,
boiled and sieved
1$\frac{3}{4}$ quantities Almond paste (see page 33)
1 (25-cm/10-inch) square silver-coloured cake
board
$\frac{3}{4}$ quantity Royal icing (see page 34)
1$\frac{1}{2}$ quantities Fondant moulding paste (see page
35)
peach (or red and yellow) food colourings

1. Brush the cake with apricot jam and cover with almond paste (see page 33). Leave to dry.
2. Position the cake on the board, securing with a little royal icing. Tint two-thirds of the moulding paste peach, kneading until evenly coloured. Use to cover the cake (see page 35). Leave to dry.
3. Reserve one quarter of the remaining paste. Use the rest to mould ten small, six medium and two large roses and six white leaves (see page 54). Tint the reserved portion pale peach and use to make one large and two medium roses.
4. Make a template by cutting a strip of paper the same size as one side of the cake i.e. about 20 cm/8 inches by 7 cm/2$\frac{3}{4}$ inches. Fold the strip in half across, then in half twice more in the same way. Open the strip out to give eight equal sections. Mark an X at the top of each fold mark. Carefully place the template to one side of the cake and prick through the paper at each X. Repeat this on the three remaining sides. These marks will be the guides for piping the first set of loops.
5. Trace the word 'Congratulations' on greaseproof paper (U.S. waxed paper) and prick it out diagonally across the centre of the cake.

Trace off the appropriate words of greeting.

CONGRATULATIONS

HAPPY ANNIVERSARY

6. With royal icing and a No. 2 writing tube, pipe over the word 'Congratulations'. When dry, pipe over again.

7. With the same tube, carefully pipe eight shallow loops at the top edge of each side of the cake, joining the pricked marks.

8. Pipe more loops over these, starting halfway along the first loop previously iced. When these are dry, pipe 2 small dots at the top of each of the second set of loops. At each corner only, pipe three small dots at the top of the first set of loops.

9. With a No. 4 writing tube, pipe a row of medium-sized dots all around the base of the cake. At every third dot, and with the same tube, pipe two smaller dots, one above the other. At each corner pipe two small dots on the cake board. Finally, using the No. 2 tube, link the lines of three dots with loops.

10. Arrange two medium and two small white modelled roses and two leaves at one corner of the cake. Arrange the remaining roses and leaves diagonally opposite. Secure the decorations with a little royal icing.

Serves about 16

Snow white wedding cake

There is a very striking built-up border to this otherwise simple cake, which lends itself very well to transferring the design to smaller upper tiers.

CAKE
1 (20-cm/8-inch) square Dark rich fruit cake (see pages 23–25)
COVERING AND DECORATION
225 g/8 oz (U.S. ⅔ cup) apricot jam, boiled and sieved
1¾ quantities Almond paste (see page 33)
1 (25-cm/10-inch) square silver cake board
3½ quantities Royal icing (see page 34)
1 small bought flower decoration

1. Brush the cake with apricot jam and cover with almond paste (see page 33). Leave to dry.

2. Position the cake on the board, securing with a little royal icing. Flat ice the cake with royal icing (see page 36) and leave to dry for at least 24 hours.

3. Make a template by cutting out a 20-cm/8-inch square from greaseproof paper (U.S. waxed paper). Fold in half and then in half again, to give four smaller squares. Open out. Measure 1.25 cm/½ inch in from the outside edge and draw another square, then another 1.25 cm/½ inch in and draw a further square. Draw a concave curve from the corner of the middle square up to the line of the inner square and down to the centre fold line. Repeat until there are eight curves. Make a second template with a

strip of paper about 6.5 cm/2½ inches wide and the length of the side of the cake. Mark each corner and the centre point 1.25 cm/½ inch down from the top edge. Join the marks with loops, dipping to 4 cm/1½ inches from the top edge of the template. Make further loops, just below the first ones.

4. Place the template on top of the cake and prick out the curves. Mark the central point on each top side edge. From these points, measure down 1.25 cm/½ inch and then 5 cm/2 inches on each side. Prick out the loops on all sides of the cake.

5. Using a No. 4 writing tube and royal icing, pipe over the traced design on top of the cake. Pipe another line a little inside this. Pipe a row of small dots, just inside the second piped line, following the shape of the curves. Pipe a large dot at each corner and at the centre of each side, where the dotted lines and the piped lines meet.

6. Using a No. 7 writing tube, pipe a curved square just outside the first piped curved square. Between this line and the edge of the cake, fill in with a lacy pattern using a No. 1 writing tube (see page 44).

7. Using the No. 7 tube again, pipe a large dot at each mark 5 cm/2 inches down in the centre of each side of the cake. Pipe two more dots above the first dot, leaving a slight gap each time.

8. With a medium-sized star tube, beginning at one corner, start piping a large coil, working along one side of the cake to the centre point, gradually diminishing the size of the coil as you pipe. Repeat, piping the next coil from that centre point to the next corner. Do the same on the other sides. Repeat the coil decoration immediately underneath the first at the top edge of the sides of the cake. Pipe a regular coil border around the base of the cake.

9. Using the No. 7 tube again, pipe over the top coil border, starting at one corner and piping an incomplete circle, then gradually piping diagonally down the length of the coil to the centre side point. Repeat all round the cake, piping next from the centre side point to the second corner. Pipe over the base coil border in the same way. Overpipe.

10. Using the No. 7 tube again, pipe the shallow loops on the cake sides. With a No. 4 tube, pipe the second deeper loops. Leave icing to harden.

11. On the wedding day, add the flower decoration.

To make a two-tier cake
Bake a 15-cm/6-inch square Dark rich fruit cake for the top tier. Cover with almond paste, mount on a 20-cm/8-inch square silver-coloured cake board and flat ice. Follow the same pattern for the decoration, making a 15-cm/6-inch template and reducing the size of the loops and coils accordingly. When all the icing is firm, position four pillars, each 2.5 cm/1 inch in from the corners on the larger cake and mount the smaller cake on top. Fix a small flower decoration in each corner on the small cake and a larger decoration in the centre.

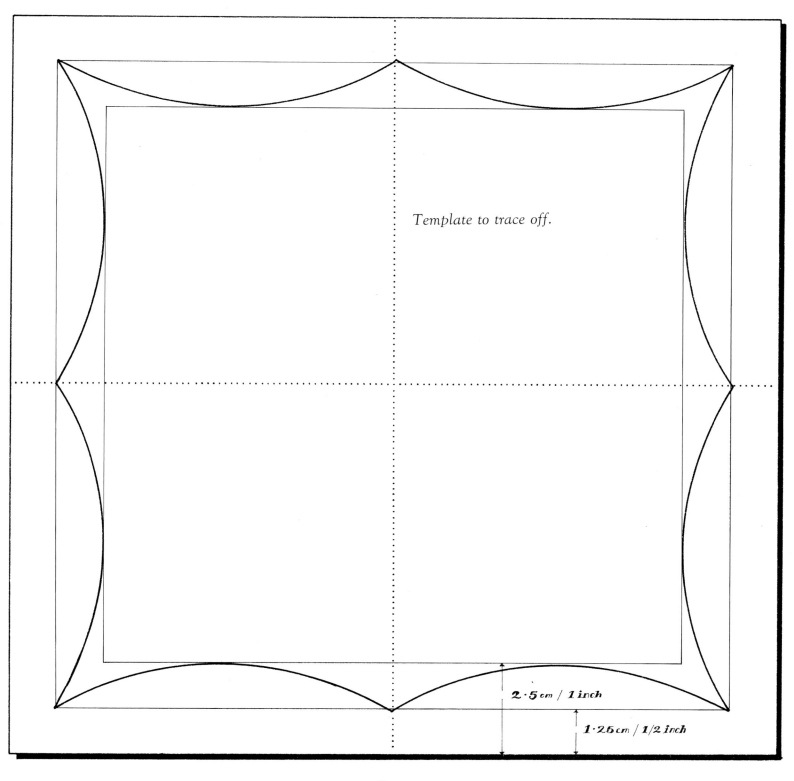

Template to trace off.

2·5 cm / 1 inch

1·25 cm / 1/2 inch

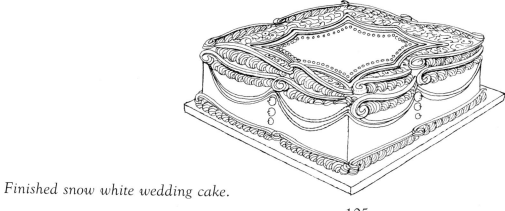

Finished snow white wedding cake.

Golden rose basket

(Illustrated opposite)

CAKE
1 (20-cm/8-inch) square Madeira cake (see page 116)
1 (25-cm/10-inch) square silver-coloured cake board
COVERING AND DECORATION
about 225 g/8 oz (U.S. $\frac{2}{3}$ cup) apricot jam, boiled and sieved
little whisked egg white
about 550 g/1$\frac{1}{2}$ lb bought Ready-to-roll icing or 1$\frac{1}{2}$ quantities Fondant moulding paste (see page 35)
1 quantity Royal icing (see page 34)
MOULDED FLOWERS
about 350 g/12 oz bought Ready-to-roll icing or $\frac{3}{4}$ quantity Fondant moulding paste (see page 35)
yellow and orange food colourings
1 (27.5-cm/11-inch) square silver-coloured cake board (optional)

1. Trim the top of the cake level if necessary then turn it over and place on the cake board. Brush the top and sides of the cake with apricot jam and the edge and narrow sides of the cake board with egg white. Roll out a little icing into strips to cover the board thinly from the edge of the cake to the edge of the board and over the sides. Smooth the icing well with the fingertips dipped in cornflour (U.S. cornstarch). Use about two-thirds of the remaining icing to cover the top and sides of the cake (see page 35).

2. Roll out the rest of the icing to a square the same size as the top of the cake and trim neatly. Place the square on a sheet of non-stick baking parchment (U.S. waxed paper) and cut in half diagonally. Separate the triangles slightly.

3. Put some of the royal icing in a piping bag fitted with a No. 2 writing tube. Fill another bag fitted with a basket weave or ribbon weave tube. Pipe three or four horizontal lines about 3 cm/1$\frac{1}{4}$ inches long with the basket weave tube on one side of the cake. Have the lines immediately above each other and leave a space the width of the tube between each line. With the writing tube, pipe a straight vertical line downwards at the end of these lines.

Stages in making Golden rose basket.

Then, with the basket weave tube again, pipe more lines as before, putting them between the first lines, starting half-way along each line and piping over the vertical line. Make another straight line in the same way and continue piping the basket weave design all round the cake. It should just touch the icing on the board and one row can be worked tipping over the top edge of the cake. Then work the same design over the two icing triangles.

4. To make the roses, tint the icing in three shades of gold with yellow and orange food colourings, and mould 40 roses of various sizes (see page 54). Lay the flowers on non-stick baking parchment (U.S. waxed paper).

5. Put the rest of the royal icing into a piping bag fitted with the writing tube and pipe a continuous twisted loop all round the base of the cake board to make a border. Leave the cake, icing triangles and roses to dry for at least 24 hours.

6. To assemble the cake, lay one of the triangular 'lids' on the cake, attaching it lightly with royal icing. Arrange moulded roses over the front half of the cake, as shown, attaching them with dots of icing where necessary. Put on the other 'lid', tilting it so that it lays gently on the flowers. Attach the lid with royal icing and then complete the basket by arranging the remaining roses in the centre of the cake where the lids join. If wished, set the whole cake and board on a second board.

Serves about 16

Note The Golden rose basket design can also be worked over a 20-cm/8-inch square Dark rich fruit cake (see page 23–25) but this should be coated with almond paste and brushed with egg white before the icing is added.

Looped ribbon cake

(Illustrated on the cover)

Bake a 20-cm/8-inch round Dark rich fruit cake (see pages 23–25) and coat with Almond paste (see page 33). Position the cake on a 25-cm/10-inch round silver-coloured cake board, flat ice with Fondant moulding paste (see page 35) and leave to dry.

Mark the centre of the cake. Make up ½ quantity Royal icing (see page 34) and tint golden yellow with food colouring. Using a small petal tube, make thirteen rose buds (see page 47) and dry off. With more yellow icing and a small star tube, pipe rosettes all round the base of the cake and the top edge. Using a No. 1 writing tube, top each rosette with a pearl. With a pin, mark off sections round the side of the cake, 1.25 cm/½ inch down from the top edge of the cake, and 5 cm/2 inches apart. Take a piece of very narrow matching golden yellow ribbon, 130 cm/52 inches long, and mark off in 10-cm/4-inch sections. Fix one end at a marked point with a dot of icing then pipe in another dot of icing and top with a rosebud. This will have to be removed temporarily when you reach the end of the piece of ribbon. Pick up the ribbon at the first marked section and fix to the side of the cake in the same way with a dot of icing and a rosebud. Continue the trimming round the cake until you reach your starting point. Remove the first rosebud, join the two ribbon ends with icing and replace the rosebud.

Fill a shallow tiny vase (a small silver mustard pot would be suitable) with a delicate toning flower arrangement and fix over the marked centre with a dot of icing.

Stages in Piping basket weave.

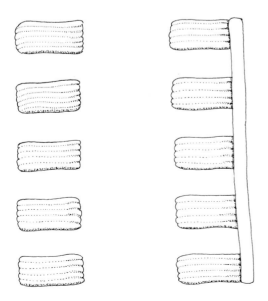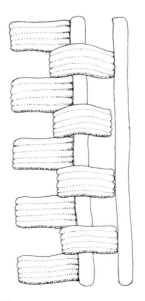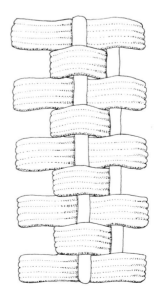

Linked rosette cake

(Illustrated on pages 10–11)

Bake a 22.5-cm/9-inch square Dark rich fruit cake (see pages 23–25) and coat with Almond paste (see page 33). Position the cake on a 27.5 cm/11 inch square gold-coloured board, flat ice with Royal icing or Fondant moulding paste (see pages 34 or 35) and leave to dry.

Taking one side of the cake at a time and using a ruler and pin, mark the very edge in ten equal divisions, making sure that you start and end with a corner mark. Using white royal icing and a small star tube, pipe a rosette on each mark. Then, 6 mm/¼ inch down the side of the cake, pipe a rosette centred between 2 rosettes in the first row and continue in this way all round the cake. Pipe rosettes around the base of the cake then a second row above every alternate rosette. Leave to dry for 2 hours.

Tint more royal icing a pale pastel shade. Using coloured icing and a No. 1 writing tube, pipe a line of icing linking one top corner rosette diagonally with the first rosette beneath it. Then continue linking the rosettes on top of the cake with those on the sides diagonally all round. Allow to dry. Overpipe with another line of coloured icing, starting half-way between one of the corner rosettes and the one next to it, down to the space between the first two rosettes on the side of the cake. Continue as before, all round the top of the cake.

With the same tube, pipe loops between the upper line of rosettes round the base of the cake, dipping the loop down to the centre of the single rosettes in between. Decorate the top with toning artificial leaves and flowers. If liked, pipe in a message diagonally from one corner to the other of the cake.

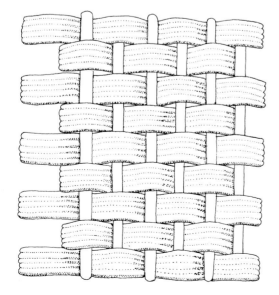

Pink daisy cake

(Illustrated on page 2)

Bake a 20-cm/8-inch round Glacé fruit cake (see page 22) and position on a 25-cm/10-inch round silver-coloured cake board. Flat ice with Fondant moulding paste tinted a deep pink (see page 35). Leave to dry.

Using ¼ quantity of white Fondant moulding paste, roll out thinly and stamp out twelve 2.5-cm/1-inch circles and nine 2-cm/¾-inch circles. Place the circles on a working surface lightly dusted with icing sugar (U.S. confectioners' sugar) and mark the centres. Place the tip of a wooden cocktail stick (U.S. toothpick) on the centre and press firmly. Continue pressing out petals all round the centre like the spokes of a wheel. Snip all round the edges of the petals just to separate them. Shape a small strip of foil into a circle and lay the daisy in this so that the centre dips down slightly in the middle. Repeat with the remaining icing circles and leave to dry.

You will need a ¼ quantity of Royal icing (see page 34) to pipe large shells all round the base of the cake with a medium-sized star tube. Mark off the edge of the cake in three even segments. Mark off the base of the cake into six equal sections, at points directly under and between the top marked sections. Paint the tips of the daisy petals with pink food colouring and the centres with yellow food colouring. Arrange groups of three flowers at each marked point on the top of the cake and two flowers at each marked point round the base of the cake, securing them with dots of icing.

Using a small leaf tube and royal icing, surround the groups of flowers with leaves. Using a No. 2 writing tube, pipe diagonal lines joining the groups of flowers on top of the cake with alternate groups at the base, and pipe small dots from the leaves down the side of the cake.

Sports motif birthday cake

(Illustrated opposite)

CAKE
1 (7-egg) quantity lemon Victoria sandwich cake mixture made by the Quick-mix method (see page 21)
MOULDED DECORATIONS
about $\frac{1}{4}$ quantity white Almond paste (see page 33)
brown and red food colourings
1 large silver-coloured cake board, about 60 cm/24 inches by 30 cm/12 inches
GLAZE
225 g/8 oz (U.S. $\frac{2}{3}$ cup) apricot jam
4 tablespoons (U.S. 6 tablespoons) water
FILLING AND DECORATION
2$\frac{1}{2}$ quantities lemon Butter icing (see page 28)
green food colouring

1. Thoroughly grease required numeral cake tins, put a strip of greaseproof paper (U.S. waxed paper) in the base of each tin and grease the paper. If it is not possible to put paper in the tins, dredge with flour and shake out the excess. Heat the oven to 180°C/350°F, Gas Mark 4.
2. Make up the cake mixture and use to fill the prepared tins evenly.
3. Bake for about 1 hour each, or until firm to the touch. Turn out carefully on to a wire rack, remove the lining paper and leave to cool.
4. To make the sporting motifs, tint the almond paste a very pale brown with food colouring. Shape part of it into eight cricket bats about 5–6 cm/2–2$\frac{1}{2}$ inches long. The handles of the bats may be painted a little darker with food colouring and left to dry. Roll the remainder of the almond paste into very thin sausages and cut into two sets of three stumps using 6–7.5-cm/2$\frac{1}{2}$–3-inch lengths, and short pieces to fit over the top for the bails. Colour the brown almond paste trimmings a deep red with red and brown food colouring and roll into four cricket balls. Leave all the decorations on a sheet of non-stick baking parchment (U.S. waxed paper) to dry. They may be made several weeks before required and stored in a sealed container.
5. If necessary, trim the cakes so they are exactly the same thickness. Transfer to the cake board.
6. To make the apricot glaze, boil the jam and water together in a pan, stirring, for 2 minutes. Sieve and leave to cool. Brush the cakes all over with glaze.
7. Make up the butter icing, adding just sufficient liquid to give a firm spreading consistency. Tint pale green with food colouring. Remove about a quarter of the icing and tint it a darker shade of green; keep closely covered in a bowl.

111

Sporting designs to copy.

8. Use the pale green icing to mask both the cakes completely, giving a fairly smooth surface to the sides and marking a pattern on the top using a round-bladed knife. Leave to set.

9. Add any remaining butter icing to the dark green icing, mix well and put into a piping bag fitted with a medium-sized star tube. Pipe a shell edge all round the base of the two cakes; then pipe another shell border around the top edges.

10. Put two crossed cricket bats and a cricket ball at the top and bottom of both the cakes and a set of stumps in between them. A name may also be piped on top in the dark green icing, if liked. Leave to set.
Serves about 12

Louise's birthday cake

(Illustrated below)

CAKE
1 (17.5-cm/7-inch) round Madeira cake (see page 116)
COVERING AND DECORATION
1 (22.5-cm/9-inch) round silver-coloured cake board
½ quantity Royal icing (see page 34)
175 g/6 oz (U.S. ½ cup) apricot jam, boiled and sieved

2 quantities Fondant moulding paste (see page 35)
yellow and green food colouring
short lengths of florists' wire
pearl stamens
little beaten egg white
about 1 metre/39 inches narrow green ribbon
small pieces of tulle
about 1 metre/39 inches of 6-mm/¼-inch wide golden yellow ribbon

1. Trim the top of the cake flat then turn it over and position on the cake board, securing with a little royal icing. Brush with apricot jam and use sufficient fondant moulding paste to cover the cake (see page 35).

2. Roll out some of the remaining white moulding paste and cut a 10-cm/4-inch fluted round. Mark one side in a diamond pattern with a knife blade and place the round over a rolling pin to dry. This makes the basket. Use more white moulding paste to mould about eight daisies each with six or seven petals (see page 53).

3. Tint further paste golden yellow and make 3–4 moulded roses, inserting short wires before the flowers are dry (see page 54). Make about 24 tiny and six slightly larger yellow flowers (see note). Insert stamens in larger flowers when completely

dry. Make yellow dot centres for the white moulded daisies.

4. With royal icing and a No. 1 writing tube, pipe out about 72 lace edgings (see page 48) on non-stick baking parchment (U.S. waxed paper), although you will only need about 36.

5. Cut a template to fit around the circumference of the cake. Fold this in half across, then fold into three, to give six equal-sized sections. Unfold, fold in half lengthways and unfold again. Mark 2.5 cm/1 inch down from the top edge on each fold mark. Draw loops to join these marks, dipping to the central fold mark each time. Place around the cake and prick out the loops on the side of the cake.

6. With the No. 1 tube again, fill in the area between the loop markings and the base of the cake with tiny random dots. Leave to dry.

7. Make the base frill by rolling out the remaining fondant. Cut into 2.5-cm/1-inch wide strips then press with the side of the ruler 6 mm/¼ inch from one side of each strip, to make the top 'gathered' edge. Then stretch the other edge evenly by pressing with a wooden cocktail stick (U.S. toothpick). Do not attempt to make the frill in one long length. Brush the base of the cake and the surface of the cake board with egg white and attach the first piece of frill. Join more pieces as necessary, smoothing over the joins with a fingertip. Apply the frill as soon as it is made, otherwise it will be brittle and difficult to handle.

8. With a small star tube and royal icing, pipe a shell border around the top of the frill. When dry, fix the green ribbon round the cake, just above the border. Join the ends together with icing.

9. Draw the name on a piece of paper and prick out on top of the cake. Tint some royal icing green to match the ribbon and pipe the name with a No. 2 tube. When dry, overpipe.

10. Cut six 1.25-cm/½-inch lengths of green ribbon. Take a sharp pointed knife and make two slits the same width as the ribbon and 6 mm/¼ inch apart just above the centre of each marked loop on the side of the cake. Insert the end of one tiny piece of ribbon in the first hole, then twist the other end and insert into the second hole, using tweezers to help if necessary. When both ends are in place, press the loop with your fingertip to flatten it. Repeat all round the cake with the other pieces of ribbon.

11. Cut twelve 1.25-cm/½-inch lengths of green ribbon and trim one end of each diagonally. Stick two pieces to the top of one loop with icing then attach three tiny yellow flowers over the join with more icing. Do this at the top of each loop all round the cake.

12. With royal icing and a No. 1 tube, pipe a tiny leaf and stem design inside each loop. Leave to dry.

13. Make up the basket decoration. Put a ball of fondant in the curved basket and press in wired roses, pieces of tulle, ribbon loops and yellow and white flowers to hide the fondant. Place on the cake and attach with royal icing. Use up any remaining flowers by attaching them to the top and sides of the cake.

14. Finally, attach the lace edging. Working only the width of one piece of edging at a time, pipe small pearls with a No. 1 tube over the pricked loops, then lift a lace motif with tweezers and press into the icing at an angle of 45 degrees. Repeat all round the cake, taking care to keep the work even. Leave to dry.

Serves about 12

Note To make the small yellow flowers for the sides of the cake and the wired yellow flowers in the basket decoration, roll out fondant moulding paste thinly and stamp out a tiny shape with a 5-petal cutter. Push out of the cutter and place on a piece of foam. Press down in the centre with the end of a paintbrush. The petals will immediately curl up. Leave to dry until hard. Special flower cutters with ejectors are now available in different sizes. Press the cutter into the fondant then lift it up with the cut shape in the end. Place over a piece of foam and press the ejector. The flower will emerge ready curled. If wire stamens are to be inserted later, prick a hole in the centre of the flower shape while the icing is still soft. When dry, insert the stamen.

Superhint *Learn to judge the right consistency of icing for the job in hand. If it is too soft for piping it will fall out of the tube and the design will not hold its shape. If too stiff, it requires a major effort to extrude and a flowing line will often break.*

Mother's Day cake

CAKE
1 (20-cm/8-inch) round Glacé fruit cake (see page 22)
COVERING AND DECORATION
175 g/6 oz (U.S. ½ cup) raspberry jam, sieved and warmed
1½ quantities Almond paste (see page 33)
1½ quantities Fondant moulding paste (using triple-distilled rose water instead of vanilla or almond flavouring) (see page 35)
red food colouring
whisked egg white
1 (32.5-cm/13-inch) round silver-coloured doily
1 (30-cm/12-inch) round silver-coloured cake board
75 g/3 oz icing sugar, sifted (U.S. scant ¾ cup sifted confectioners' sugar)
1 teaspoon triple-distilled rose water
1 metre/39 inches pink ribbon, 2 cm/¾ inch wide

1. Brush the cake with jam and cover with almond paste (see page 33). Leave to dry.
2. Tint the fondant paste pale pink with food colouring, kneading it in well. Brush the cake with egg white and flat ice with the pink fondant (see page 35), without putting it on the cake board first.
3. Lay the doily on the cake board and set the covered cake carefully on top.
4. Draw the greeting such as 'Love to Mother' or 'Happy Mother's Day' on greaseproof paper (U.S. waxed paper) and transfer the design to the top of the cake.
5. Make up a glacé icing using the sugar, rose water and enough water to give a thick consistency which will hold its shape. Take one third to a small bowl and keep closely covered. Colour the larger portion a deeper pink than the fondant icing covering the cake.
6. Put the pink icing in a paper piping bag (see page 12) fitted with a No. 2 plain tube and pipe the greeting on the cake following the design. Leave to dry.
7. Put the reserved icing in another paper piping bag fitted with a No. 1 tube and over-pipe the greeting in white. Trim the ends of the ribbon into 'V' shapes, place round the cake and tie in a bow.
Serves about 16

Superhint *The addition of even 1 teaspoon glycerine prevents royal icing from becoming too hard to cut. But do not add it to the icing for the base of a tiered wedding cake or for piping flowers or run-outs.*

Engagement chocolate cake

CAKE
1 (20-cm/8-inch) basic cake as in Frosted chocolate Christmas cake (see page 147)
COVERING AND DECORATION
100 g/4 oz (U.S. ⅓ cup) apricot jam, boiled and sieved
1 (25-cm/10-inch) gold-coloured cake board
1½ quantities Fondant moulding paste (see page 35)
1 quantity coffee Butter icing (see page 28)

1. Brush the cake with jam, set it on the cake board and cover with fondant moulding paste (see page 35).
2. Draw the word 'Congratulations' on a piece of greaseproof paper (U.S. waxed paper), together with the first names of the engaged couple. Transfer this to the top of the cake. Cut out a plain circular template to fit the top of the cake and prick round the outside edge to give a good guide for piping.
3. Put a little butter icing into a paper icing bag (see page 12) fitted with a No. 2 icing tube and pipe the greeting on the top of the cake.
4. Put the remaining icing in a piping bag fitted with a medium-sized star tube and pipe a shell border around the base of the cake where it joins the cake board, and rosettes all round the pricked line on the top edge.
Serves about 16

Superhint *Fondant moulding paste keeps for months and benefits from handling. Keep kneading until it loses its dullness and takes on a satiny shine.*

American bridal cake

(Illustrated on pages 98–99)

This spectacular tiered cake without pillars can be made in stages. Bake the small and medium-sized cakes together and the largest one separately to ensure even distribution of oven heat.

PIPED ROSES
about ¾ quantity Royal icing (see page 34)
red food colouring
MADEIRA CAKES
For 15-cm/6-inch round or hexagonal tin, or 12.5-cm/5-inch square tin

175 g/6 oz (U.S. ¾ cup) butter or margarine
175 g/6 oz caster sugar (U.S. ¾ cup granulated
sugar)
3 eggs
175 g/6 oz self-raising flour, sifted (U.S. 1½ cups
all-purpose flour sifted with 1½ teaspoons
baking powder)
1 teaspoon vanilla essence (U.S. vanilla extract)
and 1 tablespoon milk, or, finely grated rind of
1 small lemon and 1 tablespoon lemon juice
75 g/3 oz plain flour (U.S. ¾ cup all-purpose
flour), sifted

For 20-cm/8-inch round or hexagonal tin, or 17.5-cm/7-inch square tin

275 g/10 oz (U.S. 1¼ cups) butter or margarine
275 g/10 oz caster sugar (U.S. 1¼ cups granulated
sugar)
5 eggs
275 g/10 oz self-raising flour, sifted (U.S. 2½ cups
all-purpose flour sifted with 2½ teaspoons
baking powder)
1½ teaspoons vanilla essence (U.S. vanilla
extract) and 2 tablespoons (U.S. 3 tablespoons)
milk, or, finely grated rind of 1 large lemon
and 2 tablespoons (U.S. 3 tablespoons) lemon
juice
150 g/5 oz plain flour (U.S. 1¼ cups all-purpose
flour), sifted

For 25-cm/10-inch round or hexagonal tin, or 22.5-cm/9-inch square tin

350 g/12 oz (U.S. 1½ cups) butter or margarine
350 g/12 oz caster sugar (U.S. 1½ cups granulated
sugar)
6 eggs
350 g/12 oz self-raising flour, sifted (U.S. 3 cups
all-purpose flour sifted with 1 tablespoon
baking powder)
2 teaspoons vanilla essence (U.S. 1 tablespoon
vanilla extract) and 3 tablespoons (U.S. 4
tablespoons) milk, or, finely grated rind of 2
small lemons and 3 tablespoons (U.S. 4

tablespoons) lemon juice
175 g/6 oz plain flour (U.S. 1½ cups all-purpose
flour), sifted

TO FINISH THE CAKES
1 (15-cm/6-inch) and 1 (20-cm/8-inch) round
silver-coloured thin cake boards
1 (27.5–30-cm/11–12-inch) round gold-coloured
thick cake board
about 450 g/1 lb apricot jam, boiled and sieved
AMERICAN CRÈME AU BEURRE
425 g/15 oz (U.S. scant 2 cups) granulated sugar
215 ml/7½ fl oz (U.S. scant 1 cup) water
1 kg/2¼ lb (U.S. 4½ cups) unsalted butter, at room
temperature
2 kg/4½ lb icing sugar, sifted (U.S. 16 cups sifted
confectioners' sugar)
6 egg yolks
about ¾ teaspoon vanilla or lemon essence (U.S.
about 1 teaspoon vanilla or lemon extract)
DECORATIONS
about 16 gold foil rose leaves
sprays of green fern, fresh or dried

1. Tint the royal icing a deep red with food colouring and make about 75–80 large roses using a large petal tube (see page 47). Leave the roses to dry on sheets of non-stick baking parchment for at least 48 hours before placing on the finished cake, otherwise the colour might run into the soft icing.
2. To make the cakes, heat the oven to 160°C/325°F, Gas Mark 3, grease the chosen tins and line with greaseproof paper (U.S. waxed paper).
3. Cream the butter and sugar together in a bowl until really light and fluffy. Add the eggs, one at a time, beating well after each addition and adding a tablespoon of flour. Beat in either the vanilla or lemon flavouring. Fold the flours into the mixture with the liquid. When smooth, transfer to the prepared tins and level the surface.
4. Bake, allowing about 1 hour and 5–10 minutes for the small cake, 1 hour and 15–20 minutes for the medium-sized cake and about 1 hour and 25–30 minutes for the large cake, or until firm to the touch. Leave in the tins for 15 minutes. Turn out on a wire rack, leave to cool and remove the lining paper.
5. When the cakes are cold, trim the tops to make them level. Turn the cakes over. Place the small tier and the central tier on the thin cake boards and the large tier on the thick board. Brush the cakes all over with jam.
6. To make the crème au beurre, put the sugar and water in a pan and heat gently, stirring, until the sugar has dissolved. Then boil to 105°C/220°F, or boil hard for 2 minutes.
7. Put the butter into a bowl and beat until creamy. Gradually beat in half the sugar, then the egg yolks. Beat in the remaining sugar, a little at a time,

alternating with the cooling sugar syrup, to give a smooth spreading consistency. Flavour with vanilla or lemon if wished.

8. Coat all three cakes quickly with crème au beurre, smoothing the surface as much as possible using a palette knife (U.S. spatula) dipped in hot water. Leave briefly to set.

9. Put the rest of the mixture into a piping bag fitted with a medium-sized star tube and pipe a shell edging around the base of the largest cake. Stand the middle tier centrally on this cake and pipe a shell border around the base of the second cake to attach it to the large cake. Then pipe a shell border around the top edge of the large cake.

10. Position the small cake centrally on top and pipe another shell border around the base of the cake and then around the top edge of the central and top tiers. Leave to dry.

11. Pipe or spoon a small mound of icing on top of the cake then arrange a cascade of red roses beginning at the top and trailing down the sides of the cakes as shown, attaching each flower with crème au beurre. Add gold leaves and small pieces of fern to decorate between the roses.

12. Finally, attach four or five red roses with sprays of fern to the sides of the bottom cake, four or five roses and sprays of fern to the central cake and three roses and fern to the top tier. Leave to set before serving.

Stages in cutting the bridal cake into convenient portions.

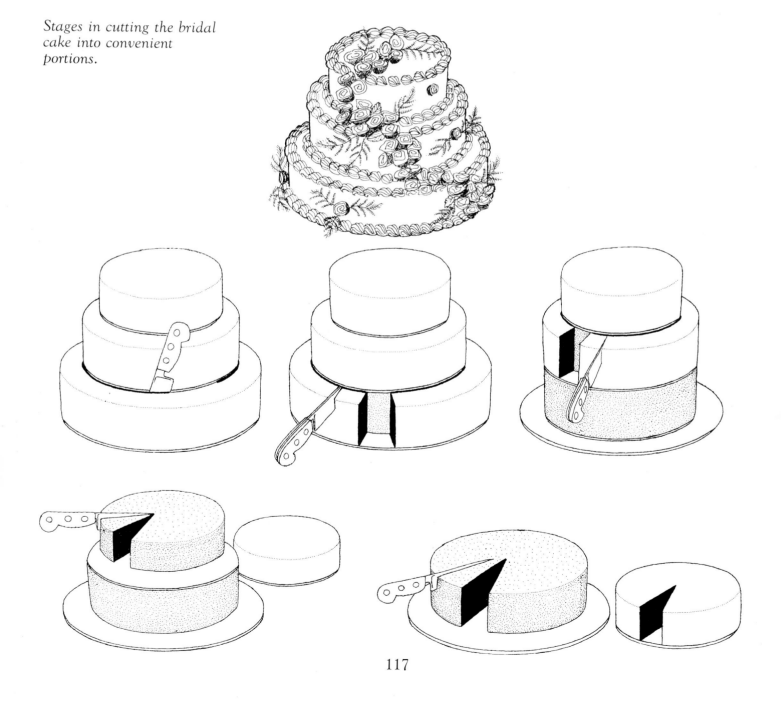

117

Ribbon and rose wedding cake

(Illustrated opposite)

Simplicity is the keynote of the fresh coloured delicate flower sprays used to decorate this magnificent three-tiered wedding cake.

CAKE
1 (15-cm/6-inch), 1 (20-cm/8-inch) and 1 (25-cm/10-inch) round Dark rich fruit cakes (see pages 23–25)
COVERING AND DECORATION
about 550 g/1¼lb (U.S. 1⅔ cups) apricot jam, boiled and sieved
4 quantities Almond paste (see page 33)
1 (20-cm/8-inch), 1 (25-cm/10-inch) and 1 (30-cm/12-inch) round silver-coloured cake boards
1 quantity Royal icing (see page 34)
4 quantities Fondant moulding paste (see page 35)
MOULDED FLOWERS
1½ quantities Fondant moulding paste (see page 35)
red and green food colouring
lengths of florist's wire
DECORATION
6 tiny sprays white silk flowers
small piece white tulle
12 pale green narrow ribbon loops
4 white narrow ribbon loops
about 3 metres/3¼ yards narrow white ribbon
7 round cake pillars

1. Brush the cakes with apricot jam and cover with almond paste (see page 33). Leave to dry.
2. Position the cakes on the boards, securing them with a little royal icing. Flat ice all the cakes with fondant moulding paste and leave to dry (see page 36).
3. Make the moulded flowers and leaves (see pages 52 to 54). Reserve about one fifth of the moulding paste for the top ornament. Of the remainder, tint one quarter pale pink, one quarter dark pink, one quarter green and leave the rest white. Make up some moulded roses and buds from pale and dark pink icing. Use the green icing to mould rose leaves and the white icing to make carnations. Leave to dry, inserting short pieces of wire before the flowers are completely hard.
4. Make up the top ornament. Lightly dust two deep fluted (6.5-cm/2½-inch) tartlet or brioche tins with cornflour (U.S. cornstarch). Roll out the reserved moulding paste to about 6 mm/¼ inch

thickness. Cut out two circles about 12.5 cm/5 inches in diameter. Press into the tins and trim off the edges cleanly with a sharp knife. Tip out of the tins to make sure that the icing is not sticking, then replace and allow to dry thoroughly.
5. Measure the circumference of all three cakes and work out the three scallop designs on greaseproof paper (U.S. waxed paper), all 4 cm/1½ inches deep at the longest point, making the same number of scallops on each cake, but remembering that they will be narrower on the second tier and even narrower on the top tier. Prick out the scallops on the side of all three cakes through the templates.
6. With royal icing and a No. 2 writing tube, pipe even-sized pearls to make a border round the base of each cake. With the No. 2 tube again, pipe pearls all round the scallop design. Leave these to dry then with a No. 1 writing tube, pipe a small dot on top of each pearl. Pipe straight extension lines from the horizontal line to the scalloped dots. Leave to dry. Tint the remaining royal icing pink and pipe out sufficient lace edging (see page 48) on non-stick baking parchment (U.S. waxed paper) to surround all three cakes, making sure you have plenty of extras in case of breakages. With a No. 1 tube and pink icing, pipe a pearl droplet between each scallop on the cake.
7. With pink icing and the No. 1 tube again, pipe small pearls along the flutes on the two parts of the top ornament. Leave to dry. Fix the two parts together with dots of royal icing to make the vase.
8. Place a small ball of moulding paste in the vase and arrange wired roses, carnations, sprays of small flowers, tulle and loops of ribbon to soften the arrangement, pressing the wires into the ball of paste.
9. Assemble the four smaller flower arrangements on the first and second tiers of the cake. With dots of royal icing, fix small balls of moulding paste directly on to each cake. Using tweezers, insert wired flowers, ribbon loops, leaves, etc. into each ball of paste, making sure to hide it.
10. With pink royal icing and a No. 1 writing tube, pipe a line around the top of each scalloped border and affix the lace work at an angle of about 45 degrees before the icing is dry. You may need a cocktail stick (U.S. toothpick) or tweezers to help you arrange the lace in a straight line. Cut lengths of white ribbon exactly to surround the circumference of each cake. Place above the lace work and fix with dots of icing. Cover each join with a tiny bow of ribbon. Leave the icing to set.
11. To assemble the cake, set four pillars on the largest cake, 5 cm/2 inches in from the edge each time, to form a square. Set the middle tier on top. Arrange three pillars on this cake about 4 cm/1½ inches in from the edge and mount the top tier. Finally, fix the top ornament in place with dabs of icing.

Ribbon and rose wedding cake.

119

Shell-bordered wedding cake

(Illustrated opposite)

A combination of graceful loops and concave scalloped circles together with strong borders of shell pattern has produced the striking design for this all-white wedding cake.

CAKE
**1 (17.5-cm/7-inch) round Dark rich fruit cake
(see pages 23–25)**
COVERING AND DECORATION
**175 g/6 oz (U.S. ½ cup) apricot jam, boiled and
sieved
1 quantity Almond paste (see page 33)
1 (20-cm/8-inch) round silver-coloured cake
board
3½ quantities Royal icing (see page 34)
tiny silver vase of fresh flowers**

1. Brush the cake with apricot jam and cover with almond paste (see page 33). Leave to dry.
2. Position the cake on the board, securing with a little royal icing. Flat ice the cake with royal icing (see page 34) and leave to dry for at least 24 hours.
3. Make a template by cutting out a 17.5-cm/7-inch circle on greaseproof paper (U.S. waxed paper). Fold the circle in half then repeat twice more. Open out to give eight equal-sized sections. Place a 4-cm/1½-inch plain cutter in the centre of the template and draw round it. From the outside edge, measure along one fold and mark at 2.5-cm/1-inch and 5-cm/2-inch points. Do the same on all fold marks. Draw curves to join these sets of marks and around the edge of the template in the same way. It should now show one small circle surrounded by three concave scalloped circles.
4. Cut a strip of paper to fit round the side of the cake, about 6.5 cm/2½ inches wide. Fold it in half lengthways, then open out. Fold it in half crossways, then repeat twice, to give eight equal-sized sections. Mark a cross where the fold marks meet at each section. Refold the strip into the eight sections, fold once more to give sixteen equal sections, then open out. From the top edge of a fold line marked with a cross, draw a gentle curve down to the unmarked centre fold, then up again to the top of the next fold line marked with a cross. Repeat along the strip to give eight deep loops. Repeat, drawing a series of loops just above and

Template for side, actual size.

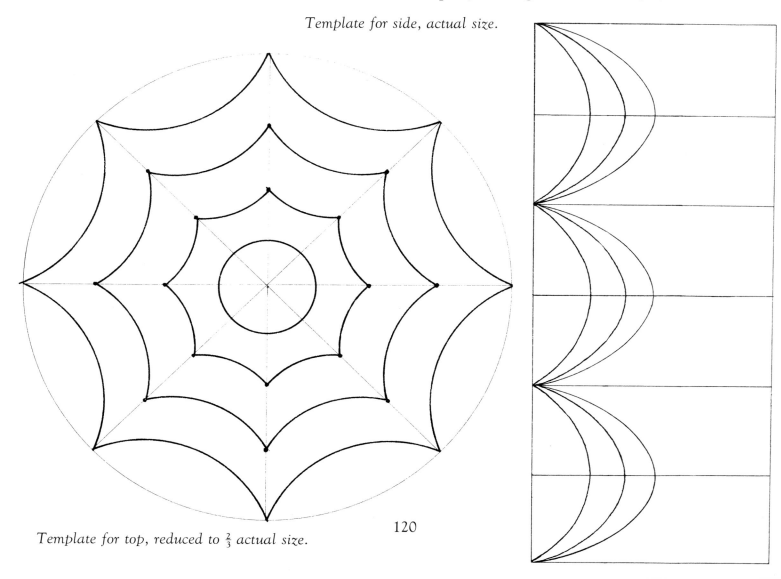

Template for top, reduced to ⅔ actual size.

120

then just below the original loops, meeting at the same point on the top edge each time.

5. Place the round template on top of the cake and prick out the design. On the sides of the cake, prick out the positions marked with a cross, and the loops.

6. Using a No. 4 writing tube and royal icing, pipe over the pricked design on the top of the cake. Dry off briefly then overpipe. Leave to dry until firm. Pipe straight lines from the inner circle, radiating out to the smallest concave circle. Pipe a continuous plain small scroll just inside the inner circle and then just outside the concave circles.

7. With the same tube, pipe rows of three loops around the side of the cake.

8. With a small star tube, pipe a medium-sized rosette at each cross mark on the side of the cake. Then pipe a slightly smaller rosette above and one below, leaving a slight gap between them. Pipe even smaller rosettes above and below the second rosettes, then a tiny rosette on either side of the first rosette.

9. With a medium-sized star tube, pipe a shell border on the top edge of the cake. Repeat the same border immediately below the first on the side of the cake. Pipe a rosette at the eight points where the loops meet.

10. Pipe a shell border round the base of the cake. Leave to harden.

11. On the wedding day, fix the flower decoration in the centre of the cake with a little icing.

To make a two-tier cake

Bake a 22.5-cm/9-inch round Dark rich fruit cake and use for the bottom tier. Coat with almond paste and flat ice with royal icing as before. Place in position on a 30-cm/12-inch round silver-coloured cake board. Make a 22.5-cm/9-inch template, drawing in only the largest set of concave curves. Prick this out on top of the cake. Complete the decoration on the top and sides as for the smaller cake. When the decorations are firm, position four pillars, 2.5-cm/1-inch in from the joining points of alternate sets of concave curves, and mount the smaller cake on top.

Superhint *Don't over-handle almond paste, as this releases the almond oil, and makes the surface oily. Handle with a sprinkling of icing sugar (U.S. confectioners' sugar) or a mixture of one third cornflour (U.S. cornstarch) and two thirds sugar, but use sparingly.*

Shell bordered wedding cake.

Peaches 'n' cream wedding cake

(Illustrated opposite)

There's quite a vogue for the warmer tones of cream or ivory in the icing for a bride's cake to match her dress, and the silk flowers used for the decoration may carry out the theme colours for the bridemaids' bouquets.

CAKES
1 (20-cm/8-inch) and 1 (25-cm/10-inch) square Dark rich fruit cakes (see pages 23–25)
COVERING AND DECORATION
450 g/1 lb (U.S. 1⅓ cups) apricot jam, boiled and sieved
4 quantities Almond paste (see page 33)
4 quantities Royal icing (see page 34)
cream food colouring (or use 6 drops lemon yellow, 3 drops brown and 3 drops strawberry pink to the full quantity of icing)
1 (25-cm/10-inch) and 1 (32.5-cm/13-inch) square gold-coloured cake boards
16 piped cream doves (see note)
extra icing sugar (U.S. confectioners' sugar)
about 12 small sprays peach-coloured silk flowers
2 small sprays cream-coloured silk flowers
24 gold-coloured leaves
short lengths of florists' wire
about 2 metres/3¼ yards peach-coloured ribbon
1 octagonal gold-coloured pillar or small vase
4 square gold-coloured pillars

1. Brush the cakes with apricot jam and cover with almond paste (see page 33). Leave to dry.

2. Tint the royal icing pale cream with food colouring. Position the cakes on the boards, securing them with a little royal icing. Flat ice the cakes (see page 36); taking the icing right to the edge of the boards all round. Leave to dry.

3. Make a template exactly the size of the top of each cake. Take the smaller one first. (Measurements in brackets apply to the larger template.) Fold in half and then in half again to give four smaller squares. Fold once more, diagonally, from the cut corner to the folded corner. Open out this last fold and make a mark 5 cm/2 inches (6.5 cm/2½ inches) along the diagonal line from the cut corner towards the centre. Then make a mark 2.5 cm/1 inch (4 cm/1½ inches) from the corner along each cut side. Join these marks to give a triangle. Draw a shallow curve from one side of the triangle to the folded edge of the square, then repeat on the other side. Prick through the paper layers to transfer the design then draw in. Prick out on top of the cakes.

4. Make a template exactly to fit the side of each cake. Mark off 2.5-cm/1-inch (4-cm/1½-inch) wide strips down each end. Fold the template in half crossways. Mark 4 cm/1½ inches down the centre fold line. Then measure 4 cm/1½ inches (9 cm/3½ inches) from the fold along the top cut edge and 2.5 cm/1 inch down. Mark this point and join it to the mark on the fold with a gentle curve. Prick through and complete the design on the other half of the template.

5. Transfer the design to the cakes. Repeat the triangle and curve design on the flooded cake board surfaces to match the top of the cakes.

6. Make the doves and leave to dry.

7. Using royal icing and a No. 2 writing tube, pipe over the triangle design and down the sides of the cake to make the corner panels. Also along the curves on top of the cake. When dry, with a No. 1 tube, pipe a random lace pattern inside the corner panels. When this is dry, using the No. 2 tube again, overpipe the first piped lines. Then, following the lines of the design, and using the smaller tube, repeat the pattern immediately outside the over-piped lines. Then pipe a continuous line of tiny scallops alongside the thinner line.

8. Using royal icing and a No. 1 tube, pipe the loop design on the sides of the cakes. First pipe a small bow in the centre of the loop then, working each time from the end of the loop towards the bow, pipe tiny teardrops above and below the marked line. Repeat on each side of both cakes.

9. With a No. 3 writing tube, pipe large pearls on each top edge between the corner designs. Pipe more pearls round the base of the cakes to match. Leave to dry. Using a No. 2 tube, link the tops of the pearls with a continuous line of icing, following the curve of the pearls. When dry, overpipe in the same way using a No. 1 tube.

10. When all the icing is dry, pipe the design on the cake boards in exactly the same way.

11. Thicken some royal icing with extra sugar and make eight small balls. Fix one to each corner of the cake board with a little more icing. While still soft, press in small flower, leaf and wired ribbon loop arrangements.

12. Make up an attractive ornament for the top of the cake, using another ball of icing. Press this into the top of the octagonal pillar or vase and insert flowers and wired ribbon loops. Lay more flowers and a ribbon bow on the upper tier, fixing them with dots of icing.

13. To finish the cakes, have ready icing and a No. 1 tube. Lift a dove and affix to a top corner of a cake with a dot of icing. Place another bird beside it. Repeat, placing pairs of birds on each corner of both cakes. When all are in position, pipe a loop of icing from the random lace to a bird's beak, on to the second bird's beak and down again to the surface of the lace. Repeat with the remaining pairs of birds.

14. To assemble the cake, place a pillar 9.5 cm/3¾ inches in from each corner of the larger cake. Mount the smaller cake on top. Fix the vase in place with dabs of icing.

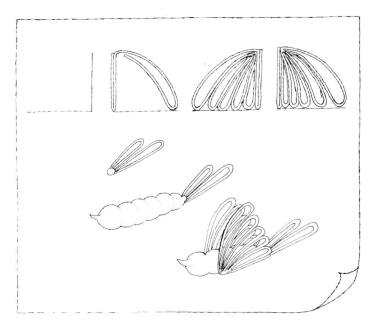

To make sugar doves

First pipe the required number of pairs of wings, making extra to allow for breakage as these are very fragile. When the wings are dry, pipe a tail, body and head unit for each dove in one continuous movement and press in a pair of wings before the icing sets. Then allow the completed doves to dry until hard.

Follow the drawings and use royal icing and a No. 1 tube. Draw pairs of opposite right angles on a sheet of non-stick baking parchment (U.S. waxed paper) having the lines extend 1.25 cm/½ inch each way from the corner every time. Starting at the end of one line, pipe to the corner and back. Then pipe from this point in a curve to the end of the other line and return, to make one 'feather'. Fill in with four more double curved loops in the same way, each decreasing in size, until you reach the corner, so that each wing has five 'feathers' all just touching each other. Make an opposite wing in the same way then repeat until the required number of pairs are piped. Leave to dry.

To make the body units, first pipe a small dot then two straight 'feathers' out from this, like making the wings, having one feather slightly longer than the other. Without breaking off, pipe the body by pressing until the icing forms a 'bulb', then the head by piping a ball on top of the body. Finally, pull the tube away sharply to make the 'beak'. While the icing is still soft, press in a pair of wings, making sure you have the top 'ridged' surface uppermost each time. Leave to dry.

Harry's christening cake

(Illustrated opposite)

To celebrate a christening, the cake can be covered in pink or blue icing. The crib is easily moulded from the same Fondant moulding paste, but be sure to reserve a small quantity of white paste for it before tinting the remainder.

CAKE
1 (20-cm/8-inch) round Dark rich fruit cake (see pages 23–25)
COVERING AND DECORATION
175–225 g/6–8 oz (U.S. ½–⅔ cup) apricot jam, boiled and sieved
1¼ quantities Almond paste (see page 33)
1 (25-cm/10-inch) round silver-coloured cake board
1½ quantities white Royal icing (see page 34)
1¼ quantities Fondant moulding paste (see page 35)
blue (or pink) food colouring
about 1.25 metre/50 inches narrow white satin ribbon

1. Brush the cake with apricot jam and cover with almond paste (see page 33). Leave to dry.
2. Position the cake on the board, securing with a little royal icing. Reserve a tiny piece of the white fondant paste to make the crib and tint the remainder pale blue with food colouring. Knead until the paste is evenly coloured with no streaks. Reserve a tiny piece of the blue paste to make the crib coverlet and use the remainder to coat the cake (see page 35). Leave to dry.
3. Make a template by cutting a 20-cm/8-inch circle from greaseproof paper (U.S. waxed paper). Fold it in half and then into three to give a cone shape. Make marks 2 cm/¾ inch in from the two outer edges. Fold the cone in half lengthways, open out again, then mark 4 cm/1½ inches in on the fold line towards the centre. Draw between these three marks to give a gentle curve, then cut along the curve. Discard the outside piece and open out the central template. Print the name of the baby on the template, allowing room for the crib.
4. Place the template carefully in the centre of the cake and prick along the scalloped edge to transfer the design to the icing. Then prick out the name of the baby and remove the template.
5. With royal icing in a paper icing bag (see page 12) fitted with a No. 2 writing tube, pipe over the marked scallop design. Pipe another scallop design inside, leaving a gap of about 3 mm/⅛ inch. Then, using the same tube, pipe the baby's name. When dry, overpipe.

Harry's christening cake.

6. With royal icing and a medium-sized star tube, pipe a shell border around the top edge of the cake then a scroll border at the bottom edge.

7. Using the No. 2 tube again, pipe a shallow loop on the side of the cake underneath every shell.

8. To make the crib, shape the reserved piece of white fondant paste into a rectangle measuring about 5 cm/2 inches long, 3 cm/1¼ inches wide and about 1.25 cm/½ inch deep. Shape a tiny piece into a canopy to fit snugly over one end of the rectangle. Roll out the reserved blue paste, to make a coverlet measuring about 5.5 cm/2¼ inches square. Use scissors to round off two corners for the foot of the coverlet. Mark the surface decoratively with a knife blade and drape over the crib. Secure on the cake with a little royal icing.

9. Cut the ribbon into two equal lengths and fix them around the cake, securing the ends with dots of royal icing.

Coming-of-age cake

(Illustrated opposite)

For a girl, nothing could be more delicate and appropriate than this design with trellis covering the moulded edge, silver balls and leaves gleaming against the background of white and pale apricot icing.

CAKE
1 (15-cm/6-inch) round Dark rich fruit cake (see pages 23–25)
COVERING AND DECORATION
175 g/6 oz (U.S. ½ cup) apricot jam, boiled and sieved
¾ quantity Almond paste (see page 33)
1 (20-cm/8-inch) octagonal silver-coloured cake board
½ quantity Royal icing (see page 34)
¾ quantity Fondant moulding paste (see page 35)
orange (or red and yellow) food colourings
silver balls
8 silver-coloured leaves
about 0.5 metres/20 inches of 3-cm/1¼-inch wide apricot ribbon

1. Brush the cake with apricot jam and cover with almond paste (see page 33). Leave to dry.

2. Position the cake on the board securing with a little royal icing. Tint the fondant moulding paste apricot with food colouring, kneading it well until no streaks are left. Use to cover the cake (see page 35). Leave to dry.

3. Make a template by cutting a 15-cm/6-inch circle from greaseproof paper (U.S. waxed paper). Draw on 5.5-cm/2¼-inch and 12-cm/4¾-inch circles then draw the figure '18' inside the smaller circle.

4. Place the template in the centre of the cake and prick out the two marked circles and the number. Carefully prick a line round the cake, 1.5 cm/⅝ inch down from the top edge.

5. With royal icing and a No. 2 writing tube, pipe small dots over the number. With a No. 4 writing tube, pipe dots round the smaller pricked circle. With the No. 2 tube again, pipe a circle of small dots, leaving a slight gap between each one, around the larger pricked circle and, in the same way, around the cake side, using the marks to guide.

6. With a No. 2 tube, pipe diagonal lines between these two rows of dots. Repeat, piping lines diagonally in the opposite direction, for a trellis.

7. Then pipe a row of dots at the side edge of the trellis and press a silver ball on every other dot.

8. Using the No. 4 tube, pipe a row of slightly larger dots around the base of the cake. With a No. 2 tube, pipe two smaller dots, one over the other, above every other larger dot. Place a silver ball on each single larger dot.

9. Arrange silver leaves on top of the cake and secure with tiny dots of icing. Place the ribbon in position and secure with icing.

_____ VARIATION _____

Young man's coming-of-age cake Make the cake and coat it with almond paste as in the main recipe. Set it on a 20-cm/8-inch square silver-coloured cake board and cover with white Fondant moulding paste (see page 35). Cut a template to fit the top of the cake, fold it in half and then in half again. Draw a straight line between the ends of the fold lines then cut along this to trim off the rounded sections of the template. Reserve one of these small sections. Position the larger square template on top of the cake, with each corner pointing towards a corner of the cake board. Prick around the outside of the template, so that the central square area is clear and the edge of the cake is marked into equal sections. Lay the reserved small piece of template, straight edge upwards, against the top edge of the side of the cake, immediately underneath one section of the top design. Prick around the lower curved edge. Repeat three more times, to give four top-and-side areas. Make up 1 quantity royal icing (see page 34) and tint pale blue with food colouring. Work the trellis pattern as in the main recipe in the four top-and-side sections of the cake, running it over the edge to fill in the sections. Then work the bead pattern all round the base of the cake, as on the girl's cake. Make a run-out figure 18 or 21 (see page 48) and leave to dry. To finish the cake, stick the numbers in the centre and decorate each corner of the central square area with a silver horseshoe.

Coming-of-age cake.

Pretty Pâtisserie

No holiday in France is complete without making at least one visit to a pâtisserie and enjoying some of the rich mouth-watering products of the pastry-cook's art. They seem to cost a frightening amount but all the ingredients are of the very best and it takes time, patience and skill acquired through years of experience to turn out these fragile masterpieces. Why not make your own? It can become a fascinating hobby just like the decoration of iced cakes. By taking a few short-cuts such as frozen puff pastry, you can easily acquire the basic techniques and soon produce very professional-looking results at a fraction of the price you would pay in an expensive pastry shop. And many of these confections can be stored in the freezer until some sufficiently important occasion.

In this chapter, the sections begin with puff pastry, that light confection of many layers which rises greatly during baking. Then we have French flan pastry, a delicately sweetened paste perfect for flans and tarts. This is followed by choux pastry, and often combined with it, to make such classic set pieces as Croque-en-bouche (see page 140). Finally, fragile snowy white meringue, to produce such intricate creations as Swans and a piped basket (see page 143).

Above: Palmiers à la crème (see page 130).
Left: Mille feuilles (see page 131).
Right: Tranche de fruits (see page 132).

Puff Pastry

With care and patience you can make puff pastry that rises evenly, has the authentic rich flavour and delicate texture. But since frozen puff pastry is so excellent, this is one aspect of the French pâtissier's art which it is hardly worth your time and trouble to acquire. I do not hesitate to recommend frozen puff pastry as the basis for these great classic recipes but, for those who want the satisfaction of doing it all themselves, here is how to make puff pastry in the traditional way.

Although modern recipes recommend using firm butter or, possibly, hard margarine, I prefer the time-honoured method used by Escoffier where the butter is folded into a clean tea towel lightly sprinkled with flour and softened by pressure with the palm of the hand before use. Fortunately, the resting time between each rolling stage is not long, so the pastry need not be frequently whisked in and out of the refrigerator to be chilled. Some cooks believe they get a better result with 'strong' flour (U.S. white bread flour) because of the high gluten content, but I think it is more important to work in a cool atmosphere, keep your hands cool and use iced water rather than cold water straight from the tap. Rolling is important for puff pastry. Use firm even strokes, keeping the dough to a neat rectangular shape, only roll it on one side and don't let the pin roll over the pastry edges.

Basic puff pastry

450 g/1 lb plain flour (U.S. 4 cups all-purpose flour)
½ teaspoon salt
450 g/1 lb (U.S. 2 cups) butter
2 teaspoons (U.S. 1 tablespoon) lemon juice
250 ml/9 fl oz (U.S. 1⅛ cups) ice cold water

1. Sift the flour and salt into a bowl and rub or cut in 50 g/2 oz (U.S. ¼ cup) of the butter. Combine the lemon juice and about two thirds of the water and stir into the flour mixture. When the dough begins to cling together, add the rest of the water and mix to a firm dough. Knead well on a lightly floured surface. Form the remaining butter into a flat cake about 15 cm/6 inches square. Roll out the dough to a neat rectangle 45 cm/18 inches by 27.5/11 inches, with a short side towards you. Place the cake of butter in the centre, fold in the two long edges of the dough over the butter, then fold down the far third of the dough, and finally fold the flap of dough nearest you up over the butter, to make a neat square parcel. Press the edges with the rolling pin to

seal. Rest the pastry in a cool place for 15 minutes until the butter is firm.
2. Roll out the dough again to a neat rectangle 45 cm/18 inches by 15 cm/6 inches. Fold down the top third of the dough, then fold up the bottom third of the dough to make a square. Seal the edges and give the dough a one quarter turn so that the folded edge is on the right. Roll and fold again in exactly the same manner. Rest the dough for 15 minutes.
3. Repeat the rolling, folding and resting processes twice more, so that the pastry has six rollings in all after the butter is incorporated. If the butter appears as streaks in the pastry, a further rolling can be given. Keep cool before using.
Makes about 1.1 kg/2½ lb

Palmiers

(Illustrated on pages 128–129)

PASTRY
1 (226-g/8-oz) pack frozen puff pastry, defrosted, or ⅕ quantity Puff pastry (see opposite)
GLAZE
1 egg, beaten
caster sugar (U.S. granulated sugar)

1. Heat the oven to 220°C/425°F, Gas Mark 7 and dampen 2–3 baking sheets (U.S. cookie sheets).
2. Roll out the pastry to a rectangle 35 cm/14 inches by 30 cm/12 inches. Brush with beaten egg and sprinkle with sugar. Fold over the long edges to meet in the centre of the pastry. Brush with egg and sprinkle with sugar again, then fold in the long folded edges to meet in the centre. Brush with egg and sprinkle with sugar a third time, then fold the whole pastry in half lengthways.
3. Cut the roll into 2-cm/¾-inch slices and arrange these well apart and cut surfaces upwards on the prepared sheets. Brush with egg once more and sprinkle with sugar.
4. Bake for 10–15 minutes, or until golden brown. Cool on a wire rack.
Makes about 18

——————— VARIATION ———————

Palmiers à la crème Sandwich Palmiers in pairs with whipped cream and any red jam, keeping the glazed sides of the pastries outwards.

Using whipped cream
Crème Chantilly Where whipped cream is recommended in pâtisserie recipes, most French pastry-cooks would use this sweetened cream. Half-whip 150 ml/¼ pint double cream (U.S. ⅔ cup heavy cream), then add a few drops of vanilla essence (U.S. vanilla extract) and 1–2 teaspoons caster sugar (U.S. 2–3 teaspoons granulated sugar), according to taste. Complete whipping until thick enough to pipe or spread.

Mille feuilles

(Illustrated on pages 128–129)

PASTRY
1 (396-g/14-oz) pack frozen puff pastry, defrosted, or ⅓ quantity Puff pastry (see opposite)
ICING
225 g/8 oz icing sugar, sifted (U.S. 1¾ cups sifted confectioners' sugar)
2 tablespoons (U.S. 3 tablespoons) hot water few drops red food colouring
FILLING
300 ml/½ pint double cream (U.S. 1¼ cups heavy cream), whipped

1. Heat the oven to 220°C/425°F, Gas Mark 7 and dampen a baking sheet (U.S. cookie sheet).
2. Roll out the pastry to an even thickness of 1.25 cm/½ inch and cut into fingers measuring 7.5 cm/3 inches by 4 cm/1½ inches with a sharp knife. Arrange on the prepared sheet.
3. Bake for 12–15 minutes, or until well risen and golden brown. Cool on a wire rack.
4. To make the icing, place the sugar in a bowl and gradually add the water. Beat well with a wooden spoon until the icing is smooth and the correct consistency to coat the back of the spoon thickly.
5. Reserve a little icing and use the remainder to cover the tops of half the pastry fingers, choosing the neatest ones to make the tops of the mille feuilles. Colour the reserved icing a deep pink with food colouring, adding a very little extra sugar if necessary to maintain the same consistency. Place the pink icing in a small paper piping bag (see page 12) or syringe fitted with a plain writing tube. While the white icing is still soft, snip off the end of the bag and pipe three or four lines of pink icing along the length of each pastry finger. Draw the tip of a pointed knife or skewer quickly across the width of the iced surface at 1.25-cm/½-inch intervals diagonally in opposite directions, to give a feathered effect. Leave to set.

6. Place the whipped cream in a piping bag fitted with a star tube and use to cover the remaining pastry fingers. Sandwich the cream-topped fingers and the iced fingers together. Serve chilled.
Makes about 8

_____ VARIATION _____

To make smaller mille feuilles, split each pastry finger into two layers and sandwich together again with cream. To make them even richer, spread the bottom half with raspberry jam before piping with cream.
Custard mille feuilles Omit the whipped cream and put the pastry fingers together with Diplomat cream, following.

FILLING VARIATIONS

Diplomat cream Measure 150 ml/¼ pint (U.S. ⅔ cup) cold milk. Take 1 tablespoon and mix with 1 tablespoon custard powder (U.S. 4 teaspoons Bird's English Dessert Mix) and 1 tablespoon sugar. Heat the remaining milk and, when boiling, pour on to the blended mixture, stirring vigorously. Return to the pan and bring to the boil, stirring constantly. Simmer for 2 minutes, then cool, covering closely with greaseproof paper (U.S. waxed paper) to prevent a skin forming. Whip 150 ml/¼ pint double cream (U.S. ⅔ cup heavy cream) and fold into the cold custard.

Chocolate diplomat cream Melt 25 g/1 oz plain chocolate (U.S. scant ¼ cup semi-sweet chocolate pieces) and stir into the custard before it cools.

Coffee diplomat cream Stir 1 tablespoon coffee essence (U.S. sweetened concentrated coffee flavoring) into the custard before it cools.

Tranche de fruits

(Illustrated on pages 128–129)

PASTRY
1 (396-g/14-oz) pack frozen puff pastry,
defrosted, or ⅓ quantity Puff pastry (see page
130)
EGG WASH
1 egg
1 tablespoon milk
CRÈME PÂTISSIÈRE
1 egg
15 g/½ oz plain flour (U.S. 2 tablespoons all-
purpose flour), sifted
25 g/1 oz caster sugar (U.S. 2 tablespoons
granulated sugar)
150 ml/¼ pint (U.S. ⅔ cup) milk
25 g/1 oz (U.S. 2 tablespoons) butter
few drops vanilla essence (U.S. vanilla extract)
FILLING
a selection of canned or fresh fruit such as
peach slices, apricot halves, banana slices,
cherries, pineapple rings
GLAZE
1 teaspoon arrowroot
300 ml/½ pint (U.S. 1¼ cups) fruit juice or water
1 tablespoon apricot jam, sieved

1. Heat the oven to 220°C/425°F, Gas Mark 7 and
dampen a baking sheet (U.S. cookie sheet).
2. Roll out the pastry thinly to a neat rectangle
35 cm/14 inches by 22 cm/9 inches. Cut off a 2.5-
cm/1-inch border from all four sides. Place the
pastry rectangle on the prepared sheet. Beat
together the egg and milk to make the egg wash.
Brush the edges of the rectangle with egg wash and
place the pastry strips neatly along the four edges to
form a double-layered edge, overlapping at the
corners. (The centre of the box remains a single
layer.) Brush all over with egg wash and prick the
centre with a fork.
3. Bake for 15–20 minutes, or until well risen and
golden brown. Press down the centre of the box
while the pastry is still hot if necessary. Cool on a
wire rack.
4. To make the crème pâtissière, beat the egg, flour
and sugar together. Heat the milk to boiling point
then pour into the flour mixture, stirring briskly.
Return the mixture to the pan, place over gentle
heat and bring just to the boil, stirring all the time,
until the mixture is smooth and thick. Remove
from the heat and beat in the butter and vanilla
essence. Leave to cool.
5. To assemble the tranche, place the pastry case on
a serving dish and spread the crème pâtissière in the
base. Arrange the chosen fruit decoratively in rows
on top.

6. To make the glaze, moisten the arrowroot with a
little of the fruit juice. Heat the rest of the juice in a
pan. Add the blended arrowroot and the jam and
stir briskly until the mixture boils, thickens and
clears. When cool but still liquid, use to cover the
fruit evenly. Serve chilled.
Serves 8

Gâteau aux marrons

(Illustrated opposite)

PASTRY
1 (396-g/14-oz) pack frozen puff pastry,
defrosted, or ⅓ quantity Puff pastry (see page
130)
FILLING
100 g/4 oz plain chocolate (U.S. ⅔ cup semi-
sweet chocolate pieces)
225 g/8 oz (U.S. 1 cup) unsweetened chestnut
purée
300 ml/½ pint double cream (U.S. 1¼ cups heavy
cream)
50 g/2 oz icing sugar, sifted (U.S. scant ½ cup
sifted confectioners' sugar)
DECORATION
few flaked almonds (U.S. slivered almonds)

1. Heat the oven to 220°C/425°F, Gas Mark 7 and
dampen three baking sheets (U.S. cookie sheets).
2. Roll out the pastry thinly and cut into three 17.5-
cm/7-inch circles. Transfer to the prepared sheets
and prick evenly with a fork.
3. Bake for 12–15 minutes, or until well risen and
golden brown. Cool on a wire rack.
4. Meanwhile, melt the chocolate in a bowl over a
pan of hot water. Place half the melted chocolate in
a bowl with the chestnut purée, cream and sugar.
Whisk until thick enough to hold its shape.
5. Trim the pastry circles to an even size and cover
one with some of the chestnut mixture. If liked,
spread almost to the edges, then pipe round the
edge with the mixture in a bag fitted with a large star
tube. Place the second pastry circle on top and
cover with more of the chestnut mixture in the
same way.
6. Spread the last pastry circle with the remaining
melted chocolate and mark decoratively with a
fork. Place on top of the gâteau and decorate with
the rest of the chestnut mixture using the same tube
and making a scroll border. Spike with almonds,
spacing them out evenly round the border. This
gâteau is best served soon after making.
Serves 8

*Above: Galette jalousie. Centre: Gâteau aux
marrons. Below: Cornets à la crème.*

Cornets à la crème

(Illustrated on page 133)

PASTRY
1 (227-g/8-oz) pack frozen puff pastry, defrosted, or ⅕ quantity Puff pastry (see page 130)
EGG WASH
1 egg
1 tablespoon milk
FILLING
about 75 ml/3 fl oz (U.S. ⅓ cup) strawberry jam, sieved
150 ml/¼ pint double cream (U.S. ⅔ cup heavy cream), whipped

1. Heat the oven to 230°C/450°F, Gas Mark 8, grease ten cream horn tins and dampen a baking sheet (U.S. cookie sheet).
2. Roll out the pastry to a rectangle 30 cm/12 inches by 25 cm/10 inches and cut into 2.5-cm/1-inch strips. Dampen one edge of each strip and, starting at the point of one prepared tin, wind a strip spirally to cover the tin, overlapping the dampened edge 6 mm/¼ inch on each preceding twist. Cover the remaining tins with pastry in the same way and place them all on the prepared sheet.
3. Beat the egg and milk together to make the egg wash and use to brush the pastry cornets.
4. Bake for 10–12 minutes, or until well risen and golden brown. Remove the horn tins carefully while the pastry is still warm, easing them out with the tip of a knife as they do tend to stick. Cool on a wire rack.
5. Place a teaspoon of jam in the base of each cornet then pipe with cream to fill. Place a little jam in a small paper piping bag (see page 12), snip off the end and pipe a swirl of jam on the cream in each cornet.
Makes 10

Galette jalousie

(Illustrated on page 133)

PASTRY
1 (396-g/14-oz) pack frozen puff pastry, defrosted, or ⅓ quantity Puff pastry (see page 130)
FILLING
350 g/12 oz mincemeat (U.S. 1 cup fruit mincemeat)
50 g/2 oz glacé cherries (U.S. ¼ cup candied cherries)
25 g/1 oz flaked almonds (U.S. ¼ cup slivered almonds)
2 tablespoons (U.S. 3 tablespoons) sherry
GLAZE
little milk

1. Heat the oven to 220°C/425°F, Gas Mark 7 and dampen a baking sheet (U.S. cookie sheet).
2. Roll out the pastry to a rectangle 32.5 cm/13 inches by 30 cm/12 inches and cut in half lengthways. Place one half on the prepared sheet.
3. Mix together the mincemeat, cherries, almonds and sherry and spread over the pastry on the baking sheet to within 2.5 cm/1 inch of the edge all round. Brush these borders with milk. Fold the second piece of pastry in half lengthways and cut across the fold at 1.25-cm/½-inch intervals, leaving a 2.5-cm/1-inch margin on the other three sides. Carefully open out the pastry and lay over the mincemeat mixture. Seal the edges firmly together all round and brush the pastry with milk.
4. Bake for 20–25 minutes, or until well risen and golden brown. Serve warm or cold.
Serves 6–8

_____ VARIATION _____

Fruit jalousie Use sweetened apricot or apple purée, made from 750 g/1½ lb fruit then sieved and well reduced to a very solid consistency, in place of the mincemeat. Mix the purée with 50 g/2 oz (U.S. ⅓ cup) seedless raisins and 1 tablespoon Kirsch before spreading on the pastry. Omit the cherries, nuts and sherry.

Serving pâtisserie in perfect condition
Many of these confections are filled with whipped cream, jam or fruit masked with a glaze. Although fresh fruit is placed over a layer of crème pâtissière, there is a tendency for fillings to soften the delicate airy layers of puff pastry. Make up your pâtisserie only as far ahead of serving (or freezing) as necessary, and keep chilled or in a cool place until required.

French flan pastry

Pâte sucrée, as the pâtissier calls it, is made by a classic method which involves mixing the ingredients by hand on a marble slab, although nowadays a laminated working surface is often used. This is the method I have given here because it is part of the fun of producing such exquisite results to do everything in the classic way. But there is a short-cut you may prefer to adopt:
Place the flour in a bowl, drop the butter, egg yolks and sugar in the centre and work with a wire pastry maker or large fork until the mixture forms a ball of dough. Turn out on a lightly floured surface and knead until smooth. Wrap and chill for 1–2 hours before use.
  This pastry is suitable for flans and large tarts (usually called gâteaux), tartelettes, barquettes (boats) and as a firm base for very elaborate confections such as Gâteau St. Honoré.

Basic French flan pastry

150 g/5 oz plain flour (U.S. 1¼ cups all-purpose flour), sifted
75 g/3 oz (U.S. ⅓ cup) butter or block margarine
2 egg yolks
50 g/2 oz caster sugar (U.S. ¼ cup granulated sugar)

1. Place the flour on a cold surface and make a large well in the centre. Put in the butter, egg yolks and sugar.
2. Squeeze the yolks, fat and sugar together with the fingertips of one hand and draw in the flour gradually, keeping it tidily together with a spatula. Mix to a soft dough, working the pastry well to ensure smoothness.
3. Wrap and chill for 1–2 hours before use.
Makes about 350 g/12 oz

Gâteau flamande

(Illustrated on page 137)

PASTRY
1 quantity French flan pastry (see opposite)
FILLING
2 tablespoons (U.S. 3 tablespoons) Kirsch
8 crystallized or glacé cherries (U.S. candied cherries), sliced
FRANGIPANE
100 g/4 oz (U.S. ½ cup) butter
100 g/4 oz caster sugar (U.S. ½ cup granulated sugar)
2 eggs, beaten
100 g/4 oz (U.S. 1 cup) ground almonds
25 g/1 oz plain flour (U.S. ¼ cup all-purpose flour), sifted
1 tablespoon Kirsch
DECORATION
25 g/1 oz flaked almonds (U.S. ¼ cup slivered almonds), toasted
100 g/4 oz icing sugar, sifted (U.S. scant 1 cup sifted confectioners' sugar)
1 tablespoon water
8 crystallized or glacé cherries (U.S. 8 candied cherries)

1. Heat the oven to 190°C/375°F, Gas Mark 5 and have ready a 20-cm/8-inch flan ring, standing on a baking sheet (U.S. cookie sheet).
2. Roll out the pastry and use to line the ring. Pour the Kirsch over the cherries and allow to stand for 5 minutes.
3. To make the frangipane, cream the butter and sugar together in a bowl until light and fluffy. Gradually beat in the egg, then stir in the almonds, flour and liqueur. Place the soaked cherries in the pastry case and cover with the frangipane. Scatter half the almonds on top.
4. Bake for about 45 minutes, or until firm to the touch and golden brown. Cool and remove the flan ring.
5. Combine the sugar and water and use to cover the gâteau. Scatter the remaining almonds on top and arrange the cherries round the edge.
Serves 8

Venitiennes

ICING
1 egg white
150 g/5 oz icing sugar, sifted (U.S. generous
1 cup sifted confectioners' sugar)
pinch of plain flour (U.S. all-purpose flour)
GLAZE
225 g/8 oz (U.S. ⅔ cup) apricot jam
1 teaspoon lemon juice
2 tablespoons (U.S. 3 tablespoons) water
PASTRY
1 quantity French flan pastry (see page 135)

1. Heat the oven to 190°C/375°F, Gas Mark 5 and have ready 2–3 ungreased baking sheets (U.S. cookie sheets).
2. To make the icing, whisk the egg white until frothy, then gradually add the sugar, beating well after each addition. Sprinkle in the flour and continue beating until the mixture will stand in peaks. Place in a plastic container with seal until required.
3. Place the ingredients for the glaze in a pan and bring slowly to the boil, stirring. Simmer for 5 minutes, then sieve, return to the pan and boil gently for 5 minutes.
4. Roll out the pastry to a rectangle measuring 30 cm/12 inches by 20 cm/8 inches. Cut into 5-cm/2-inch squares using a floured knife. Spread the squares with icing then arrange slightly apart on the sheets. Place the glaze in a paper icing bag (see page 12), snip off the end and pipe a cross on each square and then a diagonal cross.
5. Bake for 10 minutes, or until the pastry edges are pale golden. Leave on the trays for a few minutes, then cool on a wire rack.
Makes about 24

Barquettes St. André

FILLING
15 g/½ oz (U.S. 1 tablespoon) butter
450 g/1 lb cooking apples, quartered, cored and sliced
strip of lemon rind
100 g/4 oz (U.S. ½ cup) sugar
ICING
1 egg white
150 g/5 oz icing sugar, sifted (U.S. generous 1 cup sifted confectioners' sugar)
pinch of plain flour (U.S. all-purpose flour)
PASTRY
1 quantity French flan pastry (see page 135)

1. To make the filling, rub the butter over the sides and base of a small pan. Add the apples and lemon rind, cover with a sheet of buttered greaseproof paper (U.S. waxed paper) and the pan lid. Cook gently for about 10 minutes, or until the apple is soft. Sieve and return to the pan with the sugar. Stir over gentle heat to dissolve the sugar, then cook rapidly until the mixture is of a dropping consistency. Leave to cool.
2. To make the icing, whisk the egg white until frothy, then gradually add the sugar, beating well after each addition. Sprinkle in the flour and continue beating until the mixture will stand in peaks. Place in a plastic container with seal.
3. Heat the oven to 190°C/375°F, Gas Mark 5 and have ready 12 boat-shaped moulds standing on a baking sheet (U.S. cookie sheet).
4. Roll out the pastry and use to line the moulds. Reserve the pastry trimmings. Fill the moulds with apple mixture then cover with icing. Re-roll the pastry trimmings to make strips 6 mm/¼ inch wide. Arrange two strips on each barquette in the shape of a St. Andrew's cross. Trim to fit.
5. Bake for about 10 minutes, or until the pastry is pale golden. Cool for 5 minutes, then ease the barquettes from the moulds and cool on a wire rack.
Makes 12

Tartelettes aux fruits

PASTRY
1 quantity French flan pastry (see page 135)
FILLING
1 tablespoon Kirsch
150 ml/¼ pint double cream (U.S. ⅔ cup heavy cream), whipped
pieces of fresh or canned fruit such as black and green grapes, strawberries, apricots
3 tablespoons (U.S. 4 tablespoons) apricot jam, sieved
few drops lemon juice

1. Heat the oven to 190°C/375°F, Gas Mark 5 and have ready twelve fluted tartlet moulds standing on a baking sheet (U.S. cookie sheet).
2. Roll out the pastry and use to line the moulds. Prick with a fork and bake 'blind' for 5–7 minutes, or until dry and pale golden brown.
3. Remove from the oven, leave for 5 minutes then ease from the moulds and cool on a rack.
4. Whip the Kirsch into the cream. Spread into the tartlet cases. Arrange pieces of fruit on top.
5. Warm the apricot jam with the lemon juice, stirring to blend. Brush over the tartlets to glaze.
Makes 12

Above: Tartelettes aux fruits. Centre right: Gâteau flamande. Centre left: Barquettes St. André. Below: Venitiennes.

Choux pastry

This is really hardly a pastry. The ingredients are partially cooked at the mixing stage, so baking is very quick, and even a small amount of the smooth golden paste makes a surprising number of feather-light puffs.

Basic Choux pastry

65 g/2½ oz plain flour (U.S. ⅔ cup all-purpose flour)
pinch of salt
150 ml/¼ pint (U.S. ⅔ cup) water
50 g/2 oz (U.S. ¼ cup) butter
2 eggs

1. Sift the flour and salt together. Place the water and butter in a small pan and bring to the boil. Add the dry ingredients all at once and stir quickly with a wooden spoon until the mixture forms a ball.
2. Remove the pan from the heat, add one egg, stir, then beat very thoroughly until it has been absorbed. Stir, then beat in the remaining egg until the mixture is a velvety consistency that keeps its shape when pulled into points with the spoon.
3. Leave to cool until just lukewarm and beat again thoroughly before use.

Gâteau St. Honoré

(Illustrated opposite)

PASTRY
½ quantity French flan pastry (see page 135)
1 egg, beaten
1 quantity Choux pastry (see above)
SYRUP
50 g/2 oz (U.S. ¼ cup) granulated sugar
2 tablespoons (U.S. 3 tablespoons) water
FILLING AND DECORATION
300 ml/½ pint double cream (U.S. 1¼ cups heavy cream), whipped
about 12 glacé cherries (U.S. candied cherries)
strips of angelica
100 g/4 oz icing sugar, sifted (U.S. scant 1 cup sifted confectioners' sugar)
1 teaspoon coffee essence (U.S. sweetened concentrated coffee flavoring)
1–2 teaspoons water

1. Heat the oven to 200°C/400°F, Gas Mark 6, have ready two baking sheets (U.S. cookie sheets) and grease one.
2. Roll out the flan pastry thinly and cut a 17.5-cm/7-inch circle using a plate as a guide. Place on the ungreased sheet, prick well and brush a 1.25-cm/½-inch wide band around the edge with egg.
3. Place the choux pastry in a piping bag fitted with a 1.25-cm/½-inch diameter plain tube and pipe a circle around the edge of the pastry. Pipe 10–15 small balls of choux pastry, each about the size of a walnut, on the greased sheet. Brush all with egg.
4. Bake, allowing 25 minutes for the base and 12–15 minutes for the puffs, or until crisp and golden brown. Cool on the sheets.
5. To make the syrup, dissolve the sugar in the water in a small pan, then boil briskly without stirring to 154°C/310°F, or until syrup dropped into cold water forms brittle strands. Stand the pan in a bowl of hot water to prevent the syrup setting.
6. Dip the bottom of each choux puff into the syrup and arrange close together around the top edge of the cake. Fill the centre of the gâteau with whipped cream and decorate with cherries and angelica.
7. Finally, combine the icing sugar and coffee essence with just enough water to make a thick glacé icing. Spoon a little on top of each choux puff.
Serves 6–8

Chocolate éclairs

(Illustrated opposite)

PASTRY
1 quantity Choux pastry (see opposite)
FILLING AND ICING
about 300 ml/½ pint double cream (U.S. 1¼ cups heavy cream), whipped
25 g/1 oz caster sugar (U.S. 2 tablespoons granulated sugar)
4 tablespoons (U.S. 6 tablespoons) water
225 g/8 oz icing sugar, sifted (U.S. 1¾ cups sifted confectioners' sugar)
1 tablespoon cocoa (U.S. unsweetened cocoa)

1. Heat the oven to 190°C/375°F, Gas Mark 5 and grease two baking sheets (U.S. cookie sheets).
2. Place the pastry in a piping bag fitted with a 1.25-cm/½-inch plain tube. Pipe 7.5-cm/3-inch lengths of pastry on the prepared sheets, cutting the mixture off cleanly with a knife dipped in hot water and allowing room for the éclairs to expand.
3. Bake for 30 minutes until pale golden. Split while hot and scoop out soft centre. Cool.
4. Fill the bases with cream and put on the tops.
5. To make the icing, dissolve the caster sugar in the water in a small pan, then boil to reduce by half. Cool. Sift the icing sugar and cocoa and beat in the sugar syrup until the mixture is well blended and glossy. Use to coat the tops of the éclairs.
Makes about 9

Above left: Croque-en-bouche. Above right: Gâteau St. Honoré. Centre left: Chocolate éclairs. Below right: Cream puffs.

Cream puffs

(Illustrated on page 138)

PASTRY
1 quantity Choux pastry (see page 139)
FILLING
about 300 ml/½ pint double cream (U.S. 1¼ cups heavy cream), whipped
DECORATION
sifted icing sugar (U.S. confectioners' sugar)

1. Heat the oven to 190°C/375°F, Gas Mark 5 and grease two baking sheets (U.S. cookie sheets).
2. Place the pastry in a piping bag fitted with a 1.25-cm/½-inch plain tube. Pipe about eight round balls of paste on the prepared sheets, making them 4–5 cm/1½–2 inches in diameter, and keeping them well apart.
3. Bake for about 30 minutes, or until crisp and golden brown. Pierce one side of each puff to allow steam to escape. Cool on a wire rack.
4. Pipe sufficient cream into each puff to fill the hollow. Dust the tops with sugar before serving.
Makes about 8

Croque-en-bouche

(Illustrated on page 138)

PASTRY
½ quantity French flan pastry (see page 135)
double quantity Choux pastry (see page 139)
1 egg beaten,
50 g/2 oz (U.S. ½ cup) chopped almonds
25 g/1 oz icing sugar, sifted (U.S. ¼ cup sifted confectioners' sugar)
SYRUP
175 g/6 oz (U.S. ¾ cup) granulated sugar
75 ml/3 fl oz (U.S. ⅓ cup) water
cream of tartar

1. Heat the oven to 190°C/375°F, Gas Mark 5, have ready three baking sheets (U.S. cookie sheets) and grease two of them.
2. Roll out the flan pastry and cut a round 17.5 cm/7 inches in diameter using a plate or bowl as a guide. Place on the ungreased sheet, prick well and bake for about 15 minutes, or until pale golden. Cool on a wire rack. Raise the oven temperature to 200°C/400°F, Gas Mark 6.
3. Meanwhile, place the choux pastry in a piping bag fitted with a small plain tube. Pipe out in small even-sized balls, each about the size of a walnut, on the greased sheets. Brush with egg, sprinkle with nuts and dust lightly with sugar.
4. Bake for 15–20 minutes, or until crisp. Cool on a wire rack.
5. Take half the sugar and water for the syrup and place in a pan. Heat gently to dissolve the sugar, add a small pinch of cream of tartar, then boil rapidly without stirring until the syrup is pale gold. Remove from the heat.
6. Place the pastry base on a serving dish. Take a choux puff, dip one side into the syrup and stick it to the round of pastry leaving a margin about 1.25 cm/½ inch wide from the edge. Take another puff and repeat this process, sticking it so that the edge of the puff slightly overlaps the first one. Continue to form a complete ring round the pastry base. Build up another ring on top of the first one, slightly in from the edge to make a smaller circle. Continue in this way, decreasing the number of balls in each ring until it closes completely.
7. Using the remaining sugar and water, make a syrup as before, adding cream of tartar in the same way. Boil without stirring to 154°C/310°F, or until a little syrup dropped into cold water forms hard brittle strands. Remove from the heat and place near the gâteau.
8. Lift a little of the syrup with a spoon and allow it to trickle back into the pan. The mixture is ready to use when it spins a thread from the spoon to the pan. With a fork in each hand, dip them into the syrup, back to back, then pull sharply apart to spin threads of dry caramel. As you work, wrap the threads round the gâteau.
Serves 8

Meringues

Most cooks who pride themselves on the excellence of their cakes have at some time or another made meringues. Do not be discouraged if your past results have been disappointing. It is perfectly possible to make beautiful, crisp, snowy-white meringues and to pipe the mixture into elegant shapes like those photographed, but it takes considerable patience.

First you must be prepared to add the sugar very slowly, a tablespoon at a time, and whisk the mixture for as long as 10 minutes. Secondly, the meringue must be baked on a completely non-stick surface and although you may compromise by using oiled greaseproof paper it is really worthwhile to line baking sheets with non-stick baking parchment (U.S. waxed paper). Then you can easily release the meringues with a spatula. Thirdly, great care is necessary in adjusting the oven temperature to the lowest possible setting, so that the meringue will dry out without taking colour or oozing sugar syrup.

Ideal meringue is firm enough to pipe and hold a shape, crisp outside and well aerated inside, but not dry and powdery. The commercial versions, made with dried albumen, do tend to be hard and over-dry but when you use fresh egg whites there should be a certain delicious hint of moistness and chewiness in the centre.

Meringue is the basis for many classic forms of pâtisserie. There are large oval 'shells', to be put together with whipped cream or flavoured cream; fantasies like swan 'boats' where a number of shapes are put together to resemble the actual birds, and nests to hold a delicious chestnut and chocolate filling, or fruit with a glaze. Tiny piped rosettes can be coloured and flavoured then served as biscuits (U.S. cookies), or used to top other sweets. Large meringue specialities include piped baskets which make delightful containers for fresh fruit salad and the famous Vacherin, (page 87) which is assembled with cream-filled layers like a cake. For these, meringue cuite gives a firmer basis to work with.

Basic meringue

2 egg whites
100 g/4 oz caster sugar (U.S. ½ cup granulated sugar)

1. Make sure that the whisk and bowl to be used are absolutely clean and dry with no trace of grease, and that the egg whites are completely free from yolk. If stored in the refrigerator, eggs should be taken out 2 hours before use and allowed to come up to room temperature.
2. Use a balloon whisk by hand to give the greatest possible volume, or a rotary beater which gives slightly less. A quicker result is achieved by using an electric mixer but it produces the least volume.
3. Caster sugar (U.S. granulated sugar) is the ideal choice, but it can be combined with an equal quantity of sifted icing sugar (U.S. confectioners' sugar), to produce a beautiful, really white meringue.
4. The generally accepted method is to whisk the egg whites until fairly stiff, add half the sugar and whisk until firm, glossy peaks form, then fold in the remainder of the sugar with a metal spoon. However, I have achieved better results by adding the sugar gradually, a tablespoon at a time, whisking steadily after each addition for at least 1 minute. The finished mixture should hold its shape firmly.
5. Plan to use the prepared meringue as soon as possible – the sugar content starts to dissolve if kept waiting and no amount of beating will restore the consistency, nor will adding extra sugar.
6. To produce a crisp meringue, add a pinch of cream of tartar or cornflour (U.S. cornstarch) to each egg white before adding the sugar.

Meringue cuite

Because it is partially cooked before shaping, it is possible to cook meringue cuite at a slightly higher temperature and therefore more quickly.

2 egg whites
100–115 g/4–4½ oz icing sugar, sifted (U.S. 1 cup sifted confectioners' sugar)
few drops vanilla essence (U.S. vanilla extract)

Observe rules 1 and 2 as for basic meringue.
1. Whisk the egg whites until frothy and then gradually whisk in the sugar, a tablespoon at a time. Add the vanilla last of all.
2. Place the bowl over a pan of simmering water and continue whisking over heat until the meringue holds its shape firmly. Use as soon as possible.

Meringues à la crème

(Illustrated on page 142)

MERINGUE
1½ quantities Basic meringue (see opposite)
little caster sugar (U.S. granulated sugar) to sprinkle (optional)
FILLING
300 ml/½ pint double cream (U.S. 1¼ cups heavy cream), whipped
25 g/1 oz (U.S. ¼ cup) chopped almonds, toasted

1. Heat the oven to 110°C/225°F, Gas Mark ¼ and line two baking sheets (U.S. cookie sheets) with non-stick baking parchment (U.S. waxed paper).
2. Put the meringue in a piping bag fitted with a 2-cm/¾-inch plain tube. Pipe out twelve oval shapes on the lined sheets, or spoon out the mixture and use two tablespoons to shape it into ovals. Leave plain or, if wished, sprinkle with a little sugar.
3. Bake in the coolest part of the oven for 2–4 hours, or until the meringues lift cleanly from the parchment. If the undersides are at all sticky, place on their sides and bake until dry. Cool on a rack.
4. Place the cream in a piping bag fitted with a star tube. Holding one shell in your left hand with the flat side upwards, pipe on a layer of cream and sandwich lightly together with another shell. Sprinkle nuts over the cream.
Makes 6

Miniature meringues

(Illustrated opposite)

MERINGUE
1 quantity Basic meringue (see page 141)
FLAVOURINGS
**few drops vanilla essence (U.S. vanilla extract)
½ teaspoon coffee essence (U.S. sweetened
concentrated coffee flavoring) or ½ teaspoon
instant coffee powder dissolved in ½ teaspoon
hot water and cooled
few drops red food colouring
few drops raspberry essence (U.S. raspberry
extract)**

1. Heat the oven to 110°C/225°F, Gas Mark ¼ and line two baking sheets (U.S. cookie sheets) with non-stick baking parchment (U.S. waxed paper).
2. Divide the meringue among three small bowls. Flavour one portion with vanilla essence. Colour and flavour one portion with coffee essence. Colour the remaining portion pink with red food colouring and flavour with raspberry essence.
3. Put the white vanilla meringue in a piping bag fitted with a 2-cm/¾-inch star tube. Pipe out large rosettes on a lined sheet. Rinse and dry the bag, put in the coffee-flavoured meringue and pipe out in the same way. Repeat with the raspberry-flavoured meringue. To save wasting mixture, you can add the different colours without rinsing out the bag, which will result in having a few parti-coloured meringues.
4. Dry out in the oven for 2–3 hours, or until the meringues lift easily from the parchment.
Makes about 24

Swan boats

(Illustrated opposite)

MERINGUE
1 quantity Basic meringue (see page 141)
FILLING
**100 ml/4 fl oz double cream (U.S. ½ cup heavy
cream), whipped
few strawberries, hulled**

1. Heat the oven to 110°C/225°F, Gas Mark ¼ and line two baking sheets with non-stick baking parchment (U.S. waxed paper). With a pencil, lightly draw on the following shapes – six 5-cm/2-inch diameter circles, to make the bases; six slightly curved 'banana' shapes, 6.5 cm/2½ inches long by 2 cm/¾ inch wide; six more similar shapes, curving in the opposite direction, to make pairs of wings; and six 'S' shapes, 7.5 cm/3 inches long and 1.25 cm/½ inch wide, each ending in a point, to make the necks.
2. Place the meringue in a piping bag fitted with a 1.25-cm/½-inch tube and pipe out into the marked shapes. If there is any mixture left, make a few extra wings and necks in case of breakages.
3. Dry out in the oven for 2–3 hours, or until the shapes lift easily from the parchment.
4. To assemble the 'swans', place the cream in a piping bag fitted with a small plain tube. Pipe four large dots of cream on each base – one in the centre for the strawberry, one immediately in front of this for the neck, and two on the sides, slightly forward of the centre, for the wings. Press the strawberry lightly in place first and then add the neck and wings.
Makes 6

Corbeille de fruits meringuée

(Illustrated opposite)

MERINGUE
2½ quantities Meringue cuite (see page 141)
GLAZE
**3 tablespoons (U.S. 4 tablespoons) apricot jam,
sieved**
FILLING
**prepared and well-drained fresh fruit such as
pineapple pieces, halved and seeded (U.S.
pitted) green grapes, orange segments, banana
and plum slices**

1. Heat the oven to 140°C/275°F, Gas Mark 1 and line a baking sheet (U.S. cookie sheet) with non-stick baking parchment (U.S. waxed paper). Draw on it a 17.5-cm/7-inch circle.
2. Spread one third of the meringue inside this circle. Place the remaining meringue in a piping bag fitted with a 2-cm/¾-inch star tube. Pipe two rings around the edge of the circle to build up raised sides, then pipe up in lines vertically on the outside of the basket, starting each line from the base and ending with a point by lifting the tube away.
3. Dry out in the oven for about 1 hour, or until the parchment will peel away cleanly from the meringue. Cool on a wire rack.
4. At serving time, warm the jam and brush it inside the meringue case. Arrange the chosen prepared fruit attractively to fill the basket.
Serves 6–8

Above: Corbeille de fruits meringuée. Centre left: Miniature meringues. Centre right: Meringues à la crème. Below: Swan boats.

Seasonal Cakes and Novelties

Christmas is a time of good cheer, when no-one grudges the time to make lengthy preparations for a family gathering. Even those who profess themselves to be too busy to decorate a cake at other times regularly produce a really beautiful one to grace the festive table. Fortunately, there are several ways to transform icing into a pretty snow scene, with no more effort than lifting it up into peaks with a knife blade.

Unusual decorations of a more formal type include an iced plaque with a Christmas message, which you remove when you're ready to cut the cake, and a chime of sugar bells that are easy to make and edible into the bargain. Moulded choristers of firm icing adorn another design and there's a Yule log with bark effect; so there are plenty of ideas to choose from.

Other occasions are remembered. There are suggestions for Easter, for Fireworks night and even a cottage design that has been simplified for children to make themselves. Also to please children, more fairytale fun. Moulded teddy bears enjoying an outdoor picnic and that evergreen character Noddy with Big Ears.

Once mastered, the art of modelling in icing permits you to let your fancy roam free. Create chicks in fancy dress or even pink elephants if you wish.

Novelty Birthday cakes are not forgotten. Easiest perhaps is the clock cake, with hands set at 4 o'clock, which could be altered to indicate the age of the birthday child.

Left: Santa Claus cake (see page 148).
Right: Tiny red rose basket (see page 151).

Frosted chocolate Christmas cake

(Illustrated opposite)

CAKE
100 g/4 oz (U.S. ½ cup) butter or margarine
100 g/4 oz caster sugar (U.S. ½ cup granulated sugar)
4 eggs, beaten
50 g/2 oz cocoa powder (U.S. ½ cup unsweetened cocoa)
175 g/6 oz plain flour (U.S. 1½ cups all-purpose flour)
225 g/8 oz (U.S. 2 cups) whole shelled mixed nuts such as hazelnuts, Brazil nuts, walnuts or pecans, almonds
225 g/8 oz green and yellow glacé cherries (U.S. 1 cup green and yellow candied cherries), roughly chopped
100 g/4 oz (U.S. ⅔ cup) chopped crystallized ginger
100 g/4 oz (U.S. ¼ lb) dried apple rings or apricots, roughly chopped
100 g/4 oz drained maraschino cherries (U.S. ½ cup drained cocktail cherries), roughly chopped
2 tablespoons (U.S. 3 tablespoons) syrup from jar of cherries
ICING AND DECORATION
1 (25-cm/10-inch) round silver-coloured cake board
1 quantity American frosting (see page 31)
silver balls
1 foil Christmas angel decoration

1. Heat the oven to 180°C/350°F, Gas Mark 4, grease a 20-cm/8-inch cake tin and line with greaseproof paper (U.S. waxed paper).
2. Put the butter in a bowl and beat until soft. Add the sugar and continue beating until light and fluffy. Gradually add the egg, beating well after each addition. Sift the cocoa with the flour and fold into the creamed mixture. Add the nuts, fruit and syrup and mix well. Transfer the mixture to the prepared tin, level the top then make a slight hollow with the back of a spoon so that the baked cake will be flat.
3. Bake for about 1½ hours, or until firm to the touch. Leave to cool in the tin for 30 minutes then turn out on a wire rack and remove the lining paper. Wrap and store the cake at this stage for up to 1 month. Decorate 24 hours before required.
4. Position the cake on the board. Make up the frosting and immediately swirl it over the cake to cover it completely. Scatter silver balls over the top and lightly press in the foil decoration. Leave until the surface is firm before cutting.
Serves about 12

Cauliflower cakes

CAKE
1 quantity Genoese sponge mixture (see page 16)
FILLING AND DECORATION
1½ quantities Almond paste (see page 33)
green food colouring
1 quantity vanilla Butter icing (see page 28)
GLAZE
225 g/8 oz (U.S. ⅔ cup) apricot jam
4 tablespoons (U.S. 6 tablespoons) water

1. Heat the oven to 190°C/375°F, Gas Mark 5, grease and flour a shallow tin measuring 27.5 cm/11 inches by 17.5 cm/7 inches and 4 cm/1½ inches deep. Bake the mixture for about 25 minutes. Cool in the tin. Turn out and cut into about fifteen 5-cm/2-inch rounds with a plain cutter.
2. Tint the almond paste dark green for the cauliflower leaves and roll out thinly between two sheets of non-stick baking parchment (U.S. waxed paper). Cut out as many 12.5-cm/5-inch rounds as possible. Gather up the trimmings and re-roll to make more rounds, about fifteen in all.
3. Make up the butter icing and place in a piping bag fitted with a medium-sized star tube.
4. To make the glaze, boil the jam and water together in a small pan, stirring constantly, for 2 minutes. Sieve and cool slightly. Use this glaze to brush the base and sides of each cake round.
5. Stand a cake on a round of almond paste and pipe small stars of butter icing all over the top surface for the 'flower' of the cauliflower. Using scissors, trim each round of almond paste into nine points. Fold these 'leaves' up round the cake, overlapping them where necessary. Mark veins on the leaves with a knife blade and reshape the points, allowing some to lay on the piped stars to give a realistic cauliflower appearance. Make up the remaining cakes in the same way.
Makes about 15

Frosted chocolate Christmas cake.

Santa Claus cake

(Illustrated on pages 144–145)

CAKE
1 (20-cm/8-inch) square Dark rich fruit cake
(see pages 23–25), or Glacé fruit cake (see
page 22)
COVERING AND DECORATION
225 g/8 oz (U.S. ⅔ cup) apricot jam, boiled and
sieved
1¾ quantities Almond paste (see page 33)
1 (25-cm/10-inch) square silver-coloured cake
board
¾ quantity Royal icing (see page 34)
1 egg white, beaten
2 quantities Fondant moulding paste (see page
35)
green and red food colouring
about 1 metre/39 inches of 6-mm/¼-inch wide
red satin ribbon
1 Santa Claus cake decoration
green and red icing pens

1. Brush the cake with apricot jam and cover with almond paste (see page 33). Leave to dry.
2. Position the cake on the board, securing with a little royal icing. Brush with egg white and use sufficient moulding paste to cover the cake (see page 35).
3. Thinly roll out some of the moulding paste trimmings and use to cover the exposed surface of the board, brushing this first with egg white so that the fondant will adhere. Trim the edges.
4. Colour more of the paste green and use to make eight small holly leaves (see page 52). Tint more red and make twelve tiny balls for the holly berries. Leave the cake and holly decorations to dry for 24 hours.

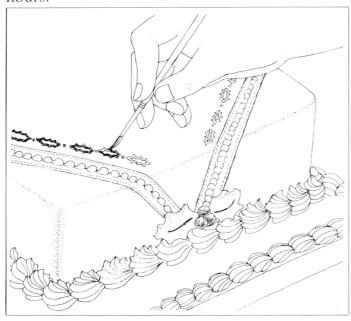

5. Mark the base of the cake in the centre of each side. Measure from one mark, up over the corner of the cake to the mark on the next side. Cut four lengths of ribbon exactly to this measurement. Also cut a square template to this measurement and lay it on the cake so that a corner point touches each mark on the cake. Prick along the lines.
6. With royal icing and a No. 1 writing tube, pipe a very thin line from the first centre point to the second along the pin pricks. Carefully position a length of ribbon and press in place. Repeat this all round the cake. Pipe a continuous row of tiny dots down the centre of each piece of ribbon. Leave to dry.
7. With the No. 1 tube again, pipe six small holly leaf outlines with a dot between each, just inside the ribbon decoration.
8. With a medium-sized star tube, pipe a twisted shell border around the base of the cake. With a small star tube, pipe a shell edging all round the edge of the board.
9. Fix a pair of holly leaves and three berries over each ribbon join. Place the Santa Claus decoration in the centre of the cake with dots of icing.
10. When all the icing is dry, carefully colour the leaf outlines with the green icing pen and the dots with the red icing pen to represent berries. If pens are not available, use a very fine paintbrush and liquid food colouring, but apply very sparingly to avoid colour spreading to the flat icing.
Serves about 20

Noel cake

(Illustrated opposite)

CAKE
1 (20-cm/8-inch) square Dark rich fruit cake
(see pages 23–25)
COVERING AND DECORATION
225 g/8 oz (U.S. ⅔ cup) apricot jam, boiled and
sieved
1¾ quantities Almond paste (see page 33)
1 (27.5-cm/11-inch) square silver-coloured
cake board
½ quantity Royal icing (see page 34)
1 egg white, beaten
2 quantities Fondant moulding paste (see page
35)
green and red food colouring
about 1 metre/39 inches narrow red ribbon
fine florists' wire
lengths of 6-mm/¼-inch wide red ribbon
silver gift tie
sprays of tiny artificial flowers
1 bought Christmas decoration or 3 sugar bells
(see page 54)
edible silver food colouring

1. Brush the cake with apricot jam and cover with almond paste (see page 33). Leave to dry.

2. Position the cake on the board, securing with a little royal icing. Brush with egg white and use sufficient moulding paste to cover the cake (see page 35).

3. Using a ruler, prick a straight line around the edge of the cake, only marking the icing occasionally to provide a guide. Using a pair of curved crimpers, pinch the cake evenly along the marked line, covering the pin pricks as you go.

4. Tint most of the remaining moulding paste green and make 22 small holly leaves (see page 52). Tint a little more bright red and roll into 16 tiny balls to make the holly berries. Leave the cake and holly decorations to dry for 24 hours.

5. Draw or trace a stylized 'Noel' on a piece of paper, then prick out on the cake. With royal icing and a No. 1 writing tube, pipe in the letters. When dry, overpipe. Pipe a line of tiny dots underneath and a few over the top.

6. With the No. 1 tube again, pipe a fine zig-zag line under each crimp mark on the side of the cake, as shown. With royal icing and a medium-sized star tube, pipe extended shells out from the base of the cake almost to the edge of the board all round. Leave to dry.

7. Loop the narrow red ribbon round the base of the cake above the shells and join the ends together with a dot of icing at a centre point on one side. Cover the join with five holly leaves and four berries, fixing them with more icing. Repeat the holly decoration on the other three sides of the cake.

8. Shape a small ball of moulding paste and fix to the top corner of the cake opposite the word Noel with royal icing. Make the decorative arrangement, if wished, by wiring loops of ribbon and gift tie and pressing them into the paste, along with sprays of flowers, the remaining holly leaves and the bells, fixing with royal icing where necessary and hiding the base completely.

9. Finally, colour the word Noel and the dots by painting them sparingly with silver food colouring using a fine brush.

Serves about 20

Noel cake.

149

Carol singers' Christmas cake

(Illustrated opposite)

CAKE
1 (20-cm/8-inch) round Dark rich fruit cake (see pages 23–25)

COVERING AND DECORATION
about 175 g/6 oz (U.S. ½ cup) apricot jam, boiled and sieved
2 quantities Almond paste (see page 33)
1½ quantities Royal icing (see page 34)
1 (25-cm/10-inch) round silver-coloured cake board
green, red and brown food colourings
2 small red candles in holders
about 1 metre/39 inches red ribbon

1. Brush the cake with apricot jam. Reserve a quarter of the almond paste and use the remainder to cover the cake (see page 33). Leave to dry.
2. Place about 3 tablespoons (U.S. 4 tablespoons) of the royal icing in a small bowl and keep closely covered. Position the cake on the board, securing with a little royal icing. Spread the rest of the royal icing over the top and sides of the cake. Mark into swirls with a knife blade and leave to set for at least 24 hours.
3. To make the decorations, pinch off a small piece of almond paste for the holly leaves, tint this green with food colouring and make two leaves (see page 52). Take two-thirds of the remaining almond paste and tint dark red. Of the almond paste that is left, tint three-quarters flesh colour by adding just 1 drop of red food colouring. Leave the last piece uncoloured.
4. First make three holly 'berries' with a tiny piece of the red paste. Then divide the large piece of red paste into three equal portions. From each portion make one cone shape for the body, two sausage shapes for the arms and a round flat 'cap' for the hat. Divide the flesh-coloured paste into three portions. From each portion make a ball for the head and two smaller balls for the hands. Make three squares from untinted paste for the hymn books and fold slightly in the centre. Assemble the carol singer figures and leave to dry for at least 8 hours.
5. Using a fine brush, paint hair, noses and eyes on the figures with brown food colouring and lips with red colouring. Finally, put the reserved royal icing into a paper piping bag (see page 12) fitted with a ribbon tube and pipe a ruff and cuffs on each figure. Arrange the carol singers, candles, holly leaves and berries on the cake and finish by looping the ribbon round the cake and tying it in a bow.
Serves 16–20

Tiny red rose basket

(Illustrated on pages 144–145)

CAKE
1 (10-cm/4-inch) round Glacé fruit cake (see page 22)

COVERING AND DECORATION
75 g/3 oz (U.S. ¼ cup) apricot jam, boiled and sieved
½ quantity Almond paste (see page 33)
1 (15-cm/6-inch) round thin silver-coloured cake board, fluted or plain
½ quantity Royal icing (see page 34)
¾ quantity Fondant moulding paste (see page 35)
1 (10-cm/4-inch) round thin silver-coloured cake board
little whisked egg white
red food colouring
4 plastic rose leaves
length silver and white lacy ribbon
1 silk butterfly

1. Brush the cake with apricot jam and cover with almond paste (see page 33). Leave to dry.
2. Position the cake on the larger cake board, secure with a little royal icing. Use two-thirds of the moulding paste to cover the cake (see page 35).
3. Cut the smaller cake board in half. Brush the underside of one piece of board with egg white and use half the remaining moulding paste to cover it. Trim the edge neatly. Using the end of a paint brush, make a line of indentations, deepest in the centre, at 1.25-cm/½-inch intervals around the side of the cake. Immediately beneath this, make another line, starting at a point half-way along the first indentation. Continue making woven wicker design over the sides and top of cake and lid.
4. Tint the rest of the paste a deep red with food colouring and use to mould one large and two medium-sized roses and two rosebuds (see page 54). Place on non-stick baking parchment (U.S. waxed paper) and leave the flowers, lid and cake to dry for at least 24 hours.
5. With royal icing and a medium-sized star tube, pipe a shell edging around the base and round the top of the cake and round the top of the lid. Leave to dry for 1 hour. Position the roses, large one in the centre, attractively around one half of the cake, fixing them with more royal icing if necessary. Press in the rose leaves. Lay the lid on the flowers at an angle and secure with dots of icing.
6. Pipe a line of royal icing up each side of the cake, ending at the 'hinge' of the lid. Lightly press on the ends of the ribbon to make the handle. Finally, attach the butterfly on the lid close to one of the roses with a dot of icing.
Serves 4

151

Miniature Christmas bell cake

(Illustrated opposite)

CAKE
1 (10-cm/4-inch) round Glacé fruit cake (see page 22)
COVERING AND DECORATION
about 100 g/4 oz (U.S. ⅓ cup) apricot jam, boiled and sieved
¼ quantity Almond paste (see page 33)
1 (15-cm/6-inch) round silver-coloured cake board
½ quantity Royal icing (see page 34)
white Christmas bell and polar bear cake decorations

1. Brush the cake with apricot jam and cover thinly with almond paste (see page 33). Dry for 24 hours.
2. Position the cake on the board, securing with a little royal icing. Flat ice the top of the cake with royal icing (see page 36).
3. When firm, spread the remaining icing around the sides of the cake and lift the surface into peaks with the tip of a round-bladed knife. Allow the icing to dry for 24 hours.
4. Finish the cake by placing the Christmas decorations on the top.
Serves 4

Miniature fruit-topped Christmas cake

(Illustrated opposite)

CAKE
1 (10-cm/4-inch) round Glacé fruit cake (see page 22)
COVERING AND DECORATION
about 100 g/4 oz (U.S. ⅓ cup) apricot jam, boiled and sieved
¼ quantity Almond paste (see page 33)
1 (15-cm/6-inch) round thin silver-coloured cake board
½ quantity Royal icing (see page 34)
30-cm/12-inch length of 4-cm/1½-inch wide red ribbon
red food colouring
moulded almond paste 'fruit' (see page 187) or bought decorations

1. Brush the cake with apricot jam and cover thinly with almond paste (see page 33). Dry for 24 hours.
2. Position the cake on the board, securing with a little royal icing. Flat ice the cake with two thin coats of royal icing (see page 34). Leave to dry for 24 hours.
3. Put some icing into a piping bag fitted with a medium-sized star tube and pipe rosettes evenly all round the top edge of the cake, leaving a gap of about 6 mm/¼ inch between each one. Pipe a further ring of rosettes about 1.25 cm/½ inch inside the first row, placing each one between two of the outer rosettes. Pipe rosettes around the base in the same way. Loop the ribbon round the cake and secure with dots of icing. Tint a little more icing bright red with food colouring and place in a paper icing bag (see page 12) fitted with a No. 1 writing tube. Pipe a zig-zag line of red icing joining the outer rosettes and the inner rosettes on top of the cake. Pipe a small dot of red icing on top of each rosette round the base of the cake. Arrange the almond paste fruit in the centre of the cake.
Serves 4

Miniature trellis Christmas cake

(Illustrated opposite)

CAKE
1 (10-cm/4-inch) round Glacé fruit cake (see page 22)
COVERING AND DECORATION
about 100 g/4 oz (U.S. ⅓ cup) apricot jam, boiled and sieved
¼ quantity Almond paste (see page 33)
1 (15-cm/6-inch) round thin silver-coloured cake board
½ quantity Royal icing (see page 34)
red food colouring
60-cm/24-inch length of 1.25 cm/½-inch wide green ribbon
small Christmas cake decoration (optional)

1. Brush the cake with apricot jam and cover thinly with almond paste (see page 33). Leave to dry for 24 hours.
2. Position the cake on the board, securing with a little royal icing. Flat ice the cake with a thin coat of royal icing and leave to dry. Take about one third of the remaining icing and tint pink with food colouring. Place in a paper piping bag (see page 12) fitted with a No. 1 writing tube. Pipe parallel lines of pink icing across the top of the cake, keeping them no more than 3 mm/⅛ inch apart. Leave to dry until firm then put half the rest of the white icing into a paper icing bag fitted with a No. 1 writing tube and

Above: Miniature holly Christmas cake. Centre left: Miniature Christmas bell cake. Centre right: Miniature fruit-topped Christmas cake. Below: Miniature trellis Christmas cake.

153

pipe a white trellis over the pink trellis, at right angles to it. Leave to dry. Put the rest of the icing into a piping bag fitted with a medium-sized star tube and pipe rosettes all round the top of the cake and the base. Cut the ribbon in half, position round the top and bottom of the side of the cake and secure with dots of icing. Finish with a Christmas cake decoration if wished. Leave the icing to set before serving.
Serves 4

Miniature holly Christmas cake

(Illustrated on page 152)

CAKE
1 (10-cm/4-inch) round Glacé fruit cake (see page 22)
COVERING AND DECORATION
about 100 g/4 oz (U.S. ⅓ cup) apricot jam, boiled and sieved
⅓ quantity Almond paste (see page 33)
red and green food colourings
1 (15-cm/6-inch) round thin silver-coloured cake board
½ quantity Royal icing (see page 34)
30-cm/12-inch length of 4-cm/1½-inch wide striped red ribbon
30-cm/12-inch length of 1.25-cm/½-inch wide striped red ribbon

1. Brush the cake with apricot jam. Reserve a small piece of the almond paste for the holly leaves and berries and use the remainder to cover the cake thinly (see page 33). Leave to dry for 24 hours.
2. Tint most of the reserved almond paste green and use to make three holly leaves (see page 52). Tint the rest red and roll into three balls for the berries.
3. Position the cake on the board, securing with a little royal icing. Flat ice the cake with two thin coats of royal icing (see page 36). Leave to dry for 24 hours.
4. Put some of the remaining royal icing into a piping bag fitted with a No. 5 plain tube and pipe a continuous overlapping scroll border round the top edge of the cake and around the base. Fix the wider ribbon around the side of the cake just under the top border and fix the narrow ribbon around the base, above the scroll. Secure with dots of icing. Put more icing into a paper icing bag (see page 12). fitted with a No. 1 writing tube and pipe small 'pearls' all round under the wide ribbon. Set the holly leaves and berries on the cake and secure with dots of icing. If wished, paint the veins on the holly leaves with a fine paint brush and food colouring. Leave the icing to dry before serving.
Serves 4

Tea-time clock cake

CAKE
100 g/4 oz (U.S. ½ cup) butter
100 g/4 oz caster sugar (U.S. ½ cup granulated sugar)
2 eggs
100 g/4 oz self-raising flour (U.S. 1 cup all-purpose flour sifted with 1 teaspoon baking powder)
finely grated rind of 1 orange
FILLING AND DECORATION
150 ml/¼ pint double cream (U.S. ⅔ cup heavy cream)
2 tablespoons caster sugar (U.S. 3 tablespoons granulated sugar)
2 tablespoons (U.S. 3 tablespoons) orange juice
50 g/2 oz icing sugar, sifted (U.S. scant ½ cup sifted confectioners' sugar)
25 g/1 oz cocoa powder (U.S. ¼ cup unsweetened cocoa), sifted
1 small pack candy-coated chocolate drops

1. Heat the oven to 190°C/375°F, Gas Mark 5, grease two 17.5-cm/7-inch shallow cake tins and line the bases with greaseproof paper (U.S. waxed paper).
2. Make up the Victoria sandwich cake mixture as the basic method on page 20, adding the orange rind before the dry ingredients. Divide the mixture between the prepared tins.
3. Bake for about 25 minutes, or until firm to the touch. Cool on a wire rack and remove the lining paper.
4. Whip the cream until thick, add the sugar and orange juice and continue whisking until holding its shape well. Choose the best cake layer for the top and spread thinly with cream. Sandwich the cakes together with the remaining cream and set on a serving plate. Mark the centre of the cake. Mix together the icing sugar and cocoa and add just enough water to make a smooth piping mixture. Place in a paper piping bag (see page 12). Snip off the tip of the bag and pipe a plain border round the outside of the cake. Arrange the chocolate drops as the numbers inside the border then pipe another circle inside these. Pipe on the hands of the clock reading at 4 o'clock (or the birthday child's age). Complete the clock face by piping in the sun, moon and stars to represent the different parts of the day. Leave the icing to set before serving.
Serves 6

Piped biscuit selection

BISCUITS
225 g/8 oz (U.S. 1 cup) butter or margarine
50 g/2 oz icing sugar, sifted (U.S. scant ½ cup
sifted confectioners' sugar)
175 g/6 oz plain flour (U.S. 1½ cups all-purpose
flour)
50 g/2 oz cornflour (U.S. scant ½ cup cornstarch)
DECORATION
pieces of crystallized ginger (U.S. candied
ginger), sliced
blanched hazelnuts (U.S. filberts), halved
sifted icing sugar (U.S. confectioners' sugar) for
sprinkling
vanilla Butter icing (see page 28)
melted chocolate

1. Heat the oven to 190°C/375°F, Gas Mark 5 and grease two baking sheets (U.S. cookie sheets).
2. Cream the butter or margarine in a bowl until soft. Add the sugar and continue beating until light and creamy. Sift the flour and cornflour together and mix in thoroughly. Place in a piping bag fitted with a large star tube.
3. Pipe the mixture out on the prepared sheets in large sizes for cookies or very small for petits fours. Make a variety of shapes – stars, bars, rounds, whirls, figures of eight, or twists. Decorate with slivers of ginger or halved nuts.
4. Bake for 10–20 minutes, depending on size, until just firm and lightly coloured. Leave on the sheets for about 3 minutes then transfer to wire racks to cool.
5. Serve plain, or sprinkle with sugar, sandwich biscuits together in pairs with butter icing, or dip half of each biscuit, either plain or filled, into melted chocolate, then leave to set on non-stick baking parchment (U.S. waxed paper).
Makes 20–35 depending on size

Jewelled Christmas treasure chest

(Illustrated on the cover)

CAKE
1 (20-cm/8-inch) square Dark rich fruit cake
(see pages 23–25)
COVERING AND DECORATION
1 (25-cm/10-inch) square gold cakeboard
about 450 g/1 lb apricot jam, boiled and sieved
1½ quantities Almond paste (see page 33)
about 550 g/1¼ lb assorted glacé fruits (U.S.
candied fruits) such as pineapple, apricots,
coloured glacé cherries, marrons glacés
12 walnut or pecan halves
10 Brazil nuts or blanched whole almonds
1 metre/39 inches of 2.5-cm/1-inch wide gold-
coloured ribbon or paper trim

1. Position the cake on the board and brush a little of the jam over the top and sides.
2. Roll out just under half the almond paste to a 20-cm/8-inch square and press firmly on top of the cake. Trim neatly.
3. Roll out the remaining almond paste and trim to give two strips, each measuring 7.5 cm/3 inches by 40 cm/16 inches. Press the strips firmly around the sides of the cake, sealing the joins neatly and allowing the top edge to protrude above the cake.
4. Round this edge off smoothly and make a decorative finish by scoring it evenly along the length with a knife blade. Score the sides of the cake diagonally with the knife in the same way. Leave to dry for 24 hours.
5. Warm a little of the remaining jam and brush it over the almond paste on top of the cake. Arrange fruits and nuts diagonally in rows on this. Warm the rest of the jam and brush the fruit and nut topping generously to give a good glaze. Finally place the ribbon around the cake and tie in a bow or secure the ends with a little icing sugar (U.S. confectioners' sugar) mixed with water.
Serves about 20

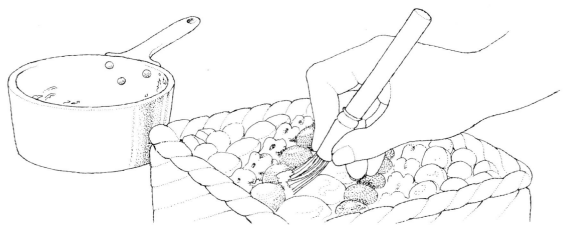

Chime of bells Christmas cake

(Illustrated opposite)

CAKE
1 (20-cm/8-inch) round Dark rich fruit cake
(see pages 23–25)
COVERING AND DECORATION
225 g/8 oz (U.S. ⅔ cup) apricot jam, boiled and
sieved
1½ quantities Almond paste (see page 33)
1 (27.5-cm/11-inch) round silver-coloured cake
board
2 quantities Royal icing (see page 34)
about ¼ quantity Fondant moulding paste (see
page 35)
red and green food colouring
2 tiny narrow red ribbon bows
2 sugar bells (see page 54)
red icing pen

1. Brush the cake with apricot jam and cover with almond paste (see page 33). Leave to dry.
2. Position the cake on the board, securing with a little royal icing. Flat ice the cake with royal icing (see page 36) and 'rough' ice the exposed surface of the board, lifting the icing into peaks with a knife blade. Leave to dry for at least 24 hours.
3. Meanwhile, tint the fondant moulding paste red to match the ribbon, roll out and cut a 10-cm/4-inch circle. Place on non-stick baking parchment (U.S. waxed paper).
4. Tint about a quarter of the remaining royal icing green and, using a leaf tube, make about 70 small leaves (see page 47). Tint a little more icing the same red as the ribbon and plaque and, using the leaf tube again, make four poinsettias by piping a flower with four 'leaf-shaped' petals first, then another four petals the same shape on top, placing them in the spaces between the first set. With green icing again, pipe in dots to make the centres of the flowers. Allow the plaque, leaves and flowers to dry for 24 hours.
5. Cut a round template the same size as the top of the cake. Fold in half and then into thirds to give six equal-sized sections. Keep the template folded and draw a straight line between the ends of the fold lines and cut along this line to trim off the curved edge. Fold the template in half again then open out just this last fold. Measure 2.5 cm/1 inch in from the cut outside edges along this fold line and mark the point. Draw a curve between the folded edges, dipping to the marked point. Prick the design through on to the other sections of paper and draw in. Carefully cut off the six outer curved sections and reserve for later use.

156

6. Open out the central template and place on the cake. Prick around the outside edge to transfer the design to the cake. Then, using one of the reserved paper pieces, place it, straight edge to the top side of the cake, immediately under a marked scallop, and prick out the design for the side loops all round the cake.

7. Using white royal icing and a No. 2 tube, work the trellis design (see page 44) into the six sections between the pricked design and the edge of the cake. Leave to dry. Meanwhile, draw the greeting on greaseproof paper (U.S. waxed paper). Prick out on the plaque and pipe in with the No. 2 tube. Dry off.

8. Using a small star tube, pipe a shell border around the inner curves of the trellis and the edge of the plaque. Using a medium-sized star tube, pipe a shell border round the edge of the cake.

9. Using the No. 2 tube again, pipe the loops on the side of the cake then, three times around each loop, pipe groups of three dots, for the 'berries'. Attach leaves around each group of dots, allowing three for the central group and two for the groups on either side.

10. Immediately underneath the six joining points of the shell borders, around the base of the cake, pipe groups of dots and attach two leaves to each, as before. Leave to dry.

11. At three points evenly round the top of the cake, where the shell borders meet, attach a poinsettia and three leaves, then at two more points attach ribbon bows. Spread a little royal icing in the centre of the cake and press on the plaque, then affix the sugar bells with tiny dots of icing.

12. Finally, using the icing pen, just touch the dots between the leaves to make them into red 'berries'. If preferred, use red liquid food colouring and a fine paint brush. Apply colour sparingly as it needs to just soak into the berry shape and not spread to the rest of the icing.

Serves about 16

Superhint *Add an exciting touch to a simple peaked Christmas cake decoration by pressing a small hand-bag mirror into the icing slightly off centre. Bring the icing up over the edge in an irregular shape to look like a pond. Arrange miniature trees and other bought decorations, such as a sleigh, around it.*

Snowmen

(Illustrated opposite)

100 g/4 oz (U.S. $\frac{1}{2}$ cup) margarine
50 g/2 oz caster sugar (U.S. $\frac{1}{4}$ cup granulated sugar)
few drops vanilla essence (U.S. vanilla extract)
100 g/4 oz plain flour (U.S. 1 cup all-purpose flour)
25 g/1 oz cocoa powder (U.S. $\frac{1}{4}$ cup unsweetened cocoa)
ICING AND DECORATION
350 g/12 oz icing sugar, sifted (U.S. $2\frac{2}{3}$ cups sifted confectioners' sugar)
3–4 tablespoons (U.S. 4–6 tablespoons) boiling water
12 currants
2 glacé cherries (U.S. candied cherries), quartered
4 small milk chocolate flakes
12 milk chocolate buttons

1. Cream the margarine and sugar together in a bowl until light and fluffy. Beat in the vanilla. Sift the flour and cocoa straight into the bowl and mix well to a dough.
2. Take one third of the mixture and divide into six equal pieces. Divide the remaining dough into six in the same way. Roll all the pieces into balls.
3. Grease one large or two smaller baking sheets (U.S. cookie sheets) and place the smaller balls about 1.25 cm/$\frac{1}{2}$ inch above the larger ones on the sheet, spacing them out well.
4. Chill for about 30 minutes. Meanwhile, heat the oven to 190°C/375°F, Gas Mark 5.
5. Bake for 12–15 minutes, or until lightly coloured. The two pieces of the biscuits should have joined together. Leave on the tin until firm then cool on a wire rack.
6. To make the icing, mix the sugar with just enough hot water to form a fairly stiff consistency. Using a teaspoon, cover each snowman shape with icing and, while still wet, press on a face made with two currants and a piece of cherry. Cut up the flakes and use pieces to make the top hats. Place two buttons down the centre of each snowman and leave to dry.
Makes 6

Snowmen.

Almond petits fours

1 egg white
50 g/2 oz caster sugar (U.S. $\frac{1}{4}$ cup granulated sugar)
75 g/3 oz (U.S. $\frac{3}{4}$ cup) ground almonds
few drops almond essence (U.S. almond extract)
DECORATION
small pieces of glacé cherry (U.S. candied cherry)
pieces of angelica

1. Heat the oven to 150°C/300°F, Gas Mark 2 and line two baking sheets (U.S. cookie sheets) with non-stick parchment (U.S. waxed paper) or rice paper.
2. Whisk the egg white stiffly then gradually add the sugar, a tablespoon at a time, whisking well after each addition, until firm and glossy. Fold in the almonds and almond essence.
3. Put the mixture into a piping bag fitted with a large star tube and pipe out small rosettes. Decorate each with a small piece of glacé cherry or angelica.
4. Bake for 15–20 minutes, or until just firm and beginning to colour. Cool on the paper. With rice paper, tear surplus paper from around each petit four. Store in an airtight container between layers of non-stick baking parchment (U.S. waxed paper).
Makes 12–18

Rum cherry truffles

175 g/6 oz plain chocolate (U.S. 1 cup semisweet chocolate pieces)
3 tablespoons single cream (U.S. 4 tablespoons light cream)
225 g/8 oz (U.S. 4 cups) soft cake crumbs (see Superhint, page 167)
50 g/2 oz (U.S. $\frac{1}{2}$ cup) ground almonds
3 tablespoons (U.S. 4 tablespoons) rum
100 g/4 oz drained maraschino cherries (U.S. $\frac{1}{2}$ cup drained cocktail cherries), chopped
COATING
sifted cocoa powder (U.S. unsweetened cocoa) or chocolate vermicelli (U.S. chocolate-flavored sprinkles or grated chocolate)

1. Melt the chocolate in the cream in a bowl over a pan of hot water. Meanwhile, mix together the cake crumbs, almonds and rum in a bowl.
2. Stir the chocolate mixture lightly and add to the rum mixture with the cherries. Stir until well combined then chill for 30 minutes or until firm.
3. Shape the mixture into small balls, each about the size of a walnut, and roll in cocoa or chocolate vermicelli. Serve in small paper cases.
Makes about 35

Honey and chocolate yule log

(Illustrated opposite)

CAKE
3 eggs
75 g/3 oz (U.S. $\frac{1}{4}$ cup) set honey
75 g/3 oz wholemeal flour (U.S. $\frac{3}{4}$ cup wholewheat flour)
caster sugar (U.S. granulated sugar) for sprinkling
FILLING AND DECORATION
150 ml/$\frac{1}{4}$ pint double cream (U.S. $\frac{2}{3}$ cup heavy cream), whipped
40 g/1$\frac{1}{2}$ oz (U.S. $\frac{1}{3}$ cup) chopped almonds, toasted
225 g/8 oz plain chocolate (U.S. 1$\frac{1}{3}$ cups semi-sweet chocolate pieces)
50 g/2 oz (U.S. $\frac{1}{4}$ cup) butter
sifted icing sugar (U.S. confectioners' sugar) for sprinkling

1. Heat the oven to 200°C/400°F, Gas Mark 6, grease a 32.5-cm/13-inch by 22.5-cm/9-inch shallow tin and line with greaseproof paper (U.S. waxed paper).

2. Whisk the eggs and honey together in a large bowl over a pan of simmering water until the mixture is pale and thick enough to fall back on itself in a firm ribbon when the beaters are lifted. Remove from the heat and continue whisking until cool. Fold in the flour lightly but thoroughly. Transfer the mixture to the prepared tin and tilt to make an even layer.

3. Bake for about 10 minutes, or until firm to the touch.

4. Meanwhile, place a damp tea cloth on a working surface, cover this with a sheet of greaseproof paper (U.S. waxed paper) and sprinkle with caster sugar. When the cake is cooked, quickly turn it out on the sugared paper and peel off the lining paper. Trim the crusty edges from the cake with a sharp knife. Using the cloth as a guide, roll up the sponge from the short end, with the paper inside. Leave until cold.

5. Whip the cream and fold in the almonds. Unroll the cake, spread with the nut cream and roll up again. Place on a wire rack.

6. Melt the chocolate with the butter in a bowl over a pan of hot water. Stir to blend then spread and swirl over the cake roll. When set, sprinkle lightly with sugar and place on a serving dish.

Serves 6–8

Honey and chocolate yule log.

160

Flake flare

(Illustrated below)

CAKE
100 g/4 oz plain flour (U.S. 1 cup all-purpose flour)
2 tablespoons cocoa powder (U.S. 3 tablespoons unsweetened cocoa)
1 teaspoon baking powder
100 g/4 oz caster sugar (U.S. ½ cup granulated sugar)
15 g/½ oz (U.S. 2 tablespoons) ground almonds
1 tablespoon mincemeat (U.S. fruit mincemeat)
4 tablespoons (U.S. 6 tablespoons) corn oil
4 tablespoons (U.S. 6 tablespoons) milk
2 eggs, separated

SYRUP
2 tablespoons caster sugar (U.S. 3 tablespoons granulated sugar)
4 tablespoons (U.S. 6 tablespoons) water
3 tablespoons (U.S. 4 tablespoons) brandy

FILLING AND DECORATION
¼ quantity Almond paste (see page 33)
green and red food colouring
3 tablespoons (U.S. 4 tablespoons) cranberry sauce

300 ml/½ pint double cream (U.S. 1¼ cups heavy cream)
150 ml/¼ pint (U.S. ⅔ cup) natural yogurt
9 small milk chocolate flakes
3 glacé cherries (U.S. candied cherries), quartered

1. Heat the oven to 200°C/400°F, Gas Mark 6, grease a 32.5-cm/13-inch by 22.5-cm/9-inch shallow cake tin and line the base with greaseproof paper (U.S. waxed paper).
2. Sift the flour, cocoa and baking powder together into a bowl. Stir in the sugar, ground almonds and mincemeat. Mix together the oil, milk and egg yolks then beat into the other ingredients for 2 minutes. Whisk the egg whites in a clean bowl until stiff, then fold into the cake mixture. Transfer to the prepared tin and level the surface.
3. Bake for about 25 minutes, or until just firm to the touch. Turn out on a wire rack and leave to cool. Remove the lining paper.
4. To make the syrup, dissolve the sugar in the water in a pan over a low heat then bring to the boil. Remove from the heat and add the brandy. Leave until just warm then spoon over the cake.
5. Tint two-thirds of the almond paste green and use to make about 14 holly leaves (see page 52). Tint the rest red and roll into about 24 holly berries.

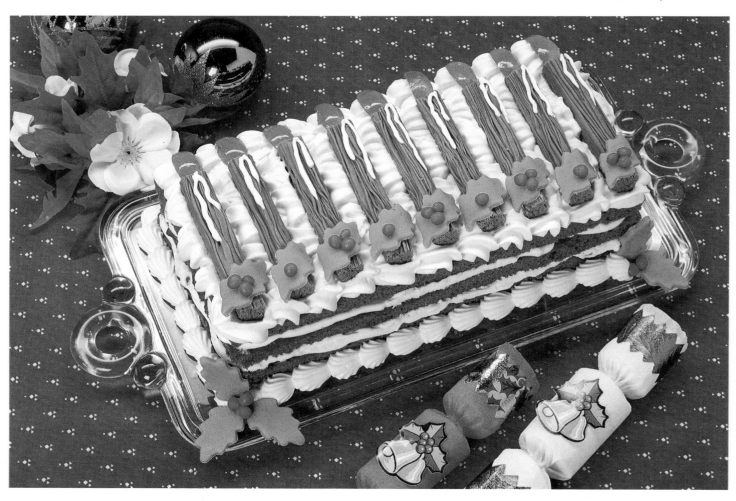

6. To assemble the gâteau, cut the cake crossways to make three equal strips. Spread two strips with cranberry sauce. Whip the cream and yogurt together until holding its shape. Spread a little over the cranberry sauce. Stack up the strips of cake on an oblong serving plate or board, with the plain layer on top.

7. Put a little cream mixture into a paper icing bag (see page 12). Put the rest into a piping bag fitted with a medium-sized star tube. Pipe cream in lines to cover the top of the cake and shells all round the base. Lay the flakes, side by side, on the lines of cream. Snip off the tip of the paper icing bag and pipe two thin lines of 'wax' on each flake 'candle'. Press pieces of cherry at one end of each flake to represent the candle flames. Arrange almond paste holly leaves and berries at the base of each 'candle' and use any remaining leaves and berries at the base corners of the gâteau.

Serves 9

Petites réligieuses ('Little Nuns')

PASTRY
1 quantity French flan pastry (see page 135)
1 quantity Choux pastry (see page 139)
FILLING
1 tablespoon rum
1 tablespoon coffee essence (U.S. sweetened concentrated coffee flavoring)
300 ml/½ pint thick sweetened custard (U.S. 1¼ cups prepared Bird's English Dessert mix)
ICING
100 g/4 oz icing sugar, sifted (U.S. scant 1 cup sifted confectioners' sugar)
2 teaspoons cocoa powder (U.S. 1 tablespoon unsweetened cocoa), sifted
1 teaspoon coffee essence (U.S. sweetened concentrated coffee flavoring)
1–2 teaspoons (U.S. 2–3 teaspoons) water
BUTTER ICING
50 g/2 oz (U.S. ¼ cup) butter
75–100 g/3–4 oz icing sugar, sifted (U.S. ¾–scant 1 cup sifted confectioners' sugar)
1½ teaspoons coffee essence (U.S. 2 teaspoons sweetened concentrated coffee flavoring)

1. Use the flan pastry to make twelve tartlet cases as instructions in recipe Tartelettes aux fruits (see page 136). Bake and cool.

2. Heat the oven to 200°C/400°F, Gas Mark 6 and grease a baking sheet (U.S. cookie sheet).

3. Put the choux pastry in a piping bag fitted with a plain tube and pipe out twelve puffs each the size of a walnut and twelve puffs about half the size,

arranging them well apart on the prepared sheet. Bake for about 15 minutes, or until crisp and golden brown. The smaller puffs may be cooked 1–2 minutes before the larger ones. Cool on a wire rack and pierce each puff at the base.

4. To make the filling, beat the rum and coffee essence into the cold custard. Pipe into the puffs.

5. To make the icing, combine the sugar, cocoa and coffee essence with enough water to make a smooth thick consistency. Use to coat the smaller puffs and leave to set.

6. Beat together the ingredients for the butter icing. Fix each large puff in a tartlet case with a dot of butter icing. Stick one iced puff on top of each larger puff with another dot of butter icing. Put the remaining butter icing in a piping bag fitted with a small star tube and pipe rosettes round the bases of the iced puffs and finish with one rosette on top.

Makes 12

Chocolate boxes

CAKE
1 quantity Genoese sponge mixture (see page 16)
ICING AND DECORATION
350 g/12 oz plain chocolate (U.S. 2 cups semi-sweet chocolate pieces)
150 g/5 oz (U.S. ⅔ cup) butter or margarine
275 g/10 oz icing sugar, sifted (U.S. 2¼ cups sifted confectioners' sugar)
2 tablespoons (U.S. 3 tablespoons) Cointreau

1. Heat the oven to 190°C/375°F, Gas Mark 5, grease and flour a shallow tin measuring 27.5 cm/11 inches by 17.5 cm/7 inches and 4 cm/1½ inches deep. Bake the mixture for about 25 minutes. Cool in the tin. Turn out and cut into 5-cm/2-inch squares.

2. Melt the chocolate in a bowl over a pan of hot water. Mark a rectangle measuring 50 cm/20 inches by 30 cm/12 inches on a sheet of non-stick baking parchment (U.S. waxed paper). Pour the melted chocolate on to the parchment and spread out thinly but evenly to cover the marked shape. Leave to set then cut into 5-cm/2-inch squares with a sharp knife. Cut small triangles from the chocolate trimmings. Chill the chocolate shapes.

3. To make the icing, beat the butter until creamy then gradually add the icing sugar and liqueur.

4. To assemble the boxes, spread a thin layer of butter icing on the four sides of each piece of cake, then press on four chocolate squares. Put the remaining butter icing into a piping bag fitted with a medium-sized star tube and pipe rosettes on top of each chocolate box. Decorate with triangles.

Makes about 15

Sweethearts' gâteau

(Illustrated below)

CAKE
2 eggs

75 g/3 oz caster sugar (U.S. ⅓ cup granulated sugar)

50 g/2 oz plain flour (U.S. ½ cup all-purpose flour)

FILLING AND DECORATION
150 ml/¼ pint double cream (U.S. ⅔ cup heavy cream)

2 tablespoons (U.S. 3 tablespoons) milk

1 tablespoon icing sugar (U.S. confectioners' sugar), sifted

1 (311-g/11-oz) can mandarin orange segments, drained

1. First make the shaped baking mould. Cut two pieces of foil, one measuring 60 cm/24 inches by 45 cm/18 inches and the other 30 cm/12 inches by 25 cm/10 inches. Fold the larger piece of foil in half lengthways, then fold it in half again, to give a rectangle measuring about 60 cm/24 inches by 11 cm/4½ inches. Fold this into three lengthways, to make a long strip 3 cm/1¼ inches wide. Form the strip into a heart shape, about 15 cm/6 inches across the widest part. Make a double fold in the ends to secure them together. Place the heart shape on the smaller piece of foil on a baking sheet (U.S. cookie sheet) and shape the base around the outside of the heart to make a firm mould. Brush the inside of the heart-shaped container with oil and dust with flour.

2. Heat the oven to 190°C/375°F, Gas Mark 5. Make up the whisked sponge as the basic method on page 16. Transfer the mixture into the foil container.

3. Bake for about 20 minutes, or until firm to the touch. Loosen the foil round the cake, turn it on to a wire rack, ease off the foil and leave the cake to cool.

4. To assemble the gâteau, whip the cream with the milk until thick then whisk in the sugar. Split the cake into two layers and place the base on a serving dish. Spread over one third of the cream. Reserve seven neat mandarin segments and arrange the remainder around the edge of the cake base on the cream. Top with the second cake layer and spread another third of the cream on top. Put the rest into a piping bag fitted with a large star tube and pipe rosettes round the edge of the cake. Arrange the reserved mandarins in the shape of a heart in the centre.

Serves 6

164

Feather iced biscuits

(Illustrated on page 2)

BISCUITS
75 g/3 oz (U.S. ⅓ cup) butter or margarine
75 g/3 oz caster sugar (U.S. ⅓ cup granulated sugar)
1 egg yolk, beaten
1 teaspoon finely grated lemon rind
175 g/6 oz plain flour (U.S. 1½ cups all-purpose flour)
½ teaspoon baking powder
DECORATION
1 quantity Glacé icing (see page 31)
few drops yellow food colouring
about 50 g/2 oz plain chocolate (U.S. about ⅓ cup semi-sweet chocolate pieces)

1. Heat the oven to 180°C/350°F, Gas Mark 4 and grease two baking sheets (U.S. cookie sheets).
2. Cream the butter and sugar together in a bowl until light and fluffy. Gradually beat in the egg yolk and lemon rind. Sift in the flour and baking powder and mix to a firm dough. Knead lightly.
3. Roll out thinly on a floured surface and stamp out rounds about 6.5 cm/2½ inches in diameter with a plain cutter, or cut out other shapes. Transfer to the prepared sheets.
4. Bake for about 12 minutes, or until pale golden. Leave on the tins for 5 minutes then cool on a wire rack.
5. Make up the icing and tint it pale yellow with food colouring. Melt the chocolate in a bowl over a pan of hot water. Cool slightly then put into a paper icing bag (see page 12).
6. Coat half the biscuits with yellow icing and, while it is still wet, snip a tiny piece off the end of the bag of chocolate and pipe three, five or seven lines across each biscuit. Using a fine skewer, feather the icing by drawing it first one way and then the other across the lines of chocolate. Do this three or five times on each biscuit. Ice the remaining biscuits in the same way. Leave to set before serving.
Makes about 30

_____ VARIATION _____

Pipe lines in 4 concentric circles and draw alternate diagonal lines outwards from the centre and inwards from the edge of the biscuits.

Sweethearts' gâteau.

Alternative method of feathering.

165

Cottage cake for children to make

(Illustrated below)

CAKE
2 bought Lemon spice bar cakes (measuring about 16 cm/6½ inches by 8 cm/3¼ inches by 5 cm/2 inches deep)
COVERING AND DECORATION
1 quantity lemon Butter icing (see page 28)
about 25 chocolate finger biscuits
about 75 g/3 oz licorice comfits (U.S. candy-coated licorice or jelly beans)
50 g/2 oz desiccated coconut (U.S. ½ cup shredded coconut, chopped)
few drops of green food colouring

1. Trim the ends of both cakes to make the corners square then cut one cake into triangles as shown in the diagram, and make a 'chimney' from one triangle.
2. Put the second cake on a serving plate and spread butter icing over the top. Sandwich the three triangles of the roof together, side by side, with more butter icing, and position on top of the cake on the plate. Cover the whole cake with butter icing and press in the chimney. Lay chocolate finger biscuits on the roof, cutting them to fit round the chimney. Use two short lengths of biscuit for the chimney stacks and make windows and a door with licorice comfits.
3. To tint the coconut, place it in a small bowl and add colouring, a drop at a time, stirring the coconut briskly with a spoon until pale green. Spread around the base of the cottage on the plate to represent grass.
Serves 8–10

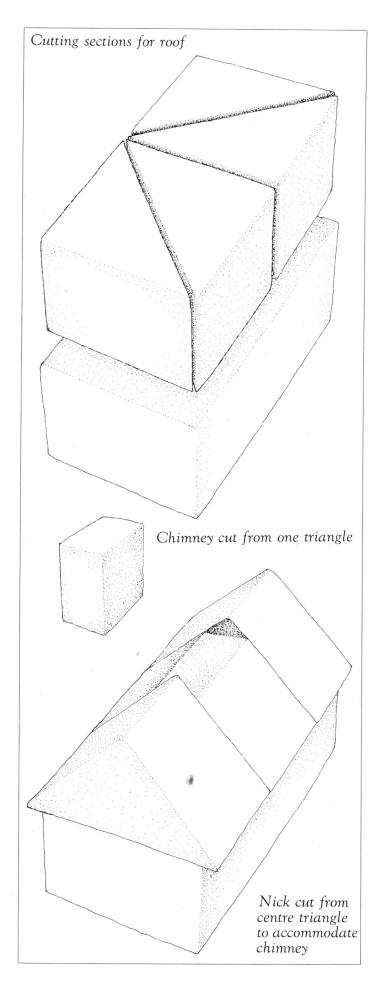

Cutting sections for roof

Chimney cut from one triangle

Nick cut from
centre triangle
to accommodate
chimney

Florentine fingers

BISCUITS
50 g/2 oz (U.S. $\frac{1}{4}$ cup) butter
**50 g/2 oz caster sugar (U.S. $\frac{1}{4}$ cup granulated
sugar)**
**40 g/1$\frac{1}{2}$ oz flaked almonds (U.S. $\frac{1}{3}$ cup slivered
almonds)**
**25 g/1 oz (U.S. scant $\frac{1}{4}$ cup) seedless raisins,
chopped**
**6 glacé cherries (U.S. candied cherries),
chopped**
**25 g/1 oz (U.S. scant $\frac{1}{4}$ cup) chopped candied
peel**
DECORATION
**175 g/6 oz plain chocolate (U.S. 1 cup semi-
sweet chocolate pieces)**

1. Heat the oven to 180°C/350°F, Gas Mark 4 and
line two or three baking sheets (U.S. cookie sheets)
with non-stick baking parchment (U.S. waxed
paper).
2. Melt the butter in a pan, stir in the sugar and
cook for a few seconds. Stir in all the other
ingredients except the chocolate and leave to cool.
Spread teaspoons of the mixture into finger shapes
on the prepared sheets, keeping them well apart.
3. Bake for 5 minutes. Flatten the florentines a little
with a palette knife (U.S. spatula) if necessary.
Return to the oven for a further 5–7 minutes, or
until golden brown. Cool until just firm, neatening
the edges by pressing them back into shape with the
knife. Transfer very carefully to a wire rack and
leave to cool.
4. Melt the chocolate in a bowl over a pan of hot
water and spread over the smooth side of each
florentine finger. As the chocolate sets, mark the
surface into wavy lines with a fork. Leave until
completely set. Undecorated Florentine fingers can
be stored in an airtight container between layers of
non-stick baking parchment (U.S. waxed paper) for
about a week.
Makes about 25

Superhint If you cut fancy shapes from slab cakes,
you are bound to be left with trimmings. Don't
throw them away. Make delicious truffles from
sponge, Victoria or Madeira off-cuts. Measure
them and use as a basis for Rum cherry truffles (see
page 159).

Simnel cake

(Illustrated below)

CAKE
**ingredients for 1 (20-cm/8-inch) round Dark
rich fruit cake (see pages 23–25)**
FILLING AND DECORATION
**1 quantity Almond paste (see page 33)
1 egg, beaten**

1. Heat the oven to 180°C/350°F, Gas Mark 4, grease a 20-cm/8-inch cake tin and line with a double thickness of greaseproof paper (U.S. waxed paper). Tie a double thickness of brown paper around the outside of the tin.

2. Make up the cake mixture and place half in the prepared tin. Take just under half the almond paste, roll out and trim to a 20-cm/8-inch circle. Lay this over the mixture in the tin and press lightly to make a level surface. Top with the remaining cake mixture and level the surface again.

3. Bake for 1 hour then reduce the oven temperature to 140°C/275°F, Gas Mark 1 and continue cooking for about a further 2 hours, or until a fine skewer or wooden cocktail stick (U.S. toothpick) inserted in the cake comes out clean. Leave in the tin for about 15 minutes then turn out on a wire rack and remove the lining paper.

4. Place the cake on a heatproof serving dish, stand this on a baking sheet (U.S. cookie sheet) and brush the top of the cake with egg. Take half the remaining almond paste and roll out to a circle as before. Trim then press on the cake and brush with egg.

5. Divide the rest of the almond paste into 11 even pieces and form each into a ball. Set these around the edge of the cake and brush with egg. Wrap the sides of the cake in foil and return to the oven for 10–15 minutes to brown the top decoration slightly. Leave to cool before serving.
Serves about 16

Note If preferred, bake the cake ahead of time, cool and seal, undecorated, in foil or plastic bag for up to 1 month. When required, decorate with almond paste topping and brown in the oven as above, or under a moderately hot grill (U.S. broiler). Watch carefully if using this method to prevent the almond paste from burning.

Simnel cake.

168

Iced Genoese fancies

CAKE
1 quantity Genoese sponge mixture (see page 16)
GLAZE
100 g/4 oz (U.S. ⅓ cup) apricot jam
2 tablespoons (U.S. 3 tablespoons) water
COATING AND DECORATION
½ quantity Almond paste (see page 33)
1 quantity Glacé icing (see page 31)
red, blue and yellow food colourings
extra sifted icing sugar (U.S. confectioners' sugar)
cake decorations such as silver balls, small orange and lemon jelly slices crystallized violets, mimosa balls or chocolate beans

1. Heat the oven to 190°C/375°F, Gas Mark 5, grease and flour a shallow tin measuring 27.5 cm/11 inches by 17.5 cm/7 inches and 4 cm/1½ inches deep. Bake the mixture for about 25 minutes. Cool in the tin. It is best to bake the sponge the day before required for decorating.

2. To make the glaze, boil the jam and water together for 2 minutes, then sieve. Turn out the cake and trim the edges with a sharp knife to give a neat rectangle 25 cm/10 inches by 15 cm/6 inches. Brush the top with glaze. Roll out most of the almond paste thinly on a sheet of non-stick baking parchment (U.S. waxed paper) to the size of the cake. Invert the cake on to it and trim the edges. Knead the trimmings into the remaining almond paste and reserve.

3. Cut the cake into various shapes as shown. Using a 5-cm/2-inch plain round cutter, stamp out six circles in two rows from one end of the cake. As cut, remove the pieces and stand them on a board, almond paste upwards. Next, divide the rest of the cake lengthwise into three strips, one 5 cm/2 inches wide; one 4 cm/1½ inches wide and the third 6 cm/2½ inches wide. Cut the first strip into three 5-cm/2-inch squares and then diagonally to give six triangles. Cut the second strip into four 4-cm/1½-inch squares. Cut the last strip into six fingers 2.5 cm/1 inch wide. Next, divide the reserved almond paste into small pieces and shape into circles, triangles, bars etc. to put on top of some of the cakes to give a raised effect. Stick them on with glaze.

4. Make up the glacé icing, keeping closely covered with cling film. Put one cake of each shape on a wire rack over a tray and spoon over white icing to coat, using the spoon and a skewer to help cover all the corners evenly. Leave until almost set, trim off the surplus drips from the base then carefully transfer cakes with a palette knife (U.S. spatula) to a board and leave to set completely.

5. Put about two-thirds of the remaining icing into a bowl (keeping the rest covered as before) and tint it pale pink with food colouring. Coat four more cakes with pink icing. Tint half the remaining pink icing a deeper pink and the rest of it with blue colouring to give a lilac colour. Coat four more cakes with deep pink icing and four with lilac icing. Now take the reserved white icing, tint it pale yellow and coat three of the remaining cakes with this colour. Finally add blue colouring to the yellow icing to make it green and use to coat the last three cakes.

6. To complete the icing, tint one or two of the remaining bowls of coloured icing a deeper colour and thicker consistency by beating in more icing sugar. Put each into a paper piping bag (see page 12) fitted with a small star tube. Pipe rosettes or shells around and across the tops of most of the cakes using colours to complement the base icing. Then add a little hot water to thin down the remaining icing slightly, put it into a paper icing bag, cut off the tip and drizzle the icing backwards and forwards over the remaining cakes. Add small cake decorations to some of the cakes and leave to set.
Makes 22

————————— VARIATION —————————

Butter-iced fancies If time is pressing, here is a much simpler way to decorate the small cakes. Coat the sides of each shape smoothly in butter icing and turn in ground hazelnuts (U.S. filberts). Stand the cakes upright, coat the tops with butter icing and pipe a border of small rosettes round the edge to neaten.

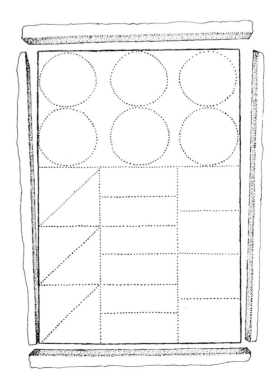

Mont Blanc nests

MERINGUE
1 quantity Basic meringue (see page 141)
FILLING
**75 g/3 oz plain chocolate (U.S. ½ cup semi-sweet
chocolate pieces)
finely grated rind of 1 orange
175 g/6 oz (U.S. ¾ cup) sweetened chestnut
purée
2 tablespoons double cream (U.S. 3 tablespoons
heavy cream)**

1. Heat the oven to 110°C/225°F, Gas Mark ¼, line two baking sheets (U.S. cookie sheets) with non-stick baking parchment (U.S. waxed paper) and draw on about six 6.5-cm/2½-inch circles.
2. Place the meringue in a piping bag fitted with a 2-cm/¾-inch star tube. Pipe a continuous line of meringue to fill one circle, then pipe around the edge to build up the sides and make a nest shape. Repeat to fill the other circles.
3. Dry out in the oven for 2–3 hours, or until the nests lift easily from the parchment. Cool on a wire rack.
4. Meanwhile, to make the filling, melt the chocolate in a bowl over a pan of hot water. Add the orange rind and chestnut purée and beat until smooth. Whip the cream and fold into the chestnut mixture.
5. At serving time, place the filling in a piping bag fitted with a large writing tube and pipe continuous random curls of chestnut mixture into the nests.
Makes about 6

Ice cream meringue boxes

MERINGUE
**1 quantity Basic meringue (see page 141) made
with half caster sugar and half soft brown
sugar (U.S. granulated sugar and light brown
sugar)
little extra caster sugar (U.S. granulated sugar)
for sprinkling**
FILLING
**500 ml/18 fl oz (U.S. 2¼ cups) coffee ice cream
150 ml/¼ pint double cream (U.S. ⅔ cup heavy
cream), whipped
12 milk chocolate buttons**

1. Heat the oven to 110°C/225°F, Gas Mark ¼, line two baking sheets (U.S. cookie sheets) with non-stick baking parchment (U.S. waxed paper) and draw twelve 6.5-cm/2½-inch squares on each.
2. Spread the meringue evenly within the marked squares and sprinkle lightly with sugar.
3. Bake for about 1¼ hours, or until the parchment peels away cleanly. Cool on the sheets.
4. If necessary, shape the ice cream into a block measuring 19 cm/7½ inches by 12.5 cm/5 inches and freeze until solid.
5. At serving time, cut the block of ice cream into six equal squares, place on small serving plates and press a meringue square against each side.
6. Put the cream into a piping bag fitted with a large star tube and pipe a rosette on each box. Top these with pairs of buttons, polishing them with a fingertip as you pick them up. Serve immediately or freeze until required.
Makes 6

Easter chocolate cake

CAKE
**2 (17.5-cm/7-inch) cake layers Chocolate
Victoria sandwich (see page 20)**
ICING AND DECORATION
**3 tablespoons cocoa powder (U.S. 4 tablespoons
unsweetened cocoa), sifted
3 tablespoons (U.S. 4 tablespoons) hot water
175 g/6 oz (U.S. ¾ cup) butter or margarine
275 g/10 oz icing sugar, sifted (U.S. 2¼ cups
sifted confectioners' sugar)
2 egg yolks
175 g/6 oz plain chocolate (U.S. 6 squares semi-
sweet chocolate)
50 g/2 oz (U.S. 2 squares) white chocolate
1 milk chocolate flake
2 fluffy 'chick' decorations
12 miniature chocolate eggs (or use ½ quantity
almond paste (see page 33) and shape into 12
eggs)**

1. Cut a 10-cm/4-inch circle out of the centre of one cake layer. Crumble the central circle.
2. To make the chocolate icing, blend the cocoa with the hot water then leave to cool. Beat the butter until soft then add the sugar, egg yolks and cocoa mixture and beat until smooth and fluffy. Stir in the cake crumbs.
3. Put the uncut cake on a serving plate and spread with icing. Top with the cake 'ring' then cover the sides, top and 'hollow' with the remaining icing.
4. Using a potato peeler, shave narrow curls from one long side of the block of dark chocolate. Make white chocolate curls in the same way.
5. Coat the cake completely in dark chocolate curls then sprinkle the white curls just over the top and in the 'nest'. Cut the flake into three unequal lengths then split each length into several thin strips using a sharp knife. Scatter these in and around the nest to look like twigs. Finish the cake by putting the chicks and eggs in the nest.
Serves 8

Easter bunny biscuits

(Illustrated below)

BISCUITS
100 g/4 oz (U.S. ½ cup) butter or margarine
75 g/3 oz caster sugar (U.S. ⅓ cup granulated sugar)
1 egg yolk
225 g/8 oz plain flour (U.S. 2 cups all-purpose flour), sifted
50 g/2 oz Bournvita (U.S. ½ cup malted chocolate drink powder)

ICING AND DECORATION
25 g/1 oz Bournvita (U.S. ¼ cup malted chocolate drink powder)
2 tablespoons (U.S. 3 tablespoons) boiling water
225 g/8 oz icing sugar, sifted (U.S. 1¾ cups sifted confectioners' sugar)
yellow food colouring
about 20 milk chocolate buttons

1. Heat the oven to 180°C/350°F, Gas Mark 4 and grease two baking sheets (U.S. cookie sheets).
2. Cream the butter and sugar together in a bowl. Beat in the egg yolk then mix in the flour and Bournvita. Knead lightly until the dough is smooth.
3. Roll out to a thickness of about 3 mm/⅛ inch and stamp out rounds with a 6.5-cm/2½-inch plain cutter. Trim the edges with the cutter to make oval or egg-shaped biscuits. Gather up the trimmings and re-roll to make more biscuits. Arrange on the prepared trays.
4. Bake for 12–15 minutes, or until the edges are pale golden. Cool on the trays until firm then transfer to a wire rack.
5. To make the dark icing, dissolve the Bournvita in the boiling water and gradually beat in three-quarters of the icing sugar. Mix a very little hot water with the remaining sugar to make a thick smooth glacé icing and tint this yellow with food colouring. Place in a paper piping bag (see page 12).
6. Spread the dark icing over all the biscuits. Snip off the end of the bag of yellow icing. Pipe a spiral on to half the biscuits, draw a skewer through it at intervals alternately out from the centre to the edge then in the opposite direction, to give a feathered pattern. Leave the other biscuits until the dark icing has set before piping on an Easter bunny outline. Finish each with a chocolate button as the tail and add a button to the feathered biscuits if wished. Leave to set and trim the edges if necessary to neaten the biscuits before serving.

Makes about 20

Easter bunny biscuits.

Noddy and his friends

(Illustrated opposite)

You will require 4 (227-g/8-oz) packs bought Ready-to-roll icing or 2 quantities Fondant moulding paste (see page 35) to cover the cake and make the figures.

Bake a deep 20-cm/8-inch round Dark rich or Glacé fruit cake (see pages 23–25 and 22). Cover with almond paste if wished. Brush the cake or the almond paste with boiled and sieved apricot jam and cover thinly with white moulding icing (see page 35).

Tint one pack of icing yellow and make up all the yellow shapes required, including the centres of the flowers. Reserve any trimmings. Tint some more icing pale pink and make the faces and flowers. Darken the remainder to red and make up the red shapes. Always reserve trimmings. Tint the remaining yellow icing brown for Big Ears' shoes, Noddy's and Mr. Plod's hair. Use reserved white icing for details on car and Big Ears. Tint a little icing pale green and make four leaves.

Gather up all remaining icing and tint some dark grey for car wheels and trim, and Mr. Plod's shoes. Finally, tint icing navy blue and make policeman's uniform, Noddy's cap and Big Ears' jacket.

Assemble the figures, paint in further details and allow to dry out for 48 hours.

Make up ¼ quantity white royal icing (see page 34). Position the cake on a large silver-coloured board, securing with a little royal icing. Using a large star tube, pipe a scroll border round the base of the cake. Place Noddy in car on centre top of cake and stand the other figures on the board. Finish with the flowers and leaves.

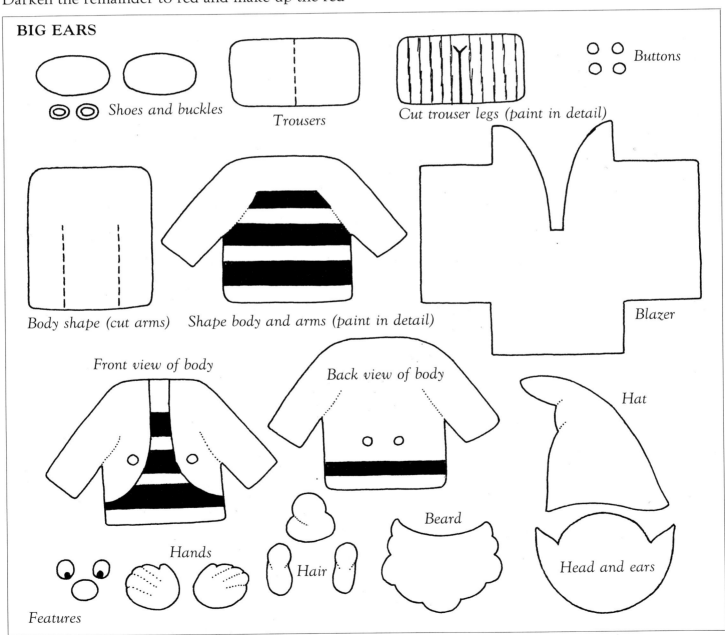

BIG EARS

Shoes and buckles

Trousers

Cut trouser legs (paint in detail)

Buttons

Body shape (cut arms)

Shape body and arms (paint in detail)

Blazer

Front view of body

Back view of body

Hat

Hands

Beard

Hair

Head and ears

Features

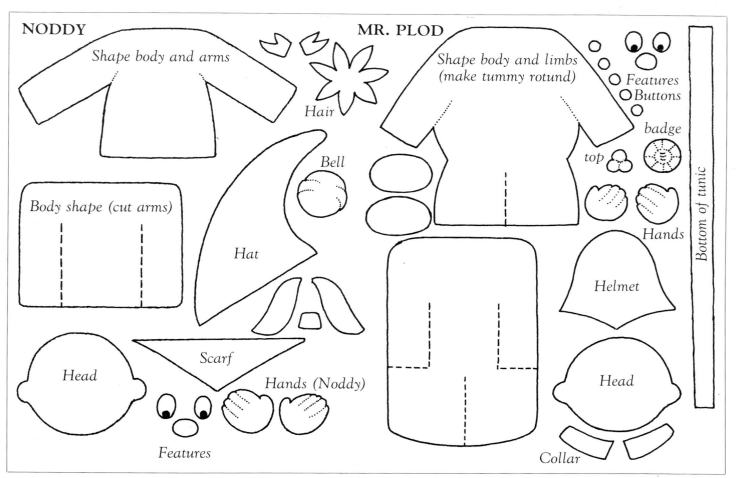

NODDY

MR. PLOD

Shape body and arms

Shape body and limbs
(make tummy rotund)

Features
Buttons

Hair

badge

Bell

top

Body shape (cut arms)

Hands

Hat

Helmet

Head

Head

Scarf

Hands (Noddy)

Bottom of tunic

Features

Collar

173

BIG EARS

Place trousers on shoes, body on trousers. Fit blazer on body and arms and trim, apply buttons. Affix head and hands, add hat, position hair and beard. Put features on face, paint in details.

NODDY

Fit body into car, position arms. Fix hands on arms then on steering wheel. Add scarf, then head. Place hat, bell and hair. Put features on face, paint in details.

MR. PLOD

Position body on boots. Add head and hands. Fix helmet, top and badge. Place buttons and collar on tunic. Fit in bottom of tunic. Put features on face, paint in details including helmet strap, hair and belt.

NODDY'S CAR

Place car body on small blocks of spare icing to support weight. Fix all wheels on body and add centres. Fit mudguards over wheels. Position steering wheel, radiator, top and grids, headlamps, door catches, bumpers and number plates. Put in seat lining and then hood.

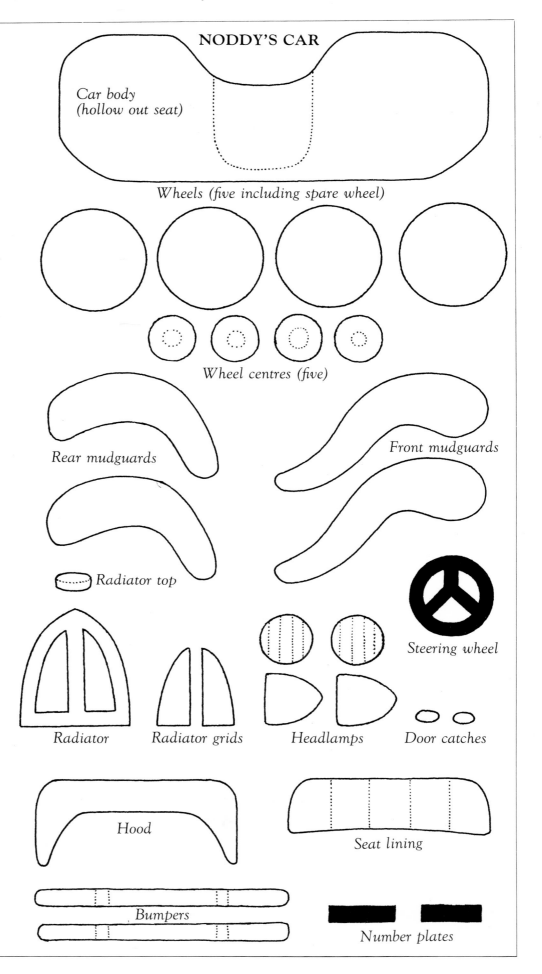

NODDY'S CAR

Car body (hollow out seat)

Wheels (five including spare wheel)

Wheel centres (five)

Rear mudguards

Front mudguards

Radiator top

Steering wheel

Radiator   Radiator grids   Headlamps   Door catches

Hood

Seat lining

Bumpers

Number plates

Catherine wheel lemon cake

(Illustrated below)

CAKE
175 g/6 oz (U.S. $\frac{3}{4}$ cup) butter or margarine
175 g/6 oz caster sugar (U.S. $\frac{3}{4}$ cup granulated sugar)
3 eggs, beaten
finely grated rind of 1 lemon
175 g/6 oz self-raising flour, sifted (U.S. $1\frac{1}{2}$ cups all-purpose flour sifted with $1\frac{1}{2}$ teaspoons baking powder)
ICING AND DECORATION
175 g/6 oz (U.S. $\frac{3}{4}$ cup) butter or margarine
350 g/12 oz icing sugar, sifted (U.S. $2\frac{2}{3}$ cups sifted confectioners' sugar)
juice of 1 lemon
1 (30-cm/12-inch) round silver-coloured cake board
small jelly diamond-shaped cake decorations

1. Cut a length of foil measuring 83 cm/33 inches and fold this into a thick strip 6.5 cm/$2\frac{1}{2}$ inches wide. Lightly grease both sides of the foil strip and a 22.5-cm/9-inch shallow cake tin, then line the base of the tin with foil or greaseproof paper (U.S. waxed paper). Place the foil strip in the tin as a coil to form a Catherine wheel. Heat the oven to 180°C/350°F, Gas Mark 4.
2. Cream the butter and sugar together in a bowl until light and fluffy. Gradually add the eggs, beating well after each addition, and lemon rind, then fold in the flour. Spoon the mixture into the tin around the coil of foil.
3. Bake for 35 minutes, or until firm to the touch. Cool in the tin for 5 minutes then loosen the foil with the aid of a knife. Carefully turn out on a wire rack and ease the cake away from the foil. While the cake is still warm, uncoil it slightly to form a larger Catherine wheel.
4. To make the icing, beat the butter and sugar together until soft and smooth, then mix in the lemon juice. Put the cake on the board and cover the top and sides and inside the coils, with icing. Mark decoratively in lines with a fork. Decorate with jelly diamonds to represent sparks shooting off the catherine wheel.
Serves 6–8

Note To make an inexpensive cake base, cover a bread board or chopping board with foil.

Catherine wheel lemon cake.

Teddy bears' picnic cake

(Illustrated opposite)

You will require two (227-g/8-oz) packs bought Ready-to-roll icing or 1 quantity Fondant moulding paste (see page 35) for the green and white icings and the same quantity for the other colours.

Bake a deep 20-cm/8-inch round Madeira cake (see page 116). Trim the top level and turn the cake upside-down on a board. Warm 175 g/6 oz (U.S. ½ cup) seedless raspberry jam and brush the cake all over. Cover thinly with white moulding icing (see page 35) and leave to dry.

Reserve sufficient white icing to make four 'plates', 2 'collars' and 1 'bib'. Tint the remainder of the first two packs of icing pale green. Roll out thinly and cut a 20-cm/8-inch square; drape this over the cake. From the trimmings, make a thin rope to surround the base of the cake and cut out a grass and bulrush decoration for the front. Affix the rope border and bulrush decoration with a little egg white. Mark border to represent grass.

Tint three-quarters of the remaining two packs of icing yellow for the four teddies and make up the basic body shape for one large teddy for the father, one slightly smaller for the mother and two others very much smaller for the children, according to the line drawings. Reserve sufficient yellow paste for the four small 'cakes'.

Colour some of the remaining icing brown and make the 'feet', bulrush tips and 'chocolate cake'. Add a little white icing to the brown icing to make the 'sausage rolls'. Use reserved white icing to make the 'plates', 'collars' and 'bib'.

Tint the remaining icing according to your creative urge, to make a coloured top for the 'cake', cherries for the small 'cakes', tie for father bear, scarf for mother bear and bow tie for one of the children. Paint details on faces, ties and bib, using food colouring and a paint brush or icing pens.

Affix the figures and picnic on the surface of the cake with a little egg white.

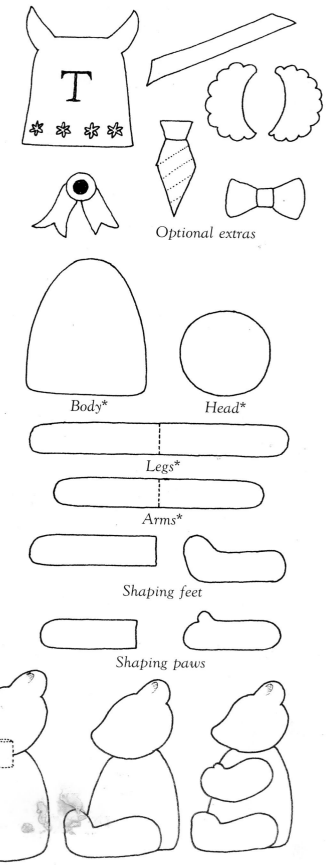

Optional extras

Body*   *Head**

Legs*

Arms*

Shaping feet

Shaping paws

Stages in assembling teddies: To make each teddy, mould the body, press a short length cut from a drinking straw into the neck, slightly protruding. Roll icing for the head into a ball, press out the muzzle shape with your thumb and pull out the ears, anchor on the straw. For each leg, turn up end of sausage shape to make a foot and on arms, shape end into a paw with a thumb. Press all the limbs gently into place.

*Make 2 large and 2 small

177

Blue butterfly cake

(Illustrated opposite)

CAKE
1 (20-cm/8-inch) square Victoria sandwich
cake (see page 20)
COVERING AND DECORATION
2 quantities Glacé icing (see page 31)
blue food colouring
1 (35-cm/14-inch) square silver-coloured cake
board
small piece of Almond paste (see page 33)
1 teaspoon seedless jam
1 tablespoon chocolate vermicelli (U.S.
chocolate sprinkles or grated chocolate)
1 sugared jelly sweet (U.S. sugared jelly candy),
about 2.5 cm/1 inch in diameter
2 whole cloves
2 (10-cm/4-inch) lengths fine silver-coloured
wire
$\frac{1}{4}$ quantity Royal icing (see page 34)

1. Cut off two opposite corners of the cake giving triangles of 7.5 cm/3 inches. Cut the cake in half diagonally through the remaining corners to form the wings of the butterfly. Without putting the cakes together, cross them over so that the long diagonal edges are on the outside. To make a larger upper wing and a smaller bottom wing, cut out a triangle of 5 cm/2 inches from each of these long outside edges, having the notches exactly opposite each other and about 10 cm/4 inches from one end. (*Instructions on cutting wing shapes illustrated overleaf.*) Place the two 'wings' on a wire rack and carefully brush off any loose crumbs. Reserve the cake trimmings.

2. Take 3 tablespoons (U.S. 4 tablespoons) of the glacé icing and place in a small bowl. Tint the larger quantity of icing pale blue with food colouring. Tint the smaller quantity of icing a much deeper blue and place in a paper piping bag (see page 12). Ice the wings one at a time. Pour half the pale blue icing over one wing and spread it evenly over the top and sides. While the icing is still wet, snip off the end of the icing bag and pipe four lines of darker icing down the wing parallel with the long edge. Using a fine skewer, feather the icing by drawing seven lines across the wing from the centre radiating to the outside edge. Repeat with the second wing and allow the icing to set.

3. Cut a slim wedge of cake from the trimmings. Arrange the wings together on the cake board, inserting the wedge of cake between the upper wings so they are slightly spread apart. Form the almond paste into a sausage shape, 7.5 cm/3 inches long, to make the body of the butterfly. Coat with jam then cover with vermicelli. Place on the cake,

178

add the sugared sweet for the head and press in the cloves to make the eyes. Make two feelers by bending the lengths of wire to give a curl at one end of each piece. Insert these into the head.

4. Tint the royal icing pale blue and place in a piping bag fitted with a small star tube. Neaten the edge of the cake by piping shells all round the base.
Serves about 16

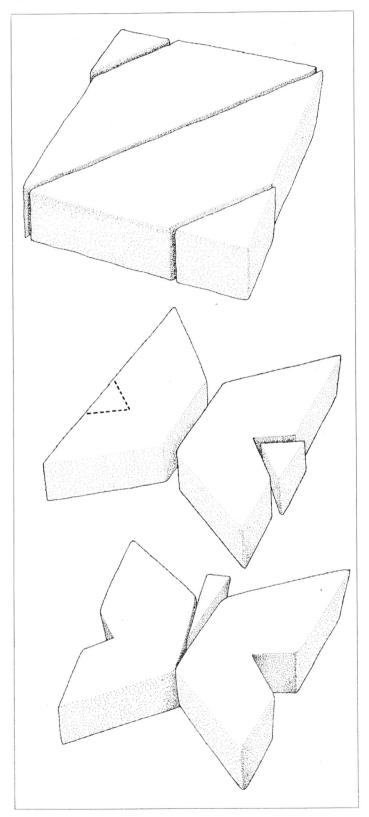

Danish pastries

The rich yeast dough from which these are made takes time, but can then be transformed into all sorts of attractive iced pastries. Prepare the dough, enclose it tightly in foil or a plastic bag and freeze. You can then leave it for several months before going on to the shaping and baking, and some cooks prefer to split the work into two sessions. All the confections based on this dough are known as Danish pastries. They are delicate enough to enjoy at a mid-morning coffee party and they also go very well indeed with a cup of hot chocolate.

The great difference between these pastries and ordinary sweet buns lies not only in the extreme richness of the dough, but also in the extravagance of the fillings and decorations. Syrupy apricots, spiced apples, almond paste, toasted almonds and all kinds of dried fruit are used, often enhanced with preserves and vanilla custard.

BASIC DOUGH
25 g/1 oz fresh yeast (U.S. 1 cake compressed yeast), or 1 tablespoon dried yeast and 1 teaspoon caster sugar (U.S. active dried yeast and granulated sugar)
about 150 ml/¼ pint (U.S. ⅔ cup) warm water (43°C/110°F)
450 g/1 lb plain flour (U.S. 4 cups all-purpose flour)
1 teaspoon salt
50 g/2 oz lard (U.S. ¼ cup shortening)
25 g/1 oz caster sugar (U.S. 2 tablespoons granulated sugar)
2 eggs, beaten
275 g/10 oz (U.S. 1¼ cups) butter

1. Blend the fresh yeast with the warm water. If using dried yeast, dissolve the sugar in the water and sprinkle the yeast on top. Leave in a warm place for about 10 minutes, or until frothy.
2. Sift the flour and salt into a bowl, rub or cut in the lard, then stir in the sugar. Add the yeast liquid and beaten eggs and mix to form a soft elastic dough, adding a little extra warm water if necessary.
3. Turn out on a floured surface and knead lightly for 5 minutes until the dough is smooth and silky. Shape into a ball, place in an oiled plastic bag and chill for 10–15 minutes.
4. Soften the butter and shape it into a block about 25 cm/10 inches by 10 cm/4 inches. Roll out the dough to a square of about 27.5 cm/11 inches and lay the piece of butter down the centre third of the dough. Fold the two flaps of dough over the butter to overlap and enclose it completely. Seal the top and bottom with the rolling pin. Turn the dough if necessary so the folded edges are at the sides and roll out into a strip three times as long as it is wide.

Fold the bottom third up over the centre third and the top third down over this. Seal the edges with the rolling pin as before. Return the dough to the oiled bag and chill for 10 minutes. Repeat the rolling, folding and chilling processes twice more, making sure you always start with the folded edge of the dough to the right hand side. Return to the oiled bag again and chill for at least 30 minutes after the last folding.

Makes sufficient dough for 32 pastries, or eight each of any four of the six varieties given below:

FILLINGS

Apricot filling Drain 1 (225-g/8-oz) can of apricot halves. Boil the syrup until reduced by half, cool, then return the apricots. Leave to stand for 2 hours. Remove for use with a slotted spoon.

Almond paste filling Almond paste (see page 33).

CUSTARD FILLING

1 egg
1 tablespoon caster sugar (U.S. granulated sugar)
1 tablespoon plain flour (U.S. all-purpose flour), sifted
1 teaspoon cornflour (U.S. cornstarch), sifted
150 ml/$\frac{1}{4}$ pint (U.S. $\frac{2}{3}$ cup) milk
few drops vanilla essence (U.S. vanilla extract)

Blend the egg, sugar, flour and cornflour together. Gradually beat in the milk until smooth. Place in a small pan and stir constantly over gentle heat until thick and smooth. Flavour with vanilla and leave to cool.

SPICY FILLING

40 g/$1\frac{1}{2}$ oz (U.S. 3 tablespoons) butter
40 g/$1\frac{1}{2}$ oz caster or icing sugar (U.S. 3 tablespoons granulated sugar or $\frac{1}{3}$ cup confectioners' sugar)
$1\frac{1}{2}$ teaspoons (U.S. 2 teaspoons) ground cinnamon or ground mixed spices

Cream the butter, sugar and spices together in a bowl until light and fluffy.

Apple filling Peel, core and chop two cooking apples. Stew gently with the minimum amount of water until reduced to a thick pulp. Beat until smooth with caster sugar or soft brown sugar (U.S. granulated sugar or light brown sugar) and ground cinnamon or ground mixed spices to taste. A few currants or chopped seedless raisins can also be added, if liked. Leave to cool.

DRIED FRUIT FILLING

25 g/1 oz (U.S. 2 tablespoons) butter
25 g/1 oz soft brown sugar (U.S. 2 tablespoons light brown sugar)
pinch of ground nutmeg or ground allspice
50 g/2 oz (U.S. $\frac{1}{3}$ cup) dried mixed fruit

Cream the butter, sugar and spice together in a bowl. Mix in the dried fruit.

GLAZE
beaten egg
TOPPINGS
clear honey
ICING
1 quantity Glacé icing (see page 31)
DECORATIONS
flaked (U.S. slivered) or chopped almonds, toasted if desired
glacé cherries (U.S. candied cherries)
redcurrant jelly
angelica

To shape and bake the pastries
While the shaped pastries are rising, heat the oven to 220°C/425°F, Gas Mark 7.

Crescents (one quarter of the dough makes eight pastries). Roll out the dough on a floured surface and trim to a 22.5-cm/9-inch circle. Cut this into eight even wedges. Put a small piece of almond paste or a little dried fruit filling in the centre of each wedge of dough, roll up carefully towards the pointed end and bend into a crescent shape. Place well apart on greased baking sheets (U.S. cookie sheets). Brush with beaten egg to glaze. Cover lightly with oiled cling film and allow to rise in a warm place for 20–30 minutes, or until puffy. Glaze again and bake for 10–15 minutes, or until well risen and golden brown. Place on a wire rack and while still warm either brush or drizzle with glacé icing and sprinkle with almonds.

Pinwheels (one quarter of the dough makes eight pastries). Roll out the dough thinly and trim to a rectangle 30 cm/12 inches by 20 cm/8 inches. Spread with dried fruit filling, also adding a few chopped nuts and chopped cherries if liked, leaving a border 1.25 cm/$\frac{1}{2}$ inch wide at one short end. Brush this border with beaten egg. Roll up like a Swiss roll (U.S. jelly roll), beginning at the other short end, pressing the border edge to seal. Cut the roll into 2.5-cm/1-inch slices. Place cut sides upwards on greased baking sheets (U.S. cookie sheets). Flatten each pinwheel a little. Glaze, cover, put to rise, glaze again and bake as for Crescents, allowing 15–20 minutes. Either brush with a little glacé icing or honey then leave plain or sprinkle with chopped almonds.

Twists (one quarter of the dough makes eight pastries). Roll out the dough as for Pinwheels and spread with dried fruit filling, cherries and/or nuts. Cut the strip in half lengthways, then fold each piece into three to make a 10-cm/4-inch square. Cut each folded piece of dough into four slices parallel to the open sides. Twist each piece across the centre or leave flat. Place on greased baking sheets (U.S. cookie sheets). Glaze, cover, put to rise, glaze again and bake as for Crescents, allowing about 15 minutes. Brush with glacé icing or honey and sprinkle with pieces of almond.

Cushions (one quarter of the dough makes eight pastries). Roll out the dough thinly and cut into eight 7.5-cm/3-inch squares. Put half an apricot or a little almond paste, custard, spicy, apple or dried fruit filling in the centre. Fold each corner into the middle, securing them together with a drop of beaten egg. Place on greased baking sheets (U.S. cookie sheets). Glaze, cover, put to rise, glaze again and bake as for Crescents, allowing 15 minutes. While still hot, drizzle with glacé icing and sprinkle with almonds, or put a little custard filling in the centre and top with a piece of cherry or angelica.

Imperial stars (one quarter of the dough makes eight pastries). Roll out the dough thinly and cut neatly into eight 7.5-cm/3-inch squares. Make a diagonal cut from each corner to within 1.25 cm/½ inch of the centre. Put a piece of almond paste in the centre of each square and fold one corner of each section into the centre so they overlap, securing them together with a little beaten egg. Place on greased baking sheets. Glaze, cover, put to rise, glaze again and bake as for Crescents, allowing 10–15 minutes. While still hot, coat thinly with glacé icing and sprinkle with almonds, or put a spoonful of custard filling in the centre and top either with a piece of cherry or a little redcurrant jelly.

Cocks' combs (one quarter of the dough makes eight pastries). Roll out the dough thinly and cut into eight rectangles measuring 12.5 cm/5 inches by 7.5 cm/3 inches. Spread almond paste, custard, apple or dried fruit filling down the centre of each piece. Brush one long edge with beaten egg and fold over the other side to enclose the filling. Make 4 or 5 cuts into the folded edge of the pastry and place on greased baking sheets (U.S. cookie sheets), curving each to open out the comb shape. Glaze, cover, put to rise, glaze again and bake as for Crescents, allowing about 15 minutes. While still hot, drizzle with glacé icing and sprinkle with almonds.

Ribbons and boards

It is usual to mount a cake centrally on a board 5 cm/2 inches larger than the cake itself, thus allowing a 2.5-cm/1-inch border all round. But this may be partly concealed by piped rosettes or shells and it adds importance to the cake if the board is 10 cm/4 inches larger than the cake, and the empty space thinly flooded with royal icing nearly to the edge. This needs finishing with a dot or pearl border. Not much icing is required and it gives an impressive appearance.

Thick boards are always more effective than thin ones and tend not to bend under the weight of a heavy cake. They are quite expensive, however, and do not look like new after use, even if you remove the cake with care. If it is impossible to recover the board, consider buying a new thin one of exactly the same size. Glue it smoothly to the slightly damaged thick board. Surround the edge to conceal the join with silver paper sold specially for the purpose, or a cake band cut exactly to fit.

If you have a good square board which is too large, it can be used again by cutting one or more cm/inches off two adjacent sides. Cover the edges all round as above to conceal the two raw edges.

Cake bands are not always popular with creative cake decorators, because they look slightly commercial, and ribbons are preferred to mask plain sides. Wide ribbons are also costly and, if in a contrasting shade to the icing, may look rather heavy. Try surrounding the cake with a wide plain ribbon of a toning shade and overbanding it with a very narrow one in a strong colour picked out from the decorations.

Tying a bow on the cake often produces a clumsy effect. It is much better to cut the ribbon just 1.25 cm/½ inch longer than the circumference of the cake and fix one end over the other with a dab of icing. Make up the bow very neatly separately and fix over the join with icing.

The effect of ribbon threaded in and out like broderie anglaise can quite easily be achieved by cutting a number of short lengths and tucking the ends of these into the icing about 2.5 cm/1 inch apart before it sets. Delicate piping details help to conceal the ruse! Lengths of ribbon can be laid on the cake itself, covering corners and running down the sides, then the edges piped to hold it very smoothly in place. Or the cake can be made to appear like an open book with a ribbon laid down the centre of one side to look like a marker. All these ideas are illustrated here to show just how to carry them out.

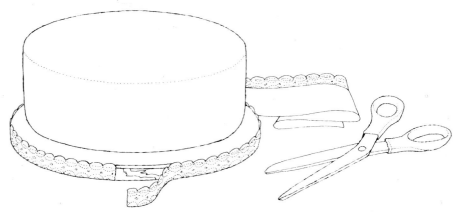

Trimmed cake band used as board edging

*Narrow ribbon in contrast colour
fixed over wider ribbon*

*Separately tied bow
fixed over join in ribbon band*

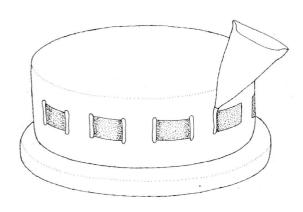

Finishing mock broderie anglais design

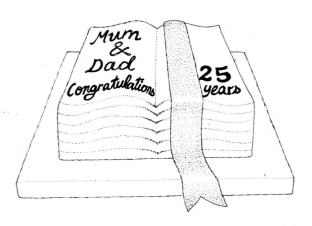

Fixing a ribbon marker over an open book cake

Eye-catching novelties

If you have little time to spare, it is not always necessary to bake and decorate a large cake for a birthday celebration. There are many ways in which you can assemble a number of small cakes to create an appropriate centrepiece for the table. Shown here is perhaps the simplest of them all with the added bonus that the cake mixture under the icing includes a proportion of a delicious healthy breakfast cereal. Work out your message, bake sufficient cup cakes to provide you with the required number of letters, and top with the icing of your choice. Then, using glacé icing (see page 31) and a plain writing tube, pipe one letter on each cake and arrange them in sequence to spell out the greeting. You can add other pretty touches as in the Birthday treat for Alison. Finish one extra cake with tiny decorations and a single candle, so that the time-honoured tradition of lighting the candle and blowing it out can be observed.

Birthday treat for Alison

CAKE
100 g/4 oz (U.S. $\frac{1}{2}$ cup) margarine
100 g/4 oz soft brown sugar (U.S. $\frac{1}{2}$ cup light
brown sugar)
2 eggs, beaten
$\frac{1}{2}$ teaspoon ground nutmeg
finely grated rind of 1 orange
100 g/4 oz self-raising flour, sifted (U.S. 1 cup
all-purpose flour sifted with 1 teaspoon baking
powder)
3 tablespoons (U.S. 4 tablespoons) orange juice
75 g/3 oz (U.S. 1$\frac{1}{2}$ cups) 'Fruit 'n fibre' cereal
DECORATION
$\frac{1}{2}$ quantity Fondant moulding paste (see page 35)
orange food colouring
50 g/2 oz icing sugar, sifted (U.S. scant $\frac{1}{2}$ cup
sifted confectioners' sugar)
1 birthday candle in holder
6 sugar flower cake decorations
silver balls
1 large silver-coloured cake board or tray
1 doily

1. Heat the oven to 190°C/375°F, Gas Mark 5 and stand about 18 paper cake cases in bun tins (U.S. muffin pans) if possible, or on a baking sheet (U.S. cookie sheet).
2. Cream the margarine and sugar until light and fluffy. Gradually beat in the egg, nutmeg and orange rind then fold in the flour, orange juice and breakfast cereal. Mix well and spoon into the cases.

Birthday treat for Alison.

184

3. Bake for about 20 minutes, or until golden brown and firm to the touch. Cool on a wire rack, still in the paper cases.

4. Tint the fondant icing pale orange with food colouring then roll out thinly and cut enough 5-cm/2-inch rounds with a plain cutter to top all the cakes. Gather up the trimmings and re-roll to make more rounds if necessary.

5. Add just enough water to the icing sugar to make a smooth glacé icing which will hold its shape. Place in a paper piping bag fitted with a No. 2 plain tube.

6. Choose one cake, insert the candle and holder in the centre then stick the sugar flowers evenly around it, fixing them with dots of icing. Pipe beads of icing between the flowers and top each with a silver ball.

7. Work out the design and pipe the required letters on the cakes. Leave to set.

8. Cover the cake board with the doily and arrange the cakes on top to make the greeting design.

9. Decorate each spare cake by piping a large pearl of white icing on the orange fondant and topping this with a silver ball.

Makes about 18 small cakes

Other birthday treats

Here are more variations for a child's birthday special using individual round cup cakes. It only works satisfactorily for birthdays between the ages of six and nine. You will need sufficient iced cakes for the number of years, to pipe with the letters of the child's name, and the word 'is'. For a boy, cover the cakes in fondant moulding paste or ready-to-roll icing tinted blue or green according to his choice. A girl might prefer pink. If, for instance, the name is Edward, and he is seven, set aside eight cakes for the letters and finish seven cakes with candles, arranging them as follows. Place three in a line across the top of the board, and four underneath to complete the figure seven. Fit in 'Edward is' at the left-hand side of the number. Other figures can of course be formed but you may need more cakes and candles.

Train novelty cake

CAKE
1 quantity cake mixture as in Birthday treat for Alison (see page 184)
DECORATION
175 g/6 oz (U.S. ½ cup) apricot jam, sieved
1 quantity Almond paste (see page 33)
2 quantities Glacé icing (see page 31)
yellow food colouring
56 milk chocolate buttons
50 g/2 oz plain chocolate (U.S. ⅓ cup semi-sweet chocolate pieces)

1. Heat the oven to 180°C/350°F, Gas Mark 4, grease a tin measuring 27.5 cm/11 inches by 17.5 cm/7 inches and about 2.5 cm/1 inch deep, and line the base with greaseproof paper (U.S. waxed paper).

2. Spread the cake mixture in the prepared tin and bake for 25 minutes, or until golden brown and just firm to the touch. Cool in the tin.

3. Turn out the cake, remove the lining paper and spread the jam over the surface. Reserve a tiny piece of almond paste and roll out the rest to a rectangle large enough to cover the cake. Put it in place and press down evenly.

4. Trim the edges of the cake with a sharp knife then cut it into 14 bars, each measuring 8 cm/3¼ inches by 4 cm/1½ inches. Top one bar cake with the reserved almond paste in the shape of a funnel, to make the engine.

5. Tint the glacé icing yellow with food colouring. Put the cakes on a wire rack over a tray and coat them with glacé icing. Before the icing is quite set, stick four chocolate buttons on each cake to represent wheels. Polish the buttons with your fingertip as you pick them up. Leave to set.

6. Melt the chocolate in a bowl over a pan of hot water and place in a paper icing bag. Snip off the end and drizzle the chocolate in a zig-zag over each cake, allowing it to trickle slightly down the sides.

7. Make a track about 130 cm/52 inches long and 10 cm/4 inches wide out of cardboard and cover with foil, pressing it smoothly over the card and underneath the edges. Place the track down the centre of the table and arrange the cake carriages in a procession along it, with the engine cake at the front.

Makes 14 small cakes

Basket of fruit cake

CAKE
1 (15-cm/6-inch) round Madeira cake (see page 116)
COVERING AND DECORATION
1 (20-cm/8-inch) round silver-coloured cake board
175 g/6 oz (U.S. ½ cup) apricot jam, boiled and sieved
2 quantities Fondant moulding paste (see page 35)
yellow and brown food colourings
2 quantities Almond paste (see page 33) to make a selection of moulded fruit including a large bunch of grapes, apples, pears, oranges, lemons, bananas and strawberries

1. Trim the top of the baked cake flat then turn it over and place on the board. Brush with jam.

2. Tint the Fondant moulding paste a golden straw colour with food colouring. Use two-thirds to flat ice the cake (see page 36).

3. While the icing is still soft, work the woven wicker design around the sides as instructed in recipe for Tiny red rose basket (see page 151).

4. Divide the reserved paste into four equal portions and roll each out into a rope about 65 cm/26 inches long. Twist the ropes together in pairs and lay one twist around the top edge and one around the base of the cake. Trim the ends and press them together neatly, smoothing over the joins with a fingertip.

5. Place the moulded bunch of grapes in the centre of the cake and arrange the rest of the fruit around it attractively.

Serves about 10

Moulded almond paste fruits

Use Almond paste (see page 33) and tint with food colouring as required, kneading it in well until the paste is evenly coloured. Remember to keep the fruit in the correct size relation and paint in the markings with food colourings using a very fine brush.

To mould apples
Tint paste green and shape into apples. Press in a spike of rosemary or the straight piece of a clove to make the stem. Dilute a little red food colouring with water and brush over about a third of the fruit on one side. Make each apple the size of a small cherry.

To mould bananas
Tint paste yellow and form into banana shapes, leaving the underneath surface flat. Pinch up two ridges running the length of each fruit and coming together at the ends. Paint in broken lines along the ridges and darken the ends of the bananas with brown food colouring. Make each banana about 5 cm/2 inches long.

To mould a bunch of grapes
Tint paste green and form each grape separately. Mould a piece of paste for the centre in the shape of the finished bunch, and press the separate grapes on to it. Push in a clove to make the stem end. You can mould a bunch of black grapes (U.S. purple grapes) in the same way but be careful not to make the paste too dark.

To mould lemons
Tint paste yellow and make into lemon shapes. Roll the fruit over the fine side of a grater to form the rind and press in a clove for the stem end.

To mould oranges
Tint paste orange and shape into the fruit. Roll over the fine side of a grater to make the rind then press in a clove for the stem end, as for lemons.

To mould pears
Tint the paste yellowish green and make into pear shapes. Dilute a little brown and red colouring together and brush over the rounded end of the fruit, drawing the strokes of the brush from the base up towards the tip, but only colouring the bottom third of the pear. Press in a spike of rosemary to make the stem.

To mould strawberries
Tint paste orangey-red and form into strawberry shapes, leaving a dip in the top of each. Roll the fruit over the fine side of a grater to mark the surface then in a little granulated sugar to represent the tiny pips (U.S. pits). Tint a little more paste green and roll out thinly. Stamp out tiny stars and press one on top of each strawberry to make the hull.

Store moulded fruit in an airtight container between layers of non-stick baking parchment (U.S. waxed paper).

Note These fruits can also be made with Fondant moulding paste (see page 32) or bought ready-to-roll icing.

Flower garden cake

CAKE
2 (20-cm/8-inch) layers Lemon feather sponge (see page 20)
FILLING AND DECORATION
lemon curd
1 (25-cm/10-inch) round silver-coloured cake board
1 quantity lemon Butter icing (see page 28)
green food colouring
1 quantity Almond paste (see page 33)
brown food colouring
12 crystallized violets and 12 crystallized primroses (see page 188)

1. Put the cake layers together with lemon curd and set on the cake board. Cut a 12.5-cm/5-inch square from a piece of greaseproof paper (U.S. waxed paper). Lay this in the centre of the cake and prick around the edge.

2. Tint the butter icing green with food colouring. Spread some around the sides of the cake and mark in vertical lines with a fork. Spread more green icing in the central square on top of the cake and mark into lines with a skewer; two lines in one direction and then two lines in the opposite direction, to represent the 'lawn'. Put the rest of the green icing into a piping bag fitted with a small star tube.

3. Tint the almond paste pale brown with food colouring. Take two-thirds and roll out into a strip 22.5 cm/9 inches long and as wide as the height of the cake. Cut into eighteen 1.25-cm/½-inch wide strips then cut one end of each strip into a point. These are the fence-posts. Roll out the remaining brown paste into a long thin strip and trim to a rectangle 35 cm/14 inches long and 5 cm/2 inches wide. Divide it in half lengthways to make two narrow strips.

4. Mark a line around the cake about two-thirds of the way up the sides. Cover the line with the two strips of paste, cutting the ends to fit neatly together. Arrange the fence-posts vertically around the sides of the cake about 2.5 cm/1 inch apart, pressing them in so that they adhere to the icing, and making sure to cover the joins in the horizontal strip of paste.

5. Carefully spread a very thin layer of lemon curd on the top edges of the cake, around the 'lawn'.

6. Use green icing to pipe a neat shell border all round the 'lawn' and around the top edge of the cake. If necessary to neaten the base of the cake, pipe small rosettes between the 'fence-posts'.

7. Using tweezers if preferred, arrange the crystallized violets and primroses on the lemon curd areas around the green 'lawn'.

Serves 8

Crystallized flowers

Several types of flower are suitable to be preserved in this way and make delightful decorations for cakes. Store carefully between layers of lightly crumpled tissue paper in an airtight container when completely dry. Pick flowers when they are just fully open, preferably on a warm sunny day. Select only unblemished blooms and handle by the stalks. These can be snipped off when the flower heads are crystallized. Make sure that the flowers you choose are edible. Some good examples are: primroses, violets, roses (either process small flowers complete or separate into petals), cherry, apple or pear blossom.

Take 25 g/1 oz (U.S. 4 tablespoons) gum arabic powder and place in a screw-topped jar. Cover with 50 ml/2 fl oz (U.S. ¼ cup) triple-distilled rose water. Shake the jar and leave in a warm place until the powder has completely dissolved, shaking the jar occasionally.

Pick up a flower by its stalk and paint it with the gum arabic liquid, covering both sides of every petal. Sprinkle the coated flower generously with caster sugar (U.S. granulated sugar) then shake off any excess. Lay the flowers on non-stick baking parchment (U.S. waxed paper) and leave until absolutely dry. This will take 2–3 days, depending upon the weather conditions.

Sugared flowers for immediate use

Choose blooms or petals as above but paint with lightly whisked egg white before coating with sugar. These flowers dry in a matter of ½–1 hour, depending upon the weather, but they do not store well for more than 3 days.

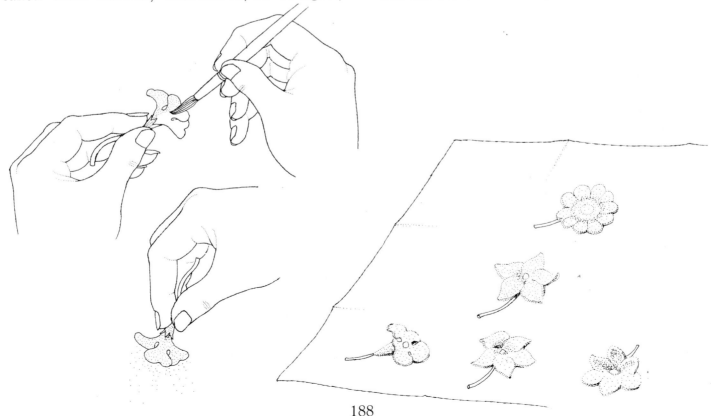

Cutting up big cakes

When confronted with a really large cake to divide into neat portions, it is important to have a cutting guide. Here are some suggestions to help you cope with this problem. Use the largest diagram for a single layer of cake that is more than 25 cm/10 inches in diameter, or one of the other diagrams for a smaller cake.

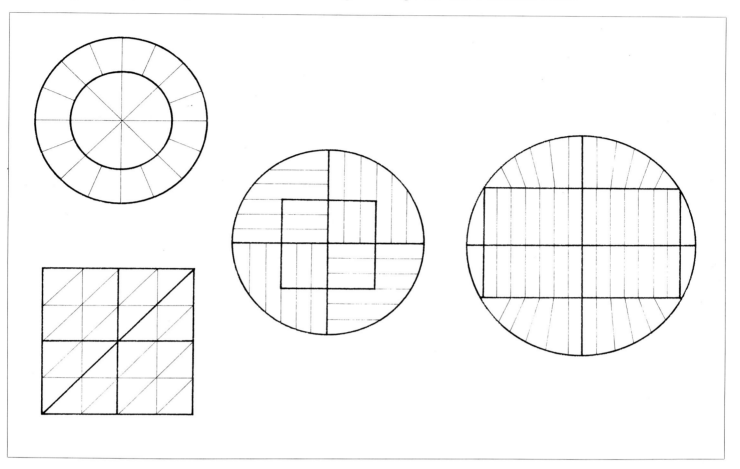

List of Stockists

Wilson's Sugarcraft,
10 Park Street,
HORSHAM, West Sussex,
RH12 1DG.

Suppliers of cake decorating materials and equipment (personal shoppers only); wedding and celebration cakes made to order. Cake decorating classes held for students of all abilities.

Sugarflair Colours Limited,
Brunel Road,
Manor Trading Estate,
BENFLEET, Essex, SS7 4PS.

Specialist manufacturers of sugarcraft colour products including icing pens, blusher powders and gold leaf or flake. (Telephone 03745 52891 for location of nearest stockist.)

Lakeland Plastics,
Alexandra Buildings,
Station Precinct,
WINDERMERE, Cumbria,
LA23 1BQ.

Suppliers of cake decorating materials and equipment (mail order only).

Index